MAIN STREET'S NEW NEIGHBORS

MELVIN K. WHITELEATHER

MAIN STREET'S NEW NEIGHBORS

J. B. LIPPINCOTT COMPANY
PHILADELPHIA AND NEW YORK

COPYRIGHT, 1945, BY
MELVIN K. WHITELEATHER

PRINTED IN THE UNITED STATES OF AMERICA

FIRST EDITION

Under Government regulations for saving paper during the war, the size and thickness of this book have been reduced below the customary peacetime standards. Only the format has been affected. The text is complete and unabridged.

*To my wife, whose intelligence and devotion
are on every page*

No foreign correspondent could wish for more thoughtful consideration from his employer than the Philadelphia *Evening Bulletin* accorded me while this book was being prepared. I therefore wish to express my sincere gratitude to that newspaper and to emphasize that the *Evening Bulletin* bears no responsibility for opinions to be found on the following pages.

CONTENTS:

OVERTURE

    1. WE GROW A NEW FACE 9

U.K. AND U.S.

    2. THE NEW ENGLISHMAN 18
    3. THE BRITISH WAY OF LIFE 23
    4. FORCES WITHIN BRITAIN 33
    5. WINSTON CHURCHILL 50

BRITISH vs. U.S. IMPERIALISM

    6. BRITISH EMPIRE EXPLAINED AGAIN 61
    7. NEAR EAST, FAR EAST 76
    8. CAN WE GET ALONG? 90

FRANCE, FRICTION AND FUMBLING

    9. FRANCE ISN'T FINISHED 98
    10. THAT DANGEROUS FRENCHMAN CHARLES DE
        GAULLE 113
    11. AFRICAN EPISODE EXTRAORDINARY 130
    12. WHY WE HAD TO BOW 162

RUSSIA, WORLD'S NEIGHBOR

    13. HOW WAR HAS AFFECTED COMMUNISM . . 172
    14. COLLABORATING WITH THE SOVIET STATE . . 187

DAS REICH

    15. Is Hitler Germany? 198
    16. The Way the Germans See It 222
    17. The Great Dilemma 229

PEACE IN OUR TIME?

    18. Achtung Minen! 248

OVERTURE

Weep not that the world changes—did it keep
A stable, changeless state, 'twere cause indeed to weep.
—BRYANT, *Mutation*

1

WE GROW A NEW FACE

The United States of America was born of revolution and we have never ceased to be proud of that fact. But now we are astonishing the world by opposing popular movements through which other people seek at least a measure of the political benefits which we ourselves have enjoyed. Whether viewed from Russia, the Balkans, Western Europe, Africa, the Near East or the Far East, we are regarded as the champions of reaction.

Moreover we have bobbed up in the grabbing class of nations, the very class upon which we have poured a century and a half of scorn. The frequent demands that we should "get something out of this war and not be fools as we were the last time," caused natural concern among our friends. The Atlantic Charter is a guidepost to which small countries constantly refer in self-protection. As one diplomat said to me: "We intend to shout its passages until we're hoarse." But none who understands, regards the Charter as anything more than a laudable aspiration which in practice will not be fulfilled.

In one way the Charter was a misfortune, for it led the masses to expect a degree of unselfishness from us which we are no longer in position to enjoy. Unselfishness is a luxury of a bygone day. Uncle Sam can no longer afford to be the tender, big-hearted man who shells out and asks nothing in return. The deeply ingrained and quite often misguided missionary spirit and, to foreigners, the amazing private generosity which makes it possible to raise fabulous sums for the relief of Zululanders, and the purchase of cocoa for people who use it to paint their shacks (this actually happened in Ruthenia), undoubtedly will linger on. But as a nation the big-handed day is over.

One of the things I sought in Moscow was an answer to this question: "Will the United States and Russia be able to get along harmoniously after the war which, by Hitler's blunder, brought them together?"

Maxim Litvinoff's reply was: "Ve're villink but vat you going to do? Go reactionary?"

The implication was that if we did, the sledding would be uphill. A leading communist might be expected to refer to "reaction." Maxim Litvinoff, however, is one of the few worldly-wise in Russia. Look back over his record of prediction at the League of Nations, subtract what was then dismissed as a sort of rabble-rousing, and you are forced to the conclusion that "Maxie" is nobody's fool.

Indeed, many more than communists look upon the United States as being reactionary. The notion that we are blocking progress, that we struggle against every force aiming at remedying conditions as they existed prior to Hitler's attack against Poland in 1939, that we shudder at blood-letting, is widespread. It may be quite uncivilized, but blood-letting remains an effective medium for people to rid themselves of what they (and not we) consider the rotten core of their national life. If they are prevented from indulging in this purifying purge, the resulting frustration can lead to consequences much less desirable than the spectacle of a modest amount of blood-letting.

Our peculiar attitude toward French Resistance, our fondness for the House of Savoy and the apparent favors for General Franco, who will get his due from his own people once the World War comes to an end, put the stamp of reaction upon us. In the case of France (in Africa) and Italy, we hid behind the appealing excuse of military necessity. Many an error in this war has been covered up with that convenient plea. In Austria we have dabbled with the Hapsburgs, of all people; in Jugoslavia and Greece, where our interests are not so direct, we have followed along behind the British who, likewise, have proceeded on the leave-things-as-they-were basis. In the Far East, where we have interests chiefly of an imperialistic nature, we have not followed such a definite line. At times we have appeared to encourage Orientals to aspire to independence, and at other times we have plumped for conservatism. Our ticklish war position in that area and the latent desire to acquire bits of Pacific territory for ourselves inspired this indecisive policy.

So the United States, once feared by Europe's crowned heads as a frightening revolutionary mass, finds itself now viewed generally as the stronghold of conservatism. It is a curious fact that despite its twelve years of liberalism at home, the Roosevelt Administration in its dealings abroad has displayed an almost hysterical fear of possible social upheaval. This explains its extreme slowness in embracing Europe's underground movements—even on the overworked excuse of military necessity. The word "underground" seemed to carry an unpalatable connotation. This fear has been shared by the British Government with the approbation of Labourite as well as Tory. Labour leaders with whom I discussed the subject were extremely chary of anything that might cause what they termed "unsettled conditions" on the Continent. The journal *The Economist*, which represents opinion in between Tory and Labour, in discussing this fear in so far as Britain was concerned, warned that "Britain is a progressive power or it is nothing. Once let it lend its name to the principles of legitimism and authority and it will be left behind by the tide of history as surely and as finally as the Talleyrands and the Metternichs, the Bourbons and the Czars."

Before definite details for a Western invasion were formally fixed at Teheran in November 1943, the Russians and leftist opinion throughout the world believed that the long delay in a land attack on the Germans in the west was caused by this same fear of social upheaval. Somehow they believed it was dictating strategy, one of the principal aims of which was explained by a story constructed on hoary lines: Hitler, Stalin and Churchill went to heaven. They were met by St. Peter who, being in a very good mood that day, decided he would grant the trio whatever they desired. What would Hitler most like to have? "I," replied Adolf, "should like to see all the people of Russia exterminated on the steppes where our armies are now fighting." St. Peter, somewhat taken back, turned to Stalin: "I," said the Russian Premier, "should like to see the Germans exterminated on the steppes of Russia where our armies are now fighting." St. Peter then turned to Churchill who had been listening quietly. "As for me," said Churchill, "I shall be very modest. Just give me a cigar and grant the wishes of the other two gentlemen."

Prime Minister Churchill stated publicly on several occasions that no move would be made in the West until the Anglo-American Staffs were satisfied that it was militarily possible. Political considerations, he said, would not be allowed to influence the decision as to when the so-called Second Front would be opened. It would have been far better from a political viewpoint if the invasion had come in 1942 instead of in 1944. There may have been a degree of over-caution on the part of the Anglo-American civil and military leaders, but anyone who witnessed the immensity of the task on June 6, 1944, could not but have been convinced that military factors alone had dictated the lateness of the attack.

An amphibious operation against an astute enemy, such as the Germans, is one of the most difficult tasks of war. Despite the years of work that finally resulted in a magnificent coördination of all land, sea and air forces, and despite the gigantic accumulation of the finest weapons of war, the margin between victory and repulse on D-Day was none too wide. Had we not waited until the Luftwaffe was beaten so badly it dared not come over the Channel and until the German Navy was made innocuous, the landing would not have been possible at all. In this matter of the western invasion, at least, nothing but the proper considerations were taken into account.

It was not only admiration for the Red Army that made the peoples of Europe and Asia look to Russia for leadership; it was the fact that Russia was encouraging popular movements while the United States and Britain were not. Russia was being quite realistic in this, but she reaped the benefits of a more disinterested policy just the same. The United States appeared unimpressed by the importance of the fact that the peoples of occupied Europe, including the pacifistic Norwegians and Netherlanders, were fighting two enemies: the foreign and the domestic. At times, in some of these countries, it was difficult to determine which was the more hated, the Germans who crossed their borders, or the natives who stooped to help them across. The domestic enemy included forces and institutions as well as persons. Our general policy was to discourage and if possible hamstring all efforts in these countries to cleanse themselves at the same time that they rid themselves of the foreign enemy.

GRABBING

If you had looked at the United States from London during the past few years, you would have got the definite impression that every last man, woman and child in the United States was laboring day and night to rook the British Empire. The British Information Service's widely distributed digests of news and comments gave that positive feeling. News of this sort from the halls of Congress, statements by members of various war agencies, and "hold everything" arguments by press and radio commentators filled much space. The greatly increased volume of space in English newspapers devoted to news from this country reflected the same national desire to retain all the bases and all the advantages which have come our way as a result of the war. United States army officers and men freely talked about what we should take after the war. In most cases we built extraordinary bases far excelling in equipment anything possessed by other armies. We were lavish. I often heard it argued that the American taxpayer had paid for all these installations, so it just did not make sense that we should turn them back to others when the end of the war came. Any Englishman who had been to Africa or the Near East or the Far East could have heard some notions, at times rather wild, about why the United States should not yield the fine air bases we have built from Africa's Atlantic Coast through India. They could have heard that the United States should go into the Near East and force the British to move over. They could not have escaped the often none too muffled tension existing between British and United States military as well as civilian establishments as a result of the efforts of one side to dig in and of the other to prevent a digging in.

In the United Kingdom, in North Africa and in Italy the British and American land, sea and air forces merged for one of the most brilliant displays of unity history has ever known. The sole criterion was military necessity. Whatever was necessary to defeat the enemy was done, regardless of uniform. But in the Near East and the Far East, defeating the enemy all too frequently was placed secondary to post-war consideration. Among members of Parliament there was apprehension about the course we intended to take. Scarcely a week went by without some member putting a question to the Churchill Government which bore directly on this subject. What about air and shipping routes after the war? What about the Near East's oil? A conservative member said to me: "The air transport service you have developed is magnificent. But we can't help wondering what it is all about when some of the most active officers take off their jackets and we discover that they are high officials of one or another of your domestic air lines!" Under the surface was a feeling that Mr. Churchill's fondness for the United States had led him into leniency. While some sections of opinion in the United States maintained that Roosevelt was a Churchill pawn, in England it was being said that Churchill was a Roosevelt lackey! The Prime Minister's statement to the House of Commons that he had not become the King's first Minister to preside over the liquidation of the British Empire was not an empty oratorical effort. It was made in reply to the criticism that he was yielding all along the line.

Among Empires with governments-in-exile either in London or Algiers, there was the same questioning of our motives. The Dutch, with their Far Eastern riches, and the French were the most concerned. When Hitler's cunning propaganda chief, Dr. Joseph Goebbels, innately the most intelligent man in the Nazi regime, taunted the British, the Belgians, the Dutch and the French, with the idea that they were being duped by the United States, he was not floundering in a void. He was playing with existing suspicions and he gave it all he had by predicting the ugly fate of matricidal death for the British Empire.

As soon as the deep shadow of impending disaster faded and a confident feeling of eventual victory crept in, Europe developed two fears involving the very countries without whose aid all Europe and the Empires attached to it would have gone down: the United States and Russia. The fears were these: Was the United States going to claim for peacetime, advantages freely granted for the purpose of defeating the common enemy, and was Russia to become a menacing colossus? On the other side of the Atlantic it looked as if a gigantic squeeze was in the making, with Europe, Britain and about everything else North, South, East, and West being caught between the Russian mass and the United States.

FREEDOM AND ECONOMICS

Why are we presenting a new face to the world? No foreign policy is entirely consistent. Each country has a broad line of policy dictated by its geographical location and a desire to keep what it possesses and to prevent it from being attacked by outsiders. But within that broad policy there are many inconsistencies, because self-interest changes from period to period in accordance with developments of thinking both at home and abroad.

The United States, however, has been almost an exception to the rule. Our broad line of policy has been much thinner than that of other great powers. We have been quite inconsistent in the bigger things as well as in the smaller ones. At times, we have shown an interest in getting territory beyond our continent for defense and trade purposes and at other times we have either disregarded such considerations altogether or have shrunk from them as if from poison. We also have tried to obtain the commercial benefits of annexation by means other than physical control. The Open Door policy in China is one example.

The reasons we always gave for not being aggressively expansionists were that we believed in the right of other peoples to rule themselves and that we were humanitarians. American idealism. Other countries were all land grabbers and what a terrible lot they were! We thanked God very piously that we were not like that. Yet, in the period in which we now are, there are no indignant voices raising a question as to whether or not it is moral for us to keep what was given to us by others to the end that we could prosecute a war in which we were as interested as were those who granted us the bases. The only arguments advanced are that we were taught a terrible lesson by the Germans and the Japanese, especially the latter, and, therefore, for our own protection, we must have bases throughout the world. We have built bases with our own money and common sense requires that we keep them. In the past we have condemned other countries, friends and foes alike, for using this same argument;

there is a great body of opinion that would deny Russia the right to keep what territory on its western border the U.S.S.R. thinks is necessary for its protection. France's insistence on her security riled our tempers from the end of the last war right down to the appearance of Hitler. While looking askance at others who claim the exclusive right to determine what their security needs are, we have insisted upon being the sole judge of what we need in the way of protection. We have followed a double standard. No one is thinking about keeping the bases turned over to us for war purposes, excepting as that may be done through negotiation. However, all too many of those who favor the retention of bases have the faulty idea that their owners are going to hand them over with a smile and a blessing. The quick negative reaction of the inhabitants of Bermuda to the prospect of becoming an American colony was not an attitude peculiar to that British island. Under the circumstances, it will take more force than a congressional resolution to get the bases.

Our broad foreign policy line has been thin and we have been able to develop idealism solely because of our unusually favorable geographical and economic positions. It has not been because the good citizens of Main Street fundamentally were better people than their neighbors on the Avenue de la Gare, Kensington High Street, Via Nomentana or Bolshaya Ulitza. We could afford to be idealistic and conduct ourselves with largesse, for it cost us nothing essential. When we contributed, unconsciously in the back of our minds was the reassuring knowledge that what we gave would soon be returned. Our neighbors could not afford such luxuries, for their means were limited; they had to watch the corners very carefully. We, however, ignored the true state of affairs and lauded our liberty to the skies quite oblivious to the fact that it stemmed from favorable economic conditions and not from fundamental differences in character or aspirations. The old world, and much of the new, have not enjoyed the freedom we have had—not because they have not willed it, but because it was not possible.

We have seen our freedom curtailed in recent years. The old position we had is slipping away. We are growing older; the world is growing smaller and however much it may be lamented, the fact is that we are daily coming closer to the situation in which older countries have long found themselves. We are beginning to watch the corners; we are beginning to look after our defense and to assume aspects of other peoples which we have condemned for a century and a half. We are talking about our "necessities" and are insisting with straight faces that we have a "right" to protect ourselves, even if at the expense of others.

Main Street has new neighbors; but the neighbors also have a new Main Street.

U.K. AND U.S.

2

THE NEW ENGLISHMAN

We have had to do with the Englishman from the beginning of our history. He is in the marrow of some of us and on the rest of us he has tattooed an unmistakable likeness of himself. We have fought with him and we have admired him. We have scorned him and we have embraced his ideals. We have made fun of him by calling him a tradition-ridden sissy and a cold fish, and yet, after he got it into what is sometimes brazenly called his thick head that we were not exactly colonials, we have always walked down the highway arm in arm with him whenever it became necessary to demonstrate to the rest of the world just where our fidelity lies. But we have never before had to do with this Englishman about whom I write.

Dunkirk and the subsequent Battle of Britain performed miracles on the people. The atmosphere changed completely. The cynicism and hopelessness that gripped the country for a full decade prior to Dunkirk lifted as the King's armorless army straggled home in little boats. Today, a bell can be heard ringing many miles away, so clear is the air. In spite of the grave problems of war's aftermath, there is no pessimism or moral dejection on the order of that existing through so many years of befuddled pre-Dunkirk leadership.

Veritably there is a new Englishman. Even the Irish, when caught off guard, will admit it and certainly there can be no better proof. The new Englishman is affable, solicitous and in danger of becoming a back-slapper, but to go as far as that would be an exaggeration excusable only on the literary grounds of emphasis. The American soldier found that he could not wear a puzzled look in Britain without having a man or woman accost him with: "Could I help you?" I found the attention so solicitous that at times I felt like putting a forestalling sign on me to read: "I'm quite all right; thank you very much." Now that was something distinctly new! It was like any small town in the United States where directions are given from any front porch and through any kitchen window and where boys walk along to show you the short cut to Mrs. Jones's house. English bobbies always have been mindful of foreigners, but this phase of their duties has passed from their shoulders to those of Mr. and Mrs. England and their children. It was even possible to strike up a lively conversation in a railway carriage! A more friendly and helpful people could not be found anywhere. Male and female, they were delightfully free and easy of manner.

Display of emotion always had been considered very bad manners. The thing to do with emotion was to squelch the dastardly thing firmly and never, never admit to even the dearest friend that such a Latin and American barbarity as emotion had welled within. Excepted, however, were certain approved times when it was regarded as proper to titter a trifle and emit a parliamentary Hear! Hear! I even believe the English of today will laugh at this description of what they used to be. Their part is to go right on being what the American soldier found them to be and not allow themselves to relax.

They have not, of course, discovered all the thrills of emotion or cast off all the reserve in such a short although intense time. But, may history bear me out, they certainly have tasted and liked some of them. An English girl who had been enjoying the company of American soldiers was asked why she liked the Americans. "Ah," she said, "because they have FIRE!" She emphasized the "fire" and punctuated her reply with meaningful gestures of her right arm and closed fist. If she found fire in the American boys and liked it, it seemed that six out of ten of her sisters between the ages of sixteen and fifty-five had found and liked the very same thing. That proportion may be high, but the truth was high enough to cause one to wonder whether this was one of the things Mr. Churchill had in mind when he said our two countries were destined to get rather mixed up with one another! That Pittsburgh G.I. whose wife complained when he became the father of quadruplets by an English girl, came close to throwing a bombshell into this aspect of our "occupation" army. When his virility became newsworthy, thousands of couples engaging in illicit relationship paused to reflect; but the only result was a tightening of their defenses and not a breaking of liaisons. As long as veterans of our British Isles "occupation" army are alive, there will exist in the United States a far more human understanding of the British than ever was possible in the past.

I sat down one evening in Algiers across the mess table from an English army captain. He did not know that I was aware of the excellent relations existing between our soldiers and English girls and women. He opened the subject by thanking the Lord that he was unmarried. He had a brother who was married and he pitied him. "After this war," he said, "there's going to be a lot of knifing in England. Our men are going to cut their women's throats. I have to read my men's mail and from what goes backward and forward I know what's going on. Some of my men have been out here three and four years, some even five. They don't have female companionship. White women are scarce. But their women back home have the Americans and it's the very devil. Last week I had trouble with one of my men. He was married six weeks before he came out here three years ago. He was very much in love with his wife and he wrote to her all that time twice a week, but last week he got a letter from her quite out of the blue that drove him almost berserk. She said, quite unabashed: "Dear Jim, I'm awfully sorry but I'm leaving you. I'm going to live with an American soldier."

"Shacking up" was by no means uncommon, with G.I.'s moving in, wearing the slippers Tommy left behind and tending the lawn and the roses and growing the Brussels sprouts. Here is an extreme example culled from among those who were not exactly living together; a woman in her 40's spent one night a week with a paunchy, unattractive man whose false teeth clicked. In return for this favor, each time she went to him she took him a bottle of Scotch (which was as hard to get in Britain as it was here) and darned his socks!

After the bulk of the American soldiers had left Britain for France, the army post office discovered that about one quarter of all the letters written by our officers and men were addressed to Britain!

When a country's men are kept away from their women for years at a time, an irresistible biological problem arises for both sexes. I have seen a few, a very few, of either sex struggling to resist. Because of their extraordinarily abnormal lives, soldiers especially suffer. In the wake of the trend created by those who have what might be called a legitimate excuse, there follows a general let-down in private morals by all too many who have no such excuse. In this respect, all armies are the same and all countries are the same. Here at home the let-down has increased with the lengthening of the war. No amount of preaching has ever changed this promiscuous mixing of the sexes a whit or ever will. Contrary to the "wise men" war is not a natural state of man—at least civilized man. The solution of this sex problem, like the solution to so many others, lies not in attacking it directly, but in an attack on its cause: war itself.

This short mention of the relationship between our soldiers and British women is an essential part of any consideration of our two countries at the present time. The matter has come up in Parliament in a guarded way and the Vicar has had a good deal to say about it a bit more openly. What I have said was not said in condemnation but with the greatest sympathy for all involved.

The new Englishman actually sees the stars and revels in the sun's rays. He has become more keenly aware that there are only 43,000,000 inhabitants in the United Kingdom. There really are human beings on this planet other than those who inhabit the British Isles! That bomb-cellar thickness of reserve which traditionally isolated the Englishman and permitted his character to grow "in" instead of "out" has been rudely shaken and pockmarked. It has been one of the curious aspects of English character that despite the Commonwealth and the Empire, despite the intimate contacts with the entire world which the English have had as the greatest trading nation in history, they have maintained that "growing in" tendency. Opinions formed by tourists of other peoples and conditions are exceedingly untrustworthy. After observing on the spot a part of that great exodus of Americans to Europe from the end of the last war to the beginning of the deluge in 1929, I was forced to doubt the value to international harmony of such casual contacts.

Nonetheless, it is an astonishing fact that although Americans have had neither the same reason nor the same opportunity to learn, they have, on the whole, a greater knowledge of Europe than have the British.

Just as there is a cleavage between the British Foreign Office and the Colonial Office, so is there one between the British who live and work at home and those who live and work in the colonies. They are not the same animal—in defiance of their common parentage and interests. The Colonial has taken his insulation with him and, as has been said many times before, wherever he goes there he creates a Little Britain. His personal security not only has been endangered but in many instances it has been at least momentarily destroyed. Yet the experience has not softened him a bit. He still is unaware that what has happened could have happened to him. He is still belligerent in mood and confident that he can and will go on as if nothing had taken place.

No people ever came so close to the brink as did the British without tumbling on over. Their heroism, stoicism and stubbornness in the face of what seemed the inevitable have been praised none too highly in poetry and prose and are destined to be still more highly praised in tomorrow's history books. The service these traits of character rendered to Western civilization at a very dark hour is measurable in our own time.

An Englishwoman with whom I discussed the sources of these traits traced them to a lack of imagination. To her it was quite clear whence came this magnificent exposition of national determination. "The real truth," she said, "is that we were so slow to catch on to what was happening while it was happening that we didn't have sense enough to be frightened. If we had realized the danger at the time, I am not sure what the results would have been. You know, it wasn't until a year or so later that we looked at each other and said: 'Blimey, we had a close call, didn't we?' "

There was perhaps partial substantiation of this explanation when the Germans renewed their heavy bombing in February of 1944 and when the robot bombs came the following June. The February bombing attacks were the heaviest in three years. Neither these attacks nor the robots in the beginning were on a scale to be compared with the height of the big blitz of 1940-41, but each created a disproportionate amount of the jitters. Consciousness had dawned by then and everyone dreaded the prospects of going through another terrible siege. London at the time was overcrowded (too many American Colonels!) making living quarters difficult to find. Suddenly in February furnished flats became plentiful. Their owners had hastened to the country. A greater exodus, this time with government encouragement, took place during the buzz-bomb period. This did not mean that the Londoner was any less brave than he was during the great test, but it did mean he had learned to leave well enough alone. It was the same mental state found in troops who have had particularly bad times in making landings. They are not quite the same after going through the first ordeal. It is interesting to speculate on what English conduct might have been had the Germans been able to throw a second and a third big blitz against the Isles.

The war has given the inhabitant of the United Kingdom a very severe shaking and as a result he is a less inhibited person. The malicious will say there is a coldly calculated reason for this loosening up in his character, especially in so far as he is affable toward Americans. It is not difficult to inject new life into the one-track mind of the malicious when Britain is concerned. The more libelous and ridiculous the charge the more widely it is accepted. The British are not cunning. They are not imaginative enough for that. They use straight power play and not razzle-dazzle. They are accused if they do and accused if they do not. Empire rulers are never right. If the British had not extended such a genuinely warm welcome to our troops, they would have been charged with gross ungratefulness and the *Congressional Record* would have been filled with denunciation.

3

THE BRITISH WAY OF LIFE

The traits of the Englishman I have described in the preceding chapter, which I chose to call a "new" side, is an obvious one observable in day-to-day reactions. For that very reason it is important. That is the side our soldiers saw; that is the side which has the greatest influence on the greatest number. I have also lumped all inhabitants of the Isles together using the term "Englishmen" as being synonymous with "British." The mendicant who sidled up to me on South Audley Street would not like that. He began with the commonplace that he had lived a while in my country and that he liked a certain five-cent cigar which he could not get in London (that told me what a long time ago it was that he had lived in my country). I appreciated the delicate manner of his "touch" thus far, but I thought his clinching argument was in extremely bad taste, in view of the common war effort which demanded that we skirt around all differences for the duration. He said, "You know I'm a foreigner in this country. I'm Scotch!" I have given no attention to the differences in character and thought existing among the English, Scotch and Welsh—leaving Eire out in accordance with its desire to remain neutral and on friendly terms with our enemies—for the reaction I have described is common to all of them, as is the British Way of Life.

Has there been no greater change in the Englishman than I have described? What about the social and economic revolution predicted for him when life in so many cities was brought to the least common denominator; when all classes were as one, fighting not for class but for life itself? What about the inevitable surge to the left, the discussion of which consumed a good amount of white paper between 1940 and 1943? During those years, not a few conservatives in the United States were seriously worried about the trend toward radical ideas which were supposed to be taking root in Britain as a consequence of the dowager's enforced mingling with the resident of London's East End and the latter's enchantment with his new position alongside the dowager which he meant never to yield. When Mr. Churchill took Mr. Ernest Bevin into the government as Minister of Labour and National Defense in 1940, it was expected that this bull-in-a-china-shop trades union leader would tear the country's social structure apart, then build a new but very changed Britain. Certainly, it was thought, the Tory Mr. Churchill would not have sought out such a man if he had not been forced to do so. Long articles were written about Mr. Bevin, and his photograph was widely reproduced as the probable future prime minister and strong man. He had in his hand a powerful weapon for changing the whole face of Britain, a weapon made necessary, to be sure, by the crisis of the moment. But how would this man use his power? The Emergency Powers Defence Act 1940, passed by the House of Commons the very afternoon of the day (May 22nd) that the Prime Minister flew to France to plead with Premier Paul Reynaud and General Weygand to carry on the fight, vested in the government full control of all persons and property in the United Kingdom. Also that same day, in a very great rush, Regulation 58A was issued, drawn under the powers granted by the Act. The Regulation gave Mr. Bevin control over every person in the United Kingdom in so far as his labor was concerned. He could push men, women and children about as he wished; and indeed he did, for all but 9,500,000 persons out of 33,000,000 between the ages of fourteen and sixty-four were placed in some form of national service in the next thirty months. Mr. Bevin, however, soon showed that he was fighting a total war and that he was not playing with social revolution. A year after he was given this tremendous power, *The Economist* complained that "Mr. Bevin is still too reluctant to use the powers that Parliament has given him over employers and managers, no less than over work people."

So, the squatty, jowly, radical Mr. Bevin was "too reluctant" to use his singular powers, even over employers and managers! Mr. Churchill took other Socialists into the government at the same time: Mr. Clement Attlee, Mr. Arthur Greenwood, Mr. Herbert Stanley Morrison, and later, Sir Stafford Cripps. These men have been distinct disappointments to the alarmists. Individually, they may not have been statesmen, but collectively they were; for they proved themselves to be Englishmen first, and Socialists second.

On the other hand, the fact that these men were not seizing their historical opportunity to break the old china in the shop stirred Leftists in the United States to great polemical heights. They said Churchill's was just another Tory government bent on holding down the lid, on keeping all the old vices and on warding off all social and economic advancement that could issue from the war. Thus the People's War was indeed a farce. When Mr. Churchill came out with his statement about not becoming the King's first minister in order to preside over the liquidation of the British Empire, it was taken as certain proof of this view. In reality, his statement proved nothing except that there is widespread misunderstanding in the United States about what the British Empire really is and the broad policies pursued therein.

The trend in the United Kingdom is toward change, not toward upheaval. It is toward social and economic adjustment and not toward revolution. An evolutionary process is unfolding, and all of Hitler's hell and all of Goebbels's damnation could not very much quicken the pace of a movement existing before the Nazi demons started their nefarious labors.

Revolution is not the British way. Since Charles the First in the seventeenth century was forced "from a corruptible crown to an incorruptible, where no disturbance can take place" as he put it when being beheaded, there has been no revolt. The Cromwell-led fight against Charles and the House of Lords firmly established the House of Commons as the English medium of government. Parliament has become a fetish, and debate within its walls possesses a sort of mystic power. Reformers, radicals and what few crackpots there are think only of accomplishing their aims through Parliament. The Parliamentary system is revered by all classes and groups. Socialists would like to see the United Kingdom function according to their notions of what a better state should be, but they would never dream of trying to get their kind of state unless that could be done through the majority of the House of Commons. The mystic power of debate is a phenomenon not quite equaled in any other country, including our own. Debate is a sacred cow. As long as it is possible to get debate on a subject in Parliament, no matter what is thereafter done about it, it seems to soothe and satisfy. Block any attempt to bring a burning question up in Parliament for debate and the spirit of Cromwell rises throughout the Kingdom overnight. Push the Hyde Park orators from their soapboxes and you really do gamble with revolution. It does not matter that these orators are fanatics and crackpots who advocate completely radical changes in religion and politics. Over the years that I have milled through the motley crowds that gather around the six to a dozen speakers to be found at Marble Arch every summer evening and on Sundays, I have never ceased to be fascinated both by the idea and by the spectacle. Yet I have never heard a sound argument advanced for any subject treated.

Along with the respect for debate goes tremendous admiration and reverence for him who can debate well. The art of debate has a strong appeal and often overshadows the subject matter. Did the speaker for the Government make his points well and how did he manage his replies to the Opposition? Did the Leader of Opposition find the weak points in the Government's policy and how well did he develop his argument? When the serious Parliamentary reporters render their accounts of the debates, they pay considerable attention to the form and do not fail to note whether it was up to standard or not. A good week in Parliament is one which has witnessed sparkling debate. Further evidence of the tremendously important role Parliament and debate play in Britain is the fact that for several years now the Leader of Opposition has been paid by the state to oppose the government! That is, he receives a salary beyond that coming to him as a Member of Parliament. It therefore behooves him to put on the best show he can when he rises to speak in the name of the Opposition. Even in the Churchill National Government there is a Leader of the Opposition, although technically there is no opposition. Such a conception is entirely foreign to our Congressional mannerisms or to the French who stick so stubbornly to doctrines and principles.

Numerous were those who became cynical about Parliament during the bad Twenties and Thirties. The war has reversed that trend. The English of today, as did their ancestors, believe so much in the powers of the Parliamentary idea that one can expect them to argue that a cannibal tribe would at once become vegetarian if given an Upper and Lower Chamber!

The British do not revolt; they debate, absorb and quietly reform. Radical notions and "isms" fail to upset the stolid British. They adopt what they want of the new and radical ideas and disregard the rest. Incorporation of the moderate and rejection of the more advanced aspects is accomplished without great shock to the community. One does not "demand" in Britain, one "advocates." What is happening today has happened before; in fact, it has been a continuous process, thus demonstrating the flexibility of the British system. Outstanding in the past were Sir Robert Peel's reforms in the middle of the last century and Disraeli's thirty years later.

Prime Minister Churchill has said of this process: ". . . One of our leading intellectuals, a great thinker . . . asked in public whether I was working for the new England or the old. It is an easy question to answer for you as well as for myself: we are working for both. The new England, or the new Britain, . . . and the old Britain have always dwelt side by side in our land, and it is by the union and interplay of the new impulses and the great traditions both working together that we have managed to solve peacefully, yet finally, problems which have ruined the unity forever of many a famous State.

"It is by this dual process that we have contrived to build up over generations that basis of life with its rights and tolerances, its individual freedom, its collective associations, and above all, its infinite power of self-improvement and national progress, that decent way of life which the broad masses of our people share and for which they now show themselves prepared to fight, and if need be to die . . ."

Such a tradition breeds hope that the British will find a solution to one of the most pressing problems confronting all peoples in capitalistic countries who hold personal liberty to be essential to well-being. It is the problem left to us in part by the Great Depression and the ideas spread by totalitarian governments, and in part by a deepening sense of need for economic readjustment. There is an interplay among them. The problem they present to the lovers of individual liberty is the same: how can government controls, necessary to prevent depressions and a lopsided piling up of wealth and power, be exercised without destroying the fundamental liberties? Out of the British predilection for absorbing and compromising should come a middle way. There are many signs that something is brewing now; at least the demands from opposing forces are not so categorical as they are in the United States. Belief in the iniquity of controls and in the inevitable fate of democracy if government continues to exercise centralized overlordship is wider in the United States than it is in Britain. All but a few in the United States decry the trend and are for letting down the war-imposed bars fast and furiously. In Britain, however, all but a few favor continuation of controls as a necessary aid to post-war readjustment for an indefinite period, and there is growing belief that many of them may have to become fixtures.

The British foresee that they, and all war-ravaged countries, will have to indulge in a considerable amount of regulation if the limited supplies of goods are to be put to use where they are most needed. Completely free trade, either domestic or foreign, will be out of the question, in this view, until a good measure of economic and social rehabilitation has been achieved. To permit a scramble for available materials would mean that the highest bidder, that is, the man with the most money, would acquire everything and the poor would have to go without. The big manufacturer would be favored as against the little one and, in general, there would be no broad and lasting recovery. The British, too, have their minds fixed on their export problem; the export industries and trades must be enabled to produce for foreign markets and therefore they must be provided with the materials necessary, even at the expense of all other manufacturers. This cannot be done without governmental direction.

The Socialists, having no fear of government controls, are all in favor of rationing and regulating to almost any degree. They believe that in the post-war period rationing will be as necessary in order to achieve fairness as it has been during the war. But they are not alone in this belief in so far as the immediate post-war period is concerned. The Federation of British Industries acknowledges that controls will be necessary, although it does so reluctantly. "Until a system of world trade is reëstablished, and possibly even thereafter," says the Federation in a report, "there is bound to be some measure of directive control of exports and imports . . . during the immediate post-war period a measure of government control over industry must be retained, to the extent and for the period which proves really necessary. Any suggestion for a more permanent system of the association of government with industry should be fully discussed with industry and, if any such regulation is found justified on economic grounds, it should be carried out by agreement and in collaboration with industry itself."

An atmosphere is encouraged in Britain in which radical notions lose their force. At all times there is a small fringe of persons who would sweep things clean at once. They serve the useful purpose of spurring the government into action. They can do that through debate in Parliament. This fringe, currently represented by a few professors, other intellectuals and union leaders scorn this flexibility which enables a prime minister to cut off the head of opposition by taking the most promising opponents into the government or by giving them substantial posts somehow serving the government. After the shock of 1940 had faded, the radical fringe came to look upon the presence of labor leaders in the Churchill Government, although it was a war-time unity government, as a clever trick on Mr. Churchill's part to keep down the forces moving toward deep change within Britain.

Another phase of this British way of doing things is the use of committees. The government, through Parliamentary urging, may be forced to consider a certain subject. Frequently, it will appoint a committee of experts composed of leading economists, professors, socialists or what not to prepare a report on the subject. The committee will go into the matter exhaustively and eventually report its findings. But the government is not bound by this. It will issue its own report drawn by its own members with the aid of permanent functionaries in the government departments concerned. This report quite frequently differs widely from the findings of the other committee the government itself has named. Eventually a bill is introduced in which parts of both reports are to be found. An example of this was the famous Beveridge Plan, which was hailed as a social revolution for Britain. It aimed at avoiding the interruption of the earning power of the masses. It did not suit the conservative elements of the Churchill Government, so another plan was put forward—and with the approval of the Labour members of the Government. The Beveridge Plan was debated in Parliament in February 1943 and at the close of the debate, the Chancellor of the Exchequer and the Home Secretary gave pledges that the Government would take some action but it would not accept the Beveridge Plan as it stood. Eighteen months later the Government plan was made public and it was fundamentally the same as Sir William Beveridge's scheme. The Government had altered the Beveridge Plan here and there. The financial benefits called for by that plan were lowered and certain changes were made in methods of procedure, but the Government adopted Sir William's intention to provide a universal system of social insurance for all ages and classes of the population.

The die-hards, moderates and radicals balance each other, and out of it all comes a middle-of-the-road policy. Any consideration of the current scene, however, must make mention of the fact that moderate Conservatives do not turn ashy pale at the mere mention of the word "Socialism" as do their counterparts in the United States. Socialism is not regarded by them as being inherently evil. Britain, by the method I have explained, has adopted Socialist features. Britain may still have an astonishing number of feudalistic remnants, among them the land tithe and the ownership of large blocks of land by a few, but that has not precluded the progressive trend toward liberalism. When I asked a prominent moderate Conservative member of the Government, who springs from a family that has served its country well, what he thought about the possibility of nationalization of land and industry, he was quite calm in reply. "Oh," he said, "there probably will be nationalization of many things but I don't see that that will change our way of life very much." Yet, in the air at the time, were schemes for nationalization of all means of communication; insurance, banks, the troublesome coal mines and even land. The Labour Party, which is the political arm of the trade unions, has an ambitious program of socialization, but its program is linked closely to Parliament. The Labour Party program is made to suit the British way of life rather than the other way around. No attempt has been made to change tradition to fit a Labour program. This is a compromise that makes it differ from the overpowering bureaucratic state, a state that would be inevitable under Socialism in countries not possessing the British Parliamentary system.

That the throwing together of the dowager and the cockney, of the banker and the greengrocer, of the bookie and the duke, of the charwoman and the chairwoman would result in a breakdown of class distinctions was very far from a sound prediction. What happened was similar to what takes place among passengers on an ocean voyage. Friendships are struck up on such voyages between persons of widely differing positions and temperaments. There is something about the fact of being together in a boat at sea and the type of life led there that throws strange people together. By the time the voyage of a week or so ends these acquaintanceships have become "eternal friendships" and there are exchanges of addresses and confidences and vows to get together ashore soon after landing. While all this is going on it seems that it is the most natural thing in the world, even a beautiful thing. But once ashore, the really natural things descend upon each party, the vows are promptly forgotten, and soon it is not possible to recall even the names of the bosom friends of the ocean. Just about as superficial as that was the effect of the British all-out effort on class differences. It made people more talkative and more mindful of one another—perhaps even the upper classes more sympathetic with the lower and thus more aware of the need for certain reforms—but the fences between the people were not broken down.

Moreover, it will take a long time to break class distinctions in Britain. The rise of laboring people to cabinet positions and of the humblest born to the House of Lords has not really been part of a leveling process. The cockney accent and the speech of miners can be heard in the House of Commons and men of mighty low but honest origins have been sent to the House of Lords by the King, but this has meant recognition of class rather than abolition of it. Such distinctions are ingrained and well developed. The upper classes may hold to themselves, but the lower classes have pride too. There is no compelling urge to jump the fences. Most crafts and trades, even menial labor, have been divided into specific compartments for generations, so that laborers come to think of themselves and their co-workers in their division as members of a distinct group or class. They have been most stubborn in resisting a breakdown of these divisions even when wartime necessity demanded it. Lack of opportunity over generations, a condition prevalent in most of the older countries, has forced boys to follow their fathers' and grandfathers' footsteps, all of which, of course, has helped to deepen the feeling of caste. They have wanted to retain their "class" distinction. Only by making higher education more widely available will this feeling eventually be broken down and that through sheer force of achievement of the newcomers. A step in that direction is being taken through a much-debated education bill. Yet the thought behind it is not concerned with a breakdown of class but with giving capable boys and girls of the lower classes greater educational opportunities. A report on the place of public schools in the general educational system was made by one of those committees set up by

Parliament. It recommended that 25 per cent of the enrollment of the exclusive and excellent public schools (in the United States, private schools) such as Eton, Harrow, and Rugby, be allocated to the underprivileged, who would be given scholarships. To this proposal one heard such remarks as this, made by persons from the very classes that would benefit: "Well, I don't know. Our boys might not feel very comfortable there. The wealthy who want to squander their money on dear schools might resent it." That remark was cogent; the problem is really a social one. One critic of the proposal to water down the exclusive public schools by forcing them to take scholarship pupils countered with this: "Make the wealthy send their sons to state schools and that would raise the social level of such schools in a way that the reverse process will never do."

It may be too much to say that the English like class distinctions. Some of them, chiefly in the middle classes, most certainly do not. What can be said is that on the whole the English are not rabidly opposed to such distinctions.

4

FORCES WITHIN BRITAIN

During my eight-month trip I traveled almost 24,000 miles, stopping in eleven different countries, political subdivisions or islands and flying over many others. Several of them I had visited many times before in the course of my thirteen years abroad from 1927 to 1940. When General Dwight D. Eisenhower was named the supreme commander for the Western invasion the last of December, 1943, I sat down in London to calculate how long it would take him to get ready. I concluded that he would not strike before the middle of the following April and possibly not until June 1st. On the basis of this calculation, I set out from England in February for Africa, the Middle East and Russia, rationing my time, acts and movements with a view to being back in England in time for the historic event. It was an evening in the early part of May when I dropped my gear down on the floor of a C54 in Casablanca, and the shiny four-motored transport plane headed out to sea for the uncomfortable all-night ride to an airport in southern England. After the snow of northern Russia and the mud of the southern part of the U.S.S.R., after the heat and glistening sand of the Persian, Egyptian and Sahara Deserts, the green patch land and profusion of roses of springtime England were a most refreshing sight. Overnight it seemed that I had been shot bleary-eyed in a rocket from one planet to another.

The radical change in landscape and the invigoratingly crisp atmosphere were not alone in announcing this apparent move from one planet to another. The intellectual waves that struck me announced it, too.

In thinking and discussing the broad aspects of major domestic and world problems of the day, London was a power house. All sorts of meetings, reports, pamphlets, books, magazine and newspaper articles dealt with that mixture of self-interest and humanitarianism always discernible in Britain. This made it seem all the more inconceivable that Britain might have become a conquered nation. For a decade before Dunkirk, there was befuddlement and stagnation. Much the same situation existed in France. Because they are doctrinaire, it is a much more painful process for the French to shake themselves free. Owing to their geographical position, however, they never had a chance to try. There was no moat separating them from the on-coming hordes as there was protecting the British. The ordeal of the French necessarily has had to be longer and more agonizing. Once the British had received their great shock, the reaction was instantaneous.

Materially, Britain has lost tremendously, and this fact forcibly must dictate her foreign course for a considerable time to come. Fortunately for her, there is a high degree of unity on this point; there are no divergent groups seeking opposed objectives abroad. Hitler's war arranged all that very nicely.

The Fascism-versus-Something-Else struggle that tore the world asunder for so many years before the war, is now a dead issue. Dislike of Communism as a doctrine is as strong as ever, but fear that Russia may spread it, happily, is fast diminishing. What reservations there are in respect to the U.S.S.R. are orthodox reservations involving straight power politics and not Communism.

Labourite as well as Tory is looking at the outside world, at the

Empire and at the Commonwealth through much the same nationalist eyes. The Socialist has become as much of a champion of the Empire and of the Commonwealth as the Conservative always has been; the Socialist has become more keenly aware of the material advantages the United Kingdom must obtain abroad. The cockney Herbert Morrison, whom Prime Minister Churchill took into his national government as Minister of Home Security, is an example of the practical Socialist. He represents what is perhaps the majority Socialist opinion. Of the Commonwealth and the Empire, Mr. Morrison says: "I want the British Commonwealth to last—not just because it is British, but because it is good, and will be better yet. Without it, the world would lose a great factor of stability and progress, just when those things will be most needed." Turning to the colonies, graded in political development all the way from some primitive community in the early stages of tutelage up to Ceylon, which has so much of the substance of self-government, and to India, which, after the war, can have full self-government for the taking, Mr. Morrison says: "We know that one of the main motives for the acquisition of many of these colonial territories was commercial. Commercial interest still plays a part, not always beneficent, in their affairs. But from an early stage, this original motive was, so far as official policy was concerned, influenced to an increasing extent by quite a different one—a motive of duty, a sense of a job to be done for the people whom we found in our care, and for the sake of our own self-respect. The colonial record has had blots and blemishes. The picture today is far from perfect. But no one can explain the progress that has taken place since the commencement of the British connection—progress in public order, health, income, education, social services and the seeds of citizenship—except by recognizing the operation of motives and policies quite other than commercial."

Now, no Conservative could better state the British case than has this Socialist product of the big city of London. Of the vital necessity to export in order to live, Mr. Morrison says: "When we look to the future we must get accustomed to certain simple, fundamental facts . . . First, if we want to keep up our standard of life, let alone to increase it, we shall have to go on importing, on much the same scale as before. . . . Second, we shall have much less interest from foreign investments because most of those investments will have been realized to beat Hitler and we shall have to reconstruct them. Thirdly, it is doubtful whether our shipping and financial services will bring us in the income they did—we certainly cannot count upon it. Fourthly and last, it therefore follows that we shall have to increase our export of goods, probably by several hundreds of millions of pounds. . . ."

Again this Socialist, with here and there a slightly different accent, talks the language of the Federation of British Industries (a counterpart of the extremely conservative National Association of Manufacturers in the United States) and of the Conservative Party. The Federation of British Industries takes the view that Britain must "for some considerable period rely upon a policy of directive imports, on the assumption that we only import from overseas countries those essential commodities for which such overseas countries are prepared to accept payment by the only means which will be open to us—i.e., by the export of our own products and such services as we can render."

A Conservative Party subcommittee on industry went more thoroughly into the subject of what Britain will have to do in the immediate post-war period. The subcommittee said that the war had radically changed Britain's export position for the worse. For many years prior to 1929, Britain had succeeded in selling more goods and services abroad than were necessary to pay for its imports and the resulting surplus had been used to increase investments overseas. But Britain had been heavily hit by the world trade slump of 1929 and from then on to the outbreak of war in 1939 grave difficulty had been experienced in selling enough abroad to pay for imports. In 1931 and 1932 and again in 1937 and 1938, the deficit was more than £50,000,000, while in the other years an adverse balance of trade had been avoided "only because the hard work and enterprise and thrift of previous generations had built up large capital investments abroad which continued to bring us a return of some £200,000,000 a year. This return reached us principally in the form of imports of foodstuffs and materials."

During the first two years of the war, the subcommittee found that a great part of these overseas investments had to be turned into cash to pay for the enormously increased supplies from overseas which were necessary for carrying on the war. This situation was eased by the United States Lend-Lease legislation and by dollar donations from Canada, but with the return of peace Britain will be faced for the first time in its history with an adverse balance of trade which the subcommittee estimated would be not less than £200,000,000 a year or nearly half the average annual value of pre-war exports. The subcommittee concluded that "No other great industrial nation faces in such acute form the absolute necessity for producing the right goods of the right quality at prices attractive to people overseas; for otherwise Britain cannot pay her way and live."

An official government report on Employment Policy stresses this same predicament: "We must continue to import from abroad a large proportion of our foodstuffs and raw materials, and to a greater extent than ever before we shall have to pay for them by the export of our goods and services. For as a result of two world wars we have had to sacrifice by far the greater part of the foreign investments which we built up over many years when we were the leading creditor country of the world. It will not, therefore, be enough to maintain the volume of our pre-war exports; we shall have to expand them greatly."

It was the knowledge of what was bound to happen to Britain's financial position that caused a good portion of the country's financial and industrial interests to hang far behind the belligerent elements of the nation during the nineteen thirties. This lagging brought forth charges that the City was Fascist. The City was anti-Communist, to be sure, and in part it was caught up in the Hitler myth that Germany's ambition was to play the "highly desirable" role of keeping Communism out of Europe. But the principal cause of the City's apathy in participating in the ideological struggle was the dwindling level of the public purse. The influence the City had on the see-nothing, hear-nothing, do-nothing policy of the Baldwin and Chamberlain Governments was great indeed. When the inevitable happened and there was no way out, the City had to go along. Now what it feared has come to pass.

It was a shock when the Dominion of Canada felt obliged to make a substantial cash contribution to keep the Motherland afloat. It was a life-saver when the United States came along with the Lend-Lease Act. If Britain did not cease to exist in her present form through direct action of Germany's military might, she will come close to disaster as one consequence of Germany's might—the loss of foreign investments—unless a solution is found to the balance of payments problem. The Nuffield College Report, issued in September, 1942, found that "Great Britain can emerge from the present war with hope of steady and speedy advancement in wealth and welfare to the extent, and only to the extent, that British industry is able to produce efficiently and cheaply a wide range of goods for consumption overseas as well as at home." The Report, which went into the problem thoroughly, found that large-scale imports of foodstuffs and raw material will have to be paid for by exports.

It is in reality a national emergency, and that is why, just as when the Germans were threatening physical destruction of the country, there is unity of all parties on this subject. It explains why the British have been uneasy about the United States, through the war, gaining a tremendous merchant shipping fleet, a dominating air transport service that encircles the globe, possible independence from British rubber as a result of the building of synthetic rubber plants and similar gains in other fields, all of which cut into Britain's ability to "pay her way and live." It is a tribute to the Joint Chiefs of Staff and to the Anglo-American agencies associated with it that despite these considerations, the war on the whole was prosecuted with nothing but victory in mind. Ships were built in the United States because it was the best place to build them. Transport planes were built in the United States for the same reason, while the British concentrated on fighting weapons. Had the British kept their post-war economic position always in view, the Allies would not have been able to throw the weight that they have against the enemy in the same length of time. Only in the Near East and the Far East was friction noticeable, but this had no important effect on the war's prosecution.

Obviously, a full solution to this national emergency cannot be found at home; Britain's food and raw materials come from abroad, and to pay for them, goods and services must be sold abroad. Hence a major part of the answer lies not in the British Isles but in the outside world. For this reason, if for no other, Britain is obliged to be in the vanguard of the search for world economic and political health through international agreements of one sort or another.

Every possible ounce of energy must be exerted to prevent a repetition of such fantastic barriers to trade as were raised between the two wars. All parties are united on the necessity for collaboration, although there are slight differences of emphasis. As a first step in this, there is a general desire to bolster the United Kingdom, as the senior member of the British Commonwealth, by forging closer economic ties within the Empire. The war brought a reawakening of the political and kinship ties that bind the United Kingdom with the Dominions as well as other units of the Empire. Advantage would be taken of this refurbished consciousness to construct an economic world of their own in so far as that might be possible. The basis for this economic unity would be a scheme whereby members of the Empire would be able to buy and sell to each other on terms better than those granted to outsiders. This is Empire preference. There is nothing new in the idea. In the economically difficult times between the two wars such preferences were embodied in an agreement signed at Ottawa in 1932. The agreement was a defensive measure against the United States Hawley-Smoot tariff act of 1930. That tariff act raised America's protection wall to its greatest height and was one of the most destructive steps taken by any government during the depression years. Nevertheless, as soon as the Ottawa restrictive agreement came into force, the United States attacked it and has since insisted upon enjoying the same privileges in Canada, Australia and other areas affected by Imperial Preference that the United Kingdom has. During a debate on postwar problems in the House of Commons in the spring of 1944, Prime Minister Churchill pointed out to members who had raised the question of Imperial Preference versus greater development of international trade, that in his negotiations with the United States he had been ever mindful of Imperial Preference.

". . . I am concerned . . . to show to the House, and also to members of my own Party, how strictly I have, during my stewardship, safeguarded the structure of Imperial Preference . . . against any danger of being swept away in the tumult of this war. At my first meeting with the President of the United States, at Argenta in Newfoundland, at the time of the so-called Atlantic Charter, and before the United States had entered the war . . . I asked for the insertion of the following words which can be read in that document: 'With due respect for their existing obligations.' Those are the limiting words, and they were inserted for the express purpose of retaining in the House of Commons, and the Dominion Parliaments, the fullest possible rights and liberties over the question of Imperial Preference. Again, in February, 1942, when the United States was our closest ally, I did not agree to Article 7 of the Mutual Aid Agreement without having previously obtained from the President a definite assurance that we were no more committed to the abolition of Imperial Preference than the American Government were committed to the abolition of their high protective tariffs. The discussions as to how a greater volume of trade and a more harmonious flow of trade can be created in the immediate post-war years in agreement, leaves us, in every respect, so far as action is concerned, perfectly free."

It is natural that the King's ministers in the United Kingdom, faced with the grave problem of the country's existence, should think it logical that the first step in tackling the problem should be made through arrangements with the King's governments in the Dominions and Crown colonies. Natural and logical, but not without difficulties, for the countries over which the King is sovereign are so diverse that their interests, both political and economic, do not always coincide with those of the United Kingdom. Disposed in their hearts as they may be to enter into such a relationship, and however much they may believe in the value to the world of the Commonwealth and of the Empire, the Dominions are not able to bind themselves too tightly to the mother country. To do so would be to risk compromising their trade relations with the world outside the Empire. Canada is especially vulnerable on this point because of her close economic ties with the United States, and she has taken the lead in trying to direct the Commonwealth's energies toward finding solutions to its problems in spheres much wider than the Commonwealth. A conference of Dominion Prime Ministers was held in London in May, 1944, to canvass all aspects of Empire relationships. The idea of developing Empire preference was discussed at that conference, but the United Kingdom viewpoint did not make much progress. Nevertheless the idea persists and no doubt there will be a return to it if satisfactory economic arrangements are not made by the world at large. The Ottawa Preferences did not cover everything, so there is a wide field still open.

A debate in the House of Commons on Commonwealth Unity preceded the Conference in May. Mr. Emanuel Shinwell, a member of the National Executive of the Labour Party and a leading Socialist, moved "That the United Kingdom should do its utmost by close coöperation and regard for the different points of view of the nations of the Commonwealth to preserve in time of peace the unity of purpose and sentiment which has held them together in time of war." Mr. Shinwell, as is his habit, was quite frank in the speech he made opening the debate on his motion. After asserting that "there can be no question of domination by the Motherland in a free, independent and coöperative Commonwealth such as we envisage," he gave a broad outline of what he thought the British should do:

"I now come to what I regard as the crux of the whole problem. Political problems, such as are envisaged in the forthcoming consultations and are associated with the Empire question, and, indeed, political problems of all kinds, can only be solved on the basis of an appreciation of economic realities. I want the House to consider, with me, these economic realities. I ventured to cross swords very humbly with General Smuts who declared that after this war we should be a poor country. Of course we shall be a poor country, of course our plight will be precarious, of course we shall have to reduce the standard of life of our people, and, of course, we shall become a second-rate, or even a third- or a fourth-rate Power unless we take appropriate steps to prevent it.

"We have to consider what our position is. No wishful thinking, no relying on our traditions, great as they are—and our resources while not inexhaustible are, nevertheless, very considerable—and no relying on our prestige in the world, which diminishes as the prestige of all countries and Empires diminishes as their economic resources and populations dwindle, will help us. We have to face the facts and unless this House and, indeed, the members of the British Commonwealth, face the facts realistically and not on the basis of sentiment or cousinly ties—all very important, indeed, but not realistic—unless they face the facts on the basis of enlightened self-interest, of what is best for ourselves, and, indeed, what is best for the world, not only will our plight be precarious, but the plight of the Dominion countries will be more precarious still. Not even Canada, and I say so with the greatest respect, in spite of her vast resources and proximity to the United States, in spite of trade associations, can afford to ignore the facts, even if there are elements in Canada who look forward to the time, twenty or thirty years hence, when Canada will be the greatest country in the world.

"Let us consider the fact that the Dominion countries can only survive by selling their primary products. . . . Australia must dispose of her wool, which is her largest export, and South Africa must dispose of her gold, which is her primary product. . . . But in order to dispose of their primary products, there must be markets to absorb them. Where are those markets? That is the problem. Markets do not emerge simply because you are anxious to export; markets only emerge if you assist in creating them, and, having created them, maintain them. In addition, the Dominion countries have created in the past, as I have already observed, secondary industries. There are apprehensions in our own country that the creation of these secondary industries may conflict with our own economic ambitions. I do not believe that the creation of secondary industries in the Dominions can harm this country unless the creation and development of those industries are accompanied by stagnation as regards population and the failure to develop resources. . . .

"Let us look at our own position. Before the war there was a decline in our import and export position. After the war we shall have, for the purpose of the revival of our industrial life, to import almost twice as much as we did before the war, and, by the same reckoning we shall have to export twice as much, and perhaps two and a half times as much. Where shall we look for this increased trade? Where are the markets? I do not object to the promotion of an Anglo-American trade agreement. Not at all. We had an Anglo-American trade agreement before the war. It is nothing new, and there is nothing unfamiliar in the process. It is perfectly true that the Anglo-American trade agreement did not prove very beneficial to this country, although we pretended it was. I do not object to agreements if they prove beneficial; that is the point. Does anyone imagine that as a result of an Anglo-American trade agreement we shall be able to export more than £40,000,000 worth of goods annually, which is pretty much what we exported before the war to the United

States, while we imported £100,000,000 worth from that country? By all means have a trade agreement with the United States, but let us look elsewhere if we are seeking for markets to absorb our products. And there is nothing exclusive in this or hostile to other nations.

"There is, within the Empire, a vast market, a goodwill market. Let us avail ourselves of the possibilities inherent in those facts. In addition, we have to recognize this possibility. America, during the war, has developed her resources with amazing efficiency. They have reached almost maximum production. But they will discover, after the war, that a problem will emerge of how to dispose of their surplus products. Where are they to find markets? In our markets and by entering into agreements, one by one, with the Dominion countries to their disadvantage and subsequently, to the disadvantage of us all? That would be unwise. There are elements in the United States who would like to have individual agreements with each of the Empire countries. I regard that as disastrous for ourselves and disastrous for the Dominion countries. Moreover, in the American market, unless they can raise the standard of life in order to coincide with their increased production, we shall discover that there is no market for us in that country.

"These are the facts that we must recognize. I approach this Empire problem in order to ascertain whether it is possible, by a process of expansion and coöperation, to find markets for our goods, and at the same time discover markets throughout the Empire, including the Colonies, for the Dominion countries. That is the proposal I am putting before the House and which, I hope, will be discussed at the forthcoming Conference. Surely there is nothing objectionable in seeking to promote increased trade within the Empire? Is that objectionable to the United States, or Soviet Russia, or China, or the United Nations as a whole? Surely it cannot be if it is to the advantage of our people."

Whether by Empire development or by wider arrangements or both, the British know that they must seek collaboration abroad. The second step through which Britain hopes to "pay her way and live" is by developing home industries more intensively than ever before so that she can continue to offer the world quality products but at lower prices and can become more alert to changing needs and new inventions. New equipment has been added during the war and British scientists have been second to none in their war resourcefulness. What the British hope to do is to avail themselves of this new equipment and of the stimulated brains of scientists to meet the problems of peace as they have met those of war.

This problem of how to live is the major force within Britain today, and it is the one with the greatest impact on Main Street. All belligerents face the task of returning to normal lives, but none, not even battered and defeated France, has a greater problem than Britain or more to lose if the answer is not found.

Britain, like all countries, has its vested interests but it is not as "set"- and "clique"-dominated as is sometimes imagined abroad. Deeply entrenched interests stubbornly resist changes, yet in spite of that there is not the same fear of socialization in Britain that there is in the United States. Concentrated wealth has been steadily diminishing because of heavy taxation. During the golden age of the last century tremendous fortunes were amassed, hence the whittling-down process takes some time. The ownership of land still is one of the big anomalies. In 1929 eleven members of the House of Lords owned approximately three million acres among them and the Duke of Sutherland alone possessed one million. At the same time there were only about one million small land owners. Large holdings in the big cities have kept up values. The city of Liverpool in 1929 wanted to buy land for improvement purposes. It was asked to pay about $6,000,000 an acre!

Large estates, suitable for agriculture, were lying fallow because their owners lacked the capital to work them efficiently. Some of these have been in cultivation since the war as a part of the effort to grow more food at home, but what will happen with the war over? It is conditions such as these that cause the Socialists to advocate nationalization of land. Landowners, although small in number, have constituted one of the forces at work within Britain. Another has been the industries, which were the backbone of Britain's commercial greatness, and the financial interests, which for so long were known as the "money market of the world." Linked with these were the shipping and communications firms. Beyond the business field was the established Church and the private schools which have done their utmost to block the widening of education and to foster the "old school tie" spirit. Their grip is being challenged; the new educational provisions are a step in that direction.

British labor is anything but radical, yet it is the main force pushing Britain along the pathway being hewn by the masses the world over; the pathway that is supposed to lead to a narrowing of the gap between income groups and hence a wider distribution of wealth. Tradition is a powerful influence in Britain, and the British labor movement is distinctly British. It has therefore developed its socialization program to conform with Parliamentary tradition and the essentially conservative temper of the country. The Labour Party and the Trades Union Congress are separate organizations, but the Party is the political arm of the Congress. The Party has one wing, however, which is not directly connected with the unions. Party and Congress constitute what is collectively known as the Labour Movement. At the polls the Party has been getting support far beyond Union membership. Since the Liberal Party wrecked itself in Lloyd George's Coalition Government during the last war, progressive-minded voters have had nowhere to turn excepting to the Labour Party. The Liberal Party still exists but it is a pitiful shell.

Britain in all her long and noble history has had but two Labour Governments, the first in 1924 and the second in 1929. Mere mention in a working class pub of the name of the man who headed those two Labour Governments brings forth immediate observations about him, observations framed in bitterness. The Prime Minister of those historic governments was Mr. Ramsay MacDonald, the vague, vain, bushy-haired, bushy-mustached, handsome clerk who moved from the denim of the miners to the mink of ladies, relishing it no end. The aim of the masses in the United States is to rise to a higher station in life (although that tendency is now changing), but the aim in Britain, where opportunity is limited, is to better the station in which one finds oneself. Ramsay MacDonald followed the American pattern and that is the basis of the bitterness against him.

The two Labour Governments did nothing exceptional. Responsibility always is sobering, a fact which those in the United States who pull their hair over the existence of the Political Action Committee of the C.I.O. would do well to keep in mind. One of the great differences between British and American labor is the fact that British labor has accepted political responsibility while the American labor movement has prided itself in not entering the political field but trying to get what it wants through established parties. The American method makes of labor a powerful pressure group which does not have to answer directly for its acts. The British method places responsibility squarely on labor, which must render an accounting at the polls. Thus British labor is forced to consider the well-being of the country as a whole rather than its own selfish interests. This system produces labor statesmen; ours does not. The recent organization of the Political Action Committee of the C.I.O. may be the forerunner of an alteration in our system, but in its present stage of development P.A.C. is little more than super-duper ward politics.

British labor has evolved what it calls "Modern Socialism." This has emerged from a long line of Socialist thinkers and men of action, but some of the theorists of the past would be most uneasy in their shabby graves if they could know the pretty pass to which Socialism has come. Labor leaders of today are conscious of the tyrannical effect of bureaucracy in a state where life is directed from the top. Life in Fascist states, no doubt, has served to raise the stop, look and listen signal. The British labor movement has been trying to go ahead with its socialization ideals and yet at the same time it has been trying to cut bureaucratic evils to a minimum and find a way to preserve individual incentive. The pattern which they think will do these two things is this: owners of an industry would be compensated when it is nationalized. Parliament would then issue a charter for the industry and a control board would be appointed to oversee the industry. Under the control board would be a manager and a staff familiar with the particular industry. The thought is that the manager or even the owner of the industry at the time of nationalization would remain, or someone else high in the organization would take that post. At least the staff would be drawn from men and women associated with the industry. The control board would be drawn from Members of Parliament just as any Parliamentary committee is. The industry manager and his staff would thus be responsible to Parliament. They could be ousted at any time when their work became unsatisfactory and any member of Parliament could bring grievances against the industry to the floor of the House of Commons at any time. The incentive to keep the brains of the industry operating at a speed necessary on one hand to prevent the industry from stagnating and on the other to maintain technological advancement and desired production would be twofold: fear of dismissal if a satisfactory job is not accomplished and the prospect of higher income if profits warrant it, for profits would go back into the industry.

A model of this manner of procedure is already in existence in London. The London Transport system operates on this plan and the Socialists point to its satisfactory functioning as a public service and a business enterprise. The man who is now the general manager is the man who formerly operated the system, a Lord. The Socialists have their eyes on a number of industries which they would nationalize in this way, but they are firm believers in getting what they want as public opinion, expressed through Parliament, sanctions it. The men directing British Labour today have no taste for one-party states, whether communistic or otherwise. They believe firmly in individual liberty and in the British way of doing things. They think they can keep both of them and still increase their material lot in life.

Another force that cannot escape mention is one that rose above all the others and recruited its strength from among the lot: the force of public conscience. For Britain always has had such a force and it has been powerful. Based partly on an ingrained sense of justice and fair play, partly on religion, partly on sentimentality and partly on ignorance, it has cried aloud when things became too intolerable in one field or another. When Britain's simultaneous reform movements drop below a hundred, it will be time to start chronicling her end. Professor André Siegfried, who specialized in Anglo-Saxon behavior, in referring to this force, used to say that "British policy frequently is dictated by a lot of old maids' societies." Such a force is too nebulous and irrational to suit a Frenchman. Bound up, too, with this force of public conscience is a rare ability to self-criticize. In no other country is there a greater amount of healthy criticism of national behavior. The Parliamentary system makes this possible. From no quarter, for example, comes more intelligent criticism of the Empire than from Britain herself. American critics of the Empire who think they are being original should know more about what the British themselves are saying.

As a sidelight, the British could profitably apply their autocriticism to their scorn of race prejudice in the United States. When confronted with one or another American criticism of British colonial policy, it is a favorite sport of the British to smile faintly and parry the criticism by asking: "And what are YOU going to do about the Negro problem?" Whereupon the American is supposed to be unhorsed. Questions about the treatment of our Negro troops in Britain were asked in Parliament on several occasions. One of the special arrangements made between our two governments before our troops started to pour into the British Isles granted the United States forces complete autonomy in handling their internal affairs. That included the right to enforce our military law without interference by the British. The Parliamentary questions were asked in connection with the shooting of Negroes convicted of rape. British girls, of course, were involved; nevertheless the thought behind the questions was that the punishment was too severe and that, in fact, it was nothing short of an intolerable demonstration on British soil of American racial prejudice. Foreign Minister Anthony Eden on one occasion was asked whether any American white soldier had ever been executed for the same crime. Mr. Eden replied that he had no information on that point.

One of the stories that went the rounds in Britain will serve to illustrate the attitude toward Negroes. During the harvest season some American troops helped farmers. A farmer was asked how he got along with the Americans. "Quite well," he replied, "quite well. They were good in the fields and they were handy with machinery. But you know I don't care so much for those white chaps they brought over here with them!"

Now the inhabitants of the British Isles are more or less free of race prejudice. A certain hotel syndicate got into hot water in the courts for refusing to take in a famous West Indian cricketer because his presence in the hotel might offend American officers who were living there. The Isles have never had to face a racial problem so their inhabitants can afford to be high-minded about the matter. But it is a different story with the English when they get out into the Empire where they are forced to rub elbows with other races. This is where the autocriticism could be used to advantage.

Parliament has refused a proposal emanating from Southern Rhodesia for a union of Northern Rhodesia and Nyasaland with Southern Rhodesia. The basis for the refusal is that Southern Rhodesia follows a policy of keeping Africans in subordinate social and political levels and Parliament will not sanction the placing of more natives under such a policy. The Union of South Africa desires to have more Imperial territory placed under its wing but this, too, is looked upon askance, for the racial bar in the Union is exceedingly strong. Parliament's attitude in these matters is cited to show how free from prejudice the British are. What is overlooked is that the people in these African territories who practice race prejudice are British. Other Europeans are involved, but the government is in British hands. When the British are out among people of color and the factors that make for prejudice are present, they practice a high degree of discrimination. I have seen people of color treated by the English with far greater scorn than is to be found anywhere in the United States. In fact, one source of minor friction wherever American and British troops worked side by side in Africa, the Near East or the Far East, was precisely the difference in the tolerant way the Americans treated the natives and the opposite methods of the British. The British felt, and frequently they were right, that theirs was the only way to get what was needed from the natives. But the fact remained that they were acting in a way that the British at home condemn.

The British, like ourselves, are experts at rationalization in foreign dealings. Together we can turn out more righteousness in the course of a calendar year than all the other nations of the globe put together. Add up our output over a century and the result turns the stomachs of the more frank peoples of the earth. To be able to take measures entirely in the national interest and place them on a footing of broad humanitarianism is an English gift which we inherited. This British penchant probably stems from a marriage of the force of public conscience with other less noble forces, to the satisfaction of all. The less noble receive approximately what they wanted but a label suitable to the righteous is placed upon the act.

5

WINSTON CHURCHILL

The eyes of anyone looking at Britain after the war began inevitably halted upon the fascinating figure of Mr. Winston Churchill. Never in history has there been a better example of the right man coming to power at the right time. The British people suspect, but they can never exactly know, just how fortunate they were that Winston Leonard Spencer Churchill, preserved by nicotine, was still impatiently champing the bit after a public life of forty years, years that appeared destined to end in frustration. He was impatient because events were moving toward what he clearly foresaw as disaster; but when he became Prime Minister in May, 1940—the post he had long wanted but seemed destined never to have—he also became imperturbable. Mr. Churchill in looks and character (without cigar, of course) so closely resembles the traditional conception of John Bull that it would seem he was John's very own favorite son. In that dark period of 1940-41, it was a question which was the father and which the son: did Winston issue from John's mold or was John fashioned in Winston's? That was how close Mr. Churchill came to being the heart and soul of the country.

We can taunt him now about that remark he made before Pearl Harbor when he was stepping gingerly through the marshland of our susceptibilities in search of material aid from us. He was obliged to proceed as if he were going through a mine field. He said, "Give us the tools and we will finish the job." Long ago it became patent that with all the tools we could have given him, he could not have finished the job. Down deep did he really think at the time that he could, or was he gambling shrewdly?

From a British viewpoint, one of Mr. Churchill's most impressive titles to greatness is the fact that he won the support of the United States. Even prior to that Japanese blunder that bombed us into the conflict, Mr. Churchill was getting along surprisingly well with us. The Lend-Lease Act saved Britain in the nick of time. When that Act was passed by Congress, Britain was down to about the last realizable asset with which to purchase the war-making wherewithal in the United States. The Lend-Lease Act was one of the master strokes of the war. Throughout the war, no one in Britain, almost literally no one, regardless of how angered he might have been with the Prime Minister, would have been willing to dispense with the services of Mr. Churchill. Times were too critical and there was none other who could preserve the absolutely necessary national unity as he did. Partisanship had to be buried in favor of the nation as a whole. That did not mean, however, that there was no partisan talk behind the scenes or that Mr. Churchill was performing precisely to the satisfaction of everyone. He was a miracle man, but he was not such a master of legerdemain that he could please all.

Oddly, it was in the field in which he scored one of his major successes where perhaps the largest volume of criticism or caution could be heard. It was his dealings with the United States that caused many heads to shake. Chiefly in his own Tory Party, but also in others, there was a feeling that Mr. Churchill was far too pro-American. It was thought that he was overawed by United States strength, both physical and moral. This strong man was felt to be strong in all things excepting when he had to deal with America. Then he bowed and scraped. He was viewed as cowering when President Roosevelt spoke. Downing Street was being run by Washington, with the Prime Minister refusing to speak out bluntly to us. The fact that Mr. Churchill was so much admired in the United States was proof of the pudding: he was a lackey of America! A Member of Parliament, and of Mr. Churchill's own party, who held this view, gave me the following explanation of this Churchillian "weakness": Mr. Churchill is the child of a very strong American mother (Jennie Jerome of New York) and a weak English father (Lord Randolph Churchill, Conservative Party leader and once Chancellor of the Exchequer). He adored his mother and looked down on his father (although he wrote a biography of his father). This adoration of his American mother he proceeded to carry over to Americans in general. Those who viewed Mr. Churchill in this light were skeptical of such utterances as he made at Harvard on September 7, 1943. Harvard on that day conferred an honorary degree on the Prime Minister and in response he said: "I am here to tell you that whatever form your system of world security may take, however the nations are grouped and ranged, whatever derogations are made from national sovereignty for the sake of the larger synthesis, nothing will work soundly or for long without the united effort of the British and American people.

"If we are together, nothing is impossible. If we are divided, all will fail. I therefore preach continually the doctrine of the fraternal associations of our two peoples not for any purpose of gaining invidious material advantages for either of them, not for territorial aggrandizement or the vain pomp of earthly domination, but for the sake of service to mankind and for the honor that comes to those who faithfully serve great causes."

The die-hards did not like this utterance because it granted too much importance to the United States. In spite of the close call Britain had, they were still under the spell of the country's glorious past. They were unwilling to admit even in the privacy of their chambers, that this glory was either of yesteryear or that it might have to be shared in the future with others, especially with ex-colonial America. When Mr. Churchill was bowing, as they put it, he was in reality being a statesman extraordinarily well grounded in the movements of history. He was not, of course, bending his proud back any more than the hour demanded. The humor in the situation lay in the fact that while it was being said in Britain that the Prime Minister was under the President's thumb, exactly the opposite was being said in the United States. And some of the President's actions were being laid to causes just as fanciful as was my M.P. friend's strong-mother, weak-father analysis of the Prime Minister's American policy. None of this came over the cables during the really bad years chiefly because no one wanted to muddy the waters. Later, it did show itself, and then through the anxiety expressed over the trade and imperialistic advantages which from London it seemed the United States was inheriting from the war.

It seems incredible that today there are still some overly ripe Tories who consider Neville Chamberlain a greater man than Winston Churchill. They are going to use their last breaths defending Chamberlain's "peace in our time," and asserting that the Chamberlain of Berchtesgaden, Godesberg and Munich was acting according to a well-thought-out plan. In doing so, they will be defending themselves and their own pleasant journeys into Nazidom which they made with a shameful degree of eagerness.

The Conservatives never have fully trusted Mr. Churchill. He is too brilliant for them, too erratic, That is the chief reason why he was descending the ladder of his public life without ever having become prime minister, when the war rescued him. He was thrust upon his own party. There was no choice but to gulp him down and trust to their iron stomachs to keep him there for the duration. Mr. Churchill's father was a pillar of the Conservative Party, but the son wavered from time to time. He first went to Parliament as a Conservative in 1900, but by 1906 he had joined the Liberals and in that year stood for Parliament under the Liberal Party banner. Subsequently he became a leading member of the party of Mr. Lloyd George. He remained with the Liberals through the 1914-18 war, but he and Mr. Lloyd George, the coalition chief of the last war, gradually grew apart in their views. Mr. Churchill was then a man without a party and indeed in 1924 he did stand for Parliament as an Independent. He was aiming at formation of a Center Party to be composed partially of Liberals and partially of Conservatives with anti-Socialism as the main plank. He failed, but only six months later he found a Conservative constituency that would have him and he went back to the party of his father, where he has since remained. This shifting around made him an irregular, and allowed him to be viewed by Conservatives much as Mr. Wendell Willkie was viewed in the United States by Republican Party bosses. Almost from the time he left office in 1929 (he was Chancellor of the Exchequer from November, 1924, to June, 1929), he became a thorn in the Conservative side again by his constant inveighing against the policy the Conservatives were following in foreign affairs. He correctly interpreted what was taking place on the Continent while his party, and indeed the country at large, followed head-on the illusion of appeasement. In view of the congenital rigidity of Conservatives, it is small wonder that Mr. Churchill had to be pushed down their throats; it is small wonder, too, that doubts about him linger on.

Mr. Churchill is a great, truly great man in adversity. When he can say, as he did on June 4, 1940: "We will defend our island whatever the cost. We will fight on the beaches and landing grounds, in the fields, in the streets, on the hills. We will never surrender . . ." when he can talk like that he reaches his greatest heights.

Mr. Churchill can throw himself into a defensive fight with such alacrity that he sweeps along with him the hearts, minds and muscles of men. His classical oratory shines with invective. He finds the turn of a phrase that thrills and commands respect, whether it is convincing or not. "Hitler," he has said, "is a monster of wickedness insatiable in his lust for blood and plunder." Speaking of the Luftwaffe in the sky, he said, "And behind all this glare, behind all this swarm I see that small group of villainous men who planned, organized and launched this cataract of horrors upon mankind." Another tribute to Hitler was, "Even the arch criminal himself, the Nazi ogre Hitler, has been frightened by the volume of world indignation which his spectacular atrocities have excited." And this one in his appeal to the Italians to overthrow Mussolini: "It is all one man— one man who, against the Crown and royal family of Italy, against the wishes of the Italian people who had no lust for this war; one man has arrayed the trustees and inheritors of ancient Rome upon the side of the ferocious pagan barbarians." When the German warships *Scharnhorst*, *Gneisenau* and *Prinz Eugen* slipped out of Brest and escaped up the Channel before the Royal Navy or the R.A.F. could do more than inflict damage, Mr. Churchill wrapped up the beginning of a phrase in nineteenth-century lace: "Whatever smart of disappointment or annoyance may remain in our breasts that the final forfeit was not exacted . . ."

It is in fighting on the defense that he is superb. He is a war lord in the best sense. He delights in the smell of gun-powder and in the action and gadgets of war. He thrills at the opportunity to plan the strategy of a global war—what an enticing problem it presents! He ignores other things to put his mind to work on instruments of war. It was Churchill who conceived of the tank in the last war, and in this one we have had the improved "Churchill tank." When it is a question of finding some new method or instrument to meet an enemy development, Churchill wants to be in on it and he can be counted on to plump for the exciting and the novel. In things pertaining to war, Churchill is like a hunting dog, absorbingly excited by every smell that comes to his nostrils, every sound that enters his alert ears, every strange bush and every strange object that comes before his eyes.

His performance on D-Day was typical of the man. He amused, thrilled and alarmed the House of Commons by throwing off all the brakes and indulging several of his fancies at once. When Commons gathered that morning, the Prime Minister was on hand bursting with late news from General Eisenhower's Headquarters. It was several hours after our British and American boys had plunged into the coast of Normandy against Hitler's vaunted Atlantic Wall. News in London about the progress was scant. Success or failure? Another Dieppe? Bitter past amphibious experiences had made the British anxious. The Prime Minister, hardly able to contain himself, rose and recounted a factual story of the preceding half dozen hours: landings had been made and more men were pouring ashore. The Germans had not prevented the landing—in fact, there had been no opposition to the expedition up to landing time. It was the story the world wanted to hear, but Supreme Headquarters had not been willing to give out so much detail. The Prime Minister had broken security restrictions; he had "scooped" the censors and the press. Who was there to say him nay? Not a few wanted to, but they limited themselves to making "suggestions." But he wasn't through with his day as a "leg" reporter. In the afternoon he flew to General Eisenhower's Headquarters, soaked up all the information he could and dashed back to Commons to make a second report as if Commons were the City Room and he the star reporter. This time, he was more discreet, but one felt he had great difficulty curbing his unbounded enthusiasm. That day he led Commons a merry pace and Commons cheered him. Then it began to worry. Every member knew this restless Prime Minister, so valuable to the world, would be on that Normandy beachhead as soon as there was an inch of cleared sand for him to stand on. Questions were asked of the Government. "Would the Government give assurances that the Prime Minister would not go to Normandy?" Churchill sent his caustic red-haired trouble-shooter Mr. Brendan Bracken, Minister of Information, into the House to make the Members feel foolish for fussing about the Old Man. Indeed, said Mr. Bracken, the Prime Minister would give no such assurances. His frequent travels had been of distinct advantage to the country, and shame on the unthinking member of the House who would request the Prime Minister to stay at home while there was excitement in Normandy! Mr. Churchill soon thereafter set out for the beachhead. Subsequently, peasants of Italy and France found a trail of cigar ashes across their countries.

When there was no war and none was immediately apparent (that left but a scant few years in his lifetime) Mr. Churchill took an interest in social reform and free trade. But war in one aspect or another has engaged his attention from the beginning of his career. He was in the army before he was first elected to Parliament in 1900. He was in the Malakand field force in 1897 and the Tirah expeditionary force a year later. Then he became a war correspondent and covered the Boer War. In World War I, between cabinet posts, he actually took a command in France. In 1911, after the *Agadir* incident with Germany, he was put into the Admiralty with quiet instructions to get the fleet in shape for war. Then, as in this war, he knocked Admirals about until he got what he wanted. Prior to 1939, he was convinced war with Germany was coming and on that score his relationship with Mr. Lloyd George cooled because the latter did not believe it. He was sent to the Admiralty again when war broke out in September 3, 1939—very late in the day—and he remained there until Mr. Chamberlain, crushed by events, was forced to resign the following May 10th. After that, as Prime Minister, and the chief British prosecutor of the war, he had a field day in grand style.

Those who prosecuted World War I also made the peace. At the time, there was no question of the wisdom of that. Later, however, when the work done in Paris turned out badly, it was widely questioned whether the war-makers should have been permitted to write the peace. Could they have written a just peace after being in the thick of the bitter struggle? Again this time it seems logical that the peace should be made in one form or another by the men who led the fight. Yet it is still a valid question whether they should be permitted to do so.

As far as Mr. Churchill is concerned, his talent lies distinctly on the war side; there he finds an outlet for his peculiar qualities and tastes, there he is magnificent.

Mr. Churchill's war Coalition cabinet is destined to come to an end soon after the last cannon is fired in Europe. Whether the Prime Minister succeeds himself as the head of a purely party government or whether he withdraws, he will have had a large hand in shaping the world order in which we are to live during the coming years.

The Conservative-Labour-Liberal Coalition is to be terminated because it is recognized that the brand of high-minded political unity existing in wartime does not carry over to peacetime. All parties during this war have had but one objective, to save the nation from defeat. To that end they have worked together remarkably well under Mr. Churchill's leadership. But differing viewpoints began to show up as soon as the threat from abroad lessened. Without unity, coalitions are but ghost governments. In 1918, Mr. Lloyd George called a general election and asked the country to support him and all Parliamentary candidates who pledged themselves to follow the Coalition cabinet which had won the war. On the basis of its war record, the Lloyd George Coalition won a tremendous success at the polls, but it soon developed that the cabinet was more or less moribund, for the wartime unity had evaporated.

The Labour Party, in September 1944, was the first of the Churchill Coalition to announce its intention to go back to party politics and fight the promised general election along party lines. Labour ministers in the Churchill Government were permitted by their party to join the war leader in 1940 on condition that they would withdraw as soon as the war ended. Those ministers have since given their word to the party that they would obey the dictum. At the time that condition was placed upon them, "the war" meant the war in Europe. The Pacific war developed later and with it came the question whether the Labour Party would extend the mandate to its ministers to include the war against Japan. The Party decided to get out as soon as the war with Germany was over because it did not want the Churchill Coalition, with its Tory influence, to dominate any more of the post-war legislation than was absolutely necessary. The nature of the war against Germany and that of the war against Japan were so different that problems of demobilization and reconversion were certain to arise before the war with Japan was over. The Labourites wanted to handle these matters in their own way. They assumed, of course, that the country, which had been voting in Tory Parliaments before the war, had changed its mind and would turn toward Labour.

The ruling out of a Coalition election left Mr. Churchill in position to lead the Tory Party campaign in the election to be held some time after Germany is defeated. His opponents in his own party have little choice but to accept him for as long as he wishes to remain. He certainly wants to stay in power until the entire war is brought to an end, but it is highly doubtful if the Prime Minister desires to stay on very long thereafter. He has fought and won the sort of battle for which he is fitted and which he loves. His only public references to his future have indicated a preference to retire and once again pick up his beloved pen. Retirement from office would not prevent him from making himself heard in the House of Commons, providing his constituency returned him to Parliament, which it most certainly would do.

Assuming that the war with Japan will not be over until after the Germans are disposed of, will Mr. Churchill be able to stay at the helm until it is all over? The Prime Minister risks his position by submitting to the Labour Party demand for a general election. Should Labour win the majority in the House of Commons that it is counting on, normal procedure would call for a Labour prime minister. It is not certain, however, that normal procedure would be followed. The matter has been under consideration for many months and it is not unlikely that if Mr. Churchill consented, he could remain as prime minister—but he would have to preside over a predominately Labour cabinet. The present government is weighted on the Tory side. Such an arrangement would enable Mr. Churchill to finish the task abroad while at the same time Labour would have the upper hand in domestic affairs. Mr. Churchill is the only man on the Conservative side of the House whom Labour would tolerate in such a capacity.

Broadly considered, there have been many striking similarities between the opposition and the support Mr. Churchill has had in Britain and those Mr. Roosevelt has had in the United States. Mr. Churchill became prime minister and has held on solely because of the war; Mr. Roosevelt was elected to a fourth term for the same reason, and his election to a third term was greatly influenced by the war, although it had not yet reached American shores. Both men won considerable support because there were no other war leaders of sufficient stature in sight to replace them.

Mr. Churchill had no serious open opposition during the anxious period when Britain was on her knees and the only question was how to keep the home front together and make winning military alliances abroad. That was not the time to quibble over method or whether a bargain was a good or bad one. But the critics raised their heads as soon as the tension eased with the entrance of the United States into the war. Some said Mr. Churchill had given away more than was necessary in order to gain support, especially the support of the United States. They said he had been victim of shrewd Yankee horse trading in the destroyers-for-bases deal and that he had bound British industry hand and foot in the Lend-Lease agreement which made it possible for American industry to seize markets all over the world.

Mr. Churchill was criticized, too, on domestic matters. As a Coalition premier, he was a compromiser in the middle of the road and this made him vulnerable to attack from his own Conservative Party for being too radical and from the Labourites for not being radical enough. As a rule, Mr. Churchill picked good administrators and his war machine functioned without the bickering and blundering that characterized so many of Mr. Roosevelt's efforts. But this did not spare the Prime Minister from criticism; it was felt that he gave too much time to details of the war and as a result, major problems on the home front dragged along.

In the United States, President Roosevelt also ran into strong opposition from his own party as well as from the Republicans, on domestic issues. He was charged with not being a good administrator and with insisting upon attending to details of the fighting part of the war to the detriment of home problems. Unlike Mr. Churchill, Mr. Roosevelt is a reformer and he was accused of trying to force through New Deal socialistic policies in the midst of war, regardless of the effect on the war's prosecution. Whenever Mr. Churchill took the road to the Left, he was driven to it by the Labour members of his Coalition Government.

In the foreign field, Mr. Roosevelt experienced much the same criticism as did his colleague in London. The darts began to fly once the war settled down and a feeling spread that victory was inescapable. The President, some said, was yielding to Prime Minister Churchill and Premier Stalin; Mr. Roosevelt was unable to make

America's ideas prevail and he was accordingly deemed unfit to sit around a table with these smart men. Mr. Roosevelt, it was said, was expending the country's patrimony for the benefit of Britain and Russia. Lend-Lease, it was argued, was a gift to an ungrateful world: even Britain would kick us in the pants as soon as possible, if not before, and nobody could contrive what the Russians were likely to do.

Thus went the similarities in the opposition to and support of the two war leaders, in so far as parallels can be drawn.

BRITISH vs. U.S. IMPERIALISM

If brothers disagree, the bystander takes advantage.
Chinese Proverb

6

BRITISH EMPIRE EXPLAINED AGAIN

The older and riper the British Empire becomes the more it seems to need explaining. Enough has been written pro and con on the subject to enable every literate in the world to have a balanced opinion. Yet there is perhaps no other subject of worldwide interest upon which there is so much unbalanced judgment. All too many persons, especially in the United States, have no desire to be exposed to the facts about it; it is much more pleasant to be swayed by emotion. Large groups of Americans hold tenaciously to the belief that the Empire is bad, and they will listen to no arguments to the contrary. Faults can be rattled off at a machine-gun staccato tempo, but few people are familiar with the good points. When the British Ambassador in Washington or a member of Parliament stands up to praise the Empire, his words are lightly dismissed. No member of Congress would dare arise on Capitol Hill to praise the Empire, but members who give it hell are applauded from the Atlantic to the Pacific.

There are several reasons for this attitude. One is our own past connection with the Empire. That our separation came about through a war of rebellion against tyranny is taught to every school child and is further perpetuated by a few organizations whose members delight in thinking of themselves as the sole true patriots in the country. This attitude persists in spite of recent historians of the colonial period who have begun to question the accuracy of the interpretation that places the cause of the rebellion upon tyranny. They now see far beyond the familiar cry of "Taxation without representation is tyranny!" Lawrence Henry Gipson, professor of history and head of the Department of History and Government at Lehigh University, who has made exhaustive studies of the colonial era, says that the American colonists did not intend to be taxed whether they had representation or not. The granting of representation in Parliament to the colonists was seriously considered in London, for, after all, the idea that taxation carried with it a right to representation was an English principle, not solely a colonial one. It was the colonists themselves, says Dr. Gipson, who objected to having representation. "The British colonials, after the futile attempt by Parliament in 1765 to extend to America the principles embodied in the British stamp tax, made plain that the only body that they would recognize as having legal competence to tax them was the local assembly of their own particular colony and that they would therefore regard taxation by Parliament, even should the undesired representation in it be granted, as nothing less than tyranny." Dr. Gipson says that the colonies at the time were not administered in a tyrannical way and he cites numerous resolutions and statements of the day to prove it, such as this statement made by Governor Dobbs before the North Carolina assembly on December 11, 1754: ". . . loaded with debts and enormous, tho' necessary taxes, [the British government] hath not only protected these colonies but indulged them in . . . the easiest taxes [spent for their own support], of any civilized nation on the Globe . . ."

As this new interpretation of the real reason for the revolution creeps into textbooks, school children will learn that the English victory over the French in the French and Indian Wars eliminated the greatest threat to the colonists and that thereafter they felt the way to expansion westward was open. The existence on a vast continent of a group of people far removed from the homeland created a dynamic situation which was bound to make itself felt. To quote Dr. Gipson again:

"One may accordingly in accepting this larger view put aside as perhaps somewhat incidental, if not irrelevant, the exact nature of the events that were to set free the American colonial from the implications of an old-world economy and also an old-world philosophy of state and to give to them freedom to work out their future no longer trammeled by the inevitable vexations and irritations incident to having that future, with all its promise, subordinated to the problems of even a benevolent parent country."

Another cause for the current American attitude toward the British Empire is the spirit of independence found in all new-world countries, which creates a feeling of sympathy for all non-independent peoples without questioning whether these peoples could survive as independents or not. This attitude opens the way to propagandists who make all manner of claims without fear of having their statements too closely scrutinized.

Another reason is the presence in the population of blocs of immigrants from countries or territories which form a part of the Empire, or which have been at odds with the Empire. Such immigrants have not learned to look at world problems through strictly American eyes; moreover they propagate opinions based upon their own narrow experiences. Still another reason is the desire on the part of a few to see the United States inherit portions of the British Empire.

The British cannot help feeling that there is a large amount of bias in attacks upon their Empire, in view of the fact that other empires receive scant attention. Do such American attacks therefore emanate from a fundamental belief in the iniquity of empires? The British one is the world's largest but it is not the oldest. The Dutch are in the business, too, and were in it before the British. The French are second only to the British in the size of their empire. The Belgians have a profitable enterprise in Africa, and the Portuguese still retain remnants of a once vast colonial domain. All of these hold on as stubbornly as do the British and they quiver whenever an Englishman, in combating American attacks, mentions the mere existence of other empires. The war in the Pacific brought consciousness to the United States of Dutch riches in the East Indies which affect the United States economically and strategically, and the Dutch are watching Uncle Sam very closely for indications as to his future course. The British and Dutch Empires in the East fought each other throughout their formative centuries but now they find themselves consorting together for survival.

The New York correspondent of the London paper, *The Economist*, puzzled by the attitude he found in the United States toward the Empire, wrote:

"Americans are on the whole not very interested in history. Temperamentally they look forward, not back. They feel themselves to be part of a young nation with new horizons opening out ahead. They are still going places. Nothing is finished yet. Everything can still be bigger than it was yesterday. The nation's emotional capital is invested in ideas of freedom and equality which they feel belong in a particular way to the United States. Whatever folk memories there may be, are all tied up with the affirmation of individual liberty—the Pilgrim Fathers, the War of Independence, the Covered Wagon, the Civil War were all connected with different aspects of human freedom. Today, when the President defines American war aims, he naturally turns to the idea of 'Four Freedoms.'

"Not by any stretch of the imagination can the people of Britain be called a young people. They have far too much self-conscious history behind them. Nor to the superficial observer is Britain an equalitarian community. It has moated granges and belted earls; in the movies, through which most Americans get their mental picture of Britain, castles and aristocrats are much in evidence. And attached to Britain is an Empire out of which the Americans fought their way to independence. It is astonishing how many do not realize that Canada, Australia and New Zealand found another way out. It is perhaps not so astonishing that the Indian crisis (1942) is naively interpreted in terms of royal absolutism, colonial servitude and stiff-necked imperialism with Mr. Churchill in the role of George the Third, Mr. Amery that of Lord North and the Congress Party that of the American Insurgents . . . 'Could not your aristocrats abandon their hold on Malaya?' Incredible though it may seem, this question has been asked in all seriousness at the end of a public meeting in the United States. It illustrates in a crude form the general vague connection in the American mind between a class-ridden society in Britain and imperialist sway over subject peoples. The depth and proportions of American ignorance in the most obvious matters of Empire policy and government are unbelievable."

True it is that Americans still are not very conscious of history or tradition, although they are becoming more and more so as age inexorably throws its blanket about them. Yet one of the basic errors they make in judging the British Empire is to regard the Empire of today as being what it was from a half century to three and a half centuries ago. No stigma was attached to the idea of empire when the British were founding theirs; indeed it was not until this century that sin became generally associated with empire. And then the motives of him who has shouted that empire is sinful needed to be closely scanned, for more than likely he was merely being covetous. The German-Italian-Japanese attempt in this century to make the world sensitive to the existence of "haves and have-nots" had nothing to do with international morality. It had to do with a proposed division of the spoils, with a shifting of colonial domains from one jurisdiction to another, and for prestige more than for economic reasons.

The backbone of present empires originally consisted of areas in which there was no organization higher than tribal society, or where political organization was on a low level and native ruling princes made treaties with the imperialists. The only armed conflict that resulted between the intruders and the natives was between "interests"—traders and pirates—not between peoples. And the intruders themselves usually were traders, not governments acting in the name of an entire people. When the traders got into trouble, they frequently had difficulty persuading their own governments to help them. In those early days, too, empires could fight each other without the conflict being felt beyond the professional fighting classes of the populations. Today, the situation is entirely different. Few backward areas remain which are not in one manner or another under the tutelage of some great power. This means that a country starting out now to build an empire or to expand an existing one runs headlong into some major power. The masses today have far greater say and far greater interest in their governments than they used to have, and science has made the world much smaller. The combination of the two conditions produces world conflict instead of the localized squabbles of old. The fury of disruptive and destructive world conflicts has bred wide indignation against war and him who starts one. Moreover, there is a sensitivity about the treatment of backward areas which did not exist when present empires came into being. These areas no longer are regarded as objects of exploitation pure and simple. The trend is toward suffrance of empires only so long as they are trustees and mentors of the natives. Empire morality today is concerned with what the holders of empires are doing to foster the advancement of their charges.

The fact that the British have an empire is not in itself blameworthy. The important thing is what they are doing with it. Are they in tune with the times? The answer is that they are. They move more slowly than many would like, but they do move. Imperialist powers are not in the habit of getting far ahead of the procession. Most critics talk as if all the colonial components of the Empire would be enjoying hilarious independence if the British were not present. It must not be forgotten that if the British were not there, some other power would be. It is indeed a question whether the colonial peoples would be as advanced today as they are if they had been under other rule. No other power, at least, would have done better. It is quite possible for an American to go into British colonies and come away utterly disgusted. It is also possible for an American to go into dependencies under the Stars and Stripes and come away equally disturbed. The glasses worn have much to do with it. I visited an American mission hospital on Bahrein Island in the Persian Gulf where the "desert doctor," Paul W. Harrison, of Nebraska, has been working among the Arabs for decades. Dr. Harrison was pleased to show me his hospital but he was somewhat concerned as to the glasses I was wearing. What color were they? He was at pains to explain that I should not judge what I was going to see by hospital standards in the United States. Indeed if I had, I would have been less favorably impressed. As it was, I marveled at his accomplishments among the natives, considering the poor materials he had at hand with which to work.

One does not have to agree with Professor Gilbert Murray when he says, in speaking about India, that "I doubt if there has ever been in human history an Empire which has tried so long and hard to divest itself of power over a subject nation" in order to appreciate the British contribution. Perhaps "contribution" is not an apt word, for whatever benefits the British have bestowed have been by-products. They did not deliberately set out to do good unto others. Their acts fall into the category of self-interest, but the value is none the less real. In spite of the fact that the bringing of Western civilization to some Africans and Orientals tends to make wretches of them, none can deny that on the whole wherever the British have been, government, sanitation and economy have been bettered. Wherever sufficient progress has been made, there has been advancement from one category to another within the Empire. The greatest progress naturally has been made by those colonies where Europeans settled in large numbers.

The Empire has evolved from beginnings made in the sixteenth century by daring traders who, like the Portuguese, Spanish, Dutch and French, sailed the seas in search of riches. Their modern counterparts are the buyers, scientists and salesmen of big corporations and combines who roam the world searching for raw materials and markets. From the time when the early traders found the spices and jewels of the East, fortunes were built and the gold rush was on. Individuals and groups of individuals sent out ships and realized handsomely on the exotic products that came back in the holds. There were risks, of course, and sometimes the ships were wrecked or fell afoul of pirates and the ships' backers went bankrupt. Traders from other countries were competing in this lucrative business and gradually it became the fashion to try to monopolize sources of supply and markets. That desire for monopoly was exactly the same then as it is today among the big industrial empires.

The Dutch in the sixteenth century had won a monopoly of trade with the Spice Islands whence came pepper, the price of which the Dutch had more than doubled. To meet this competition, the East India Company was formed of men who had been trading in the East. It was an act of defense. A century later, Queen Elizabeth chartered the Company as "The Governor and Company of Merchants of London trading with the East Indies." It was to have a monopoly of British trade in the vast area beyond the Cape of Good Hope or the Straits of Magellan. Unauthorized traders were liable to forfeiture of their ships and cargo. There were one hundred and twenty-five shareholders, whose profits rarely fell below the tidy return of 100 per cent. The Company fared so well that James the First in 1609 renewed the Charter "forever," but it could be revoked upon a three-year notice if trade ever fell so low that the Crown felt it was no longer profitable to the realm. The Company made agreements with local rulers for monopoly trade and built forts for protection against pirates. It even built small workshops. In India the Company gradually assumed ruling control over some areas, again as a means of protecting its business.

The year 1689 is usually considered the date when business got mixed up seriously with government in India. As men connected with big concerns today drop out and start their own businesses, so then men connected with the East India Company went out on their own to get a share of the fabulous profits. These were called "interlopers." Eventually the question as to whether the Crown had a right to establish a monopoly of Indian trade was raised and the courts decided it had. Interloping continued nonetheless. There were so many interlopers that they formed a new company. The dispute went into Parliament, which decided that only Parliament could prevent an Englishman from trading in the East Indies; the Crown could not. Parliament then began to tap the East India Company's profits. After its decision that any Englishman could trade if he desired, the East India Company manœuvred to regain its monopoly. It was allowed to reorganize—but it had to lend the state two million pounds. A few years later the two rival companies amalgamated, in return for which they lent the state another three million pounds. The Company thus became a good source for loans and Parliament took advantage of it at will; it even kept the Company alive for that purpose beyond a point when it should have been replaced by a formal governmental organization.

As the Company's governmental functions in India became more and more elaborate, the British Government step by step subjected the Company's acts to the will of Parliament. Indicative of the principal interest of the British Government is the fact that the monopoly of trade was taken away from the Company before its governing rights. Its India trade monopoly was removed in 1813 and its China trade monopoly in 1833, but it was allowed to continue administering territory over which it had gained control. It was not until the Indian Mutiny of 1857 that the Company was finally shorn of its extraordinary powers and its territories were taken over by the Crown. Queen Victoria became Empress of India in 1876. Thus a business that started in the sixteenth century ended in the nineteenth century with the British Government falling heir to a problem of empire that has still to be resolved.

The East India Company did not confine all of its operations to the Orient. It sold its products wherever it could and thus became involved in North America. It was the East India Company's three hundred and forty chests of tea that were dumped unceremoniously into Boston Harbor in 1773. England's colonies along the Atlantic seaboard of the North American continent were Europeans with a cultural level equal to that of England. They did not intend to be the butt of exploitation, and even before they really had sufficient strength to assert their will, they asserted it anyway. With outside help, they won. Nothing has ever prevented other parts of the Empire, including the Indians, from doing likewise except their own lack of development.

The East India Company is a good example of how the empire started and how it grew. It was not alone, for, as the centuries passed, other traders opened up different areas to colonization, thus adding to the Empire's size. Business motives varied in accordance with the development of industry in Great Britain. And as the Empire grew, the question of protection arose; from time to time other bits of territory here and there were added for strategic purposes.

Some historians divide Great Britain's Empire history into three parts. The First Empire operated on the "mercantilist" theory held by imperialist powers of the time. Colonies existed for the purpose of supplying products to the mother country and in return taking manufactured articles from the mother country. The British Empire was not to trade with the Dutch Empire; they were, in fact, to fight each other. All too many critics of empire today argue as if that condition still existed. The Second Empire began with the defeat of Napoleon and brought to Britain the golden Victorian age. The industrial revolution in Britain changed the outlook of businessmen, and the water-tight system of the First Empire gave way to free trade. Exploitation pure and simple was on its way out. New Zealand, Canada, Australia and South Africa, in order, received measures of self-government. Treaties signed by Britain had applied to the colonies too, but in the latter part of the last century, colonies were permitted to sit in on the negotiation of commercial treaties. This led to permission for the self-governing colonies to accept or reject British commercial treaties as they desired. But all political treaties negotiated by the British had to be accepted by the colonies, self-governing or not, right up to World War I.

The Third Empire issued from World War I. An Imperial Conference in 1926 cast the die and the Statute of Westminster of 1931 formally made it legal. As it exists today, the Empire has two parts which overlap occasionally: the Commonwealth of Nations and the Colonies. The Commonwealth is composed of the United Kingdom, Canada, Australia, New Zealand, South Africa and the Irish Free State. In the words accepted at the 1926 Conference, these parts of the Empire are "autonomous Communities within the British Empire, equal in status, in no way subordinate one to another in any aspect of their domestic or external affairs, though united by a common allegiance to the Crown, and freely associated as members of the British Commonwealth of Nations . . . Every self-governing member of the Empire is now the master of its destiny. In fact, if not always in form, it is subject to no compulsion whatever." The Statute of Westminster of 1931 declared that no act of the Parliament of the United Kingdom was to apply to a Dominion unless "it is expressly declared in that Act that that Dominion has requested and consented to the enactment thereof." The Statute further provided that "inasmuch as the Crown is the symbol of the free association of the members of the British Commonwealth of Nations, and as they are united by a common allegiance to the Crown, it would be in accord with the established constitutional position of all the members of the Commonwealth in relation to one another that any alteration in the law touching the Succession to the Throne or the Royal Style and Titles shall hereafter require the assent as well of the Parliaments of all the Dominions as of the Parliament of the United Kingdom."

Canada, Australia, New Zealand, South Africa and the Irish Free State were placed on a par with the United Kingdom, the mother country. They all have the same king but the acts of one do not bind another. The United Kingdom's declaration of war in 1939 did not automatically carry the other members of the Commonwealth into the conflict. Except Eire, which remained neutral, they all came along later of their own free will. They follow the United Kingdom only when they desire. In a grave matter such as the war, they desired to act with the United Kingdom. What puzzles so many people is that the desire to remain closely associated is so strong. Americans are apt to think of their own break for independence and wonder what sort of persons the Canadians, Australians, New Zealanders, and South Africans can be, that they, too, have not broken away from the mother country.

They merely solved their problems in a different way from ours, and now they find compatibility within the Empire. We paved the way for their present working arrangement, for our insurrection administered a sound lesson to the motherland. The Dominions send diplomatic representatives abroad wherever they wish. Where they do not feel it necessary to spend money on diplomatic establishments, they ask the British Foreign Office to look out for their interests. The King's direct tie with the Dominions is a Governor General, but his functions are mostly ceremonial. The United Kingdom maintains a High Commissioner in London. Shortly after the last war, the Dominions Office of the British Government was divorced from the Colonial Office as one of the acts signaling the advance of the Dominions from colonial to independent status. The Dominions Office became a sort of intermediary between the United Kingdom and the Dominions, but its functions are gradually being taken over by the Foreign Office and its elimination should not be far off. The matter of protection from foreign foes, however, was left almost entirely to the Royal Navy. In theory the British fleet is the King's and inasmuch as the King of the United Kingdom is also the King of the Dominions, it was the Monarch who was charged with protecting his domains. In practice, the Royal Navy is the United Kingdom's burden although some financial help is received from the Dominions. It is spread out over the world and in normal times it proved sufficient. But the Australians and New Zealanders found when Japan struck in this war that they were left helplessly unprotected. Canada and Australia have had a few warships of their own but by no means enough. Neither could afford to maintain a military estalishment of sufficient size to protect it from a powerful enemy. Canada has been more fortunate than any other Dominion because she has not had to rely on the Royal Navy. She knows that

United States military might would be at her side in case of attack and the world knows it too. Canada, therefore, has not been a tempting prize, but Australia, and New Zealand, lying alone in the Southwest Pacific, looked to the Japanese like a ripe apple. The United States had to rescue Australia and New Zealand, but it was a close call. The matter of future protection in that area too, greatly disturbs the peoples of those Dominions.

The Commonwealth thus is a loose affair technically held together by the Crown, which is nothing more than a symbol, but actually it is bound more by blood and sentiment than anything else. In no other way could the Commonwealth exist. The day-to-day connection is maintained through the High Commissioners, but general policy is debated and decided by Imperial Conferences called whenever it is felt one is needed.

The Colonial portion of the Empire is quite another matter. Most of the colonies are the concern of the United Kingdom government, but Australia, New Zealand and South Africa have colonial territories under their wings. Australia, for example, has taken over British New Guinea and South Africa has Zululand, while Australia, New Zealand and South Africa received mandates under the League of Nations. There is growing agitation in the Dominions for the right to control those colonies of the Empire which lie in their respective areas.

There are so many different forms of governments in the dependencies that to disentangle them all would require a full volume. Generally speaking, there are four categories: Colonies which are considered British territory with the inhabitants being British subjects; Protectorates, which are foreign territory with the native inhabitants enjoying no rights as British subjects; Protected States, whose inhabitants owe allegiance to a local Sovereign; and Mandated Territories. Within these categories are many different governmental practices which reflect the British aptitude for improvisation to meet a given situation.

The most advanced of the colonies are those which have a large percentage of white settlers. The next are those with inhabitants of other than Western culture but which have progressed to a sufficient cultural level. The lowest form, or that in which the greatest amount of control from London is in evidence, are those with peoples of primitive culture. The degree of local self-government depends upon the degree of literacy. Theoretically, each dependency is free to advance from one stage to another, like a child going through grammar school, up to Dominion status. Actually, only the colonies where whites are predominant make much progress in this direction and some are too small to be able to assume independent status. Newfoundland rose to Dominionship and then had to revert to a Crown colony when it discovered that independence was not wholly an unmixed blessing. Ceylon with its Orientals, however, is close to the top rank and Southern Rhodesia, where there are only 62,000 whites as against 1,300,000 blacks, is nearing it.

In general, where local inhabitants have had it in them, they have moved upward. The chief criticism of the British is leveled at their practices in the more backward dependencies and in India. India is like a sore thumb on the Empire; it requires special treatment and most British considerations of Empire policy leave India out as being beyond the competence of ordinary mortals. Attacks against the colonial administration reached their height while the Japanese were brushing through Burma, Malaya and other colonial dependencies, whether British, French or Dutch. It was charged that the natives were not giving help against the Japanese enemy because they saw no difference between the Japanese and the British. The British, it was said, had failed to exert themselves toward raising the standard of living and were, in fact, attempting to keep the natives in permanent subjection. The general tenor of the criticism was that if more had been done for the natives the Japanese would never have been able to accomplish the swift conquests that took them majestically southward to the Dutch Indies and the borders of Australia. Such statements were made in the heat of battle and while the problem of how to stop the Japanese staggered the imagination. Calmer consideration, however, brought realization that even if the colonial peoples had been as free as birds, they could have done little more than they did. The great fortress of Singapore fell without undue ceremony and it did not fall because natives were disgusted with the British and refused to help defend it. The Philippines fell, too, although there was supposed to be a better atmosphere existing there as between the United States and the Filipinos who fought gallantly for their islands. The Filipino fight often has been pointed to as proof of what other Orientals would have done had they been treated right. It is rather an indication that Japan's military machine would by no means have been stalled regardless of the relationship between the colonizing power and the natives.

Two things about the Empire that are not widely realized are that it is not held together by force and that no part of the Empire pays tribute to the mother country. One of the amazing things has been the small number of troops stationed in the dependencies. The United Kingdom would not have the manpower to garrison all of the dependencies sufficiently if it were a matter of holding them by force. The Royal Navy's policing of the oceans, of course, has been effective in this respect, for wherever the Navy could find waters deep enough to navigate, natives knew that it would come to shell them if they rebelled. However, the navy alone could not stop rebellion. India, for example, is a subcontinent that could not be subdued by the shelling of Bombay and Calcutta if the Indians really were prepared to take the independence they claim.

Some Empire apologists of recent times have gone so far as to say that colonies are really burdens. If that were true, the market would be glutted with cheap bits of land and millions of blacks. Such statements were based on the fact that Britain has found it necessary to vote large sums of money for some dependencies. Instead of receiving revenue from colonies, Britain sends it to the colonies. That is a fact, but it still does not prove that colonies are a burden. Profit of business transactions with the colonies still remains higher than the amount Britain votes for assistance, although Britain shares the colonial trade about equally with other countries. Colonial profit has, however, been declining, while the relationship between prosperity at home and prosperity in the colonies has been drawing closer and closer. The less the colonies are prospering and advancing, the less the colonizer receives in business returns. This is his urge to see to it that the colonial is treated fairly and to refrain from the sort of exploitation fashionable in another century.

Although Englishmen of all shades of opinion have come to the defense of the Empire in the face of accusations resulting from war experience, they have not been so blind as to insist that the status quo should or can go on forever. But they resent the free advice they hear coming across the Atlantic. As to the future, there is no division of opinion in regard to who is to continue to exercise the legal responsibilities in the Empire; all insist that Britain should not yield a single colony to another power. But there is a body of opinion receptive to the idea of sharing colonial tasks with those countries "as ready to accept responsibility as to offer advice, as ready to share burdens as benefits," to quote the words of Mr. Herbert Morrison. The true problem, however, is how to better the conditions of the natives and not how to divide up with other powers. British Socialists would have the Government take a hand in developing resources in the interests of colonial peoples. Private concerns with their narrower interests would be superseded by more impartial governmental agencies, not dissimilar to Mr. Henry Wallace's WPA idea for developing backward areas. Other schemes such as the creation of international authorities in different areas likewise do not involve changes in sovereignty. The Institute of Pacific Relations meeting in Canada in 1942 proposed an International Council for the Pacific Zone. Its purpose would be primarily defense against prowlers (with the Japanese in mind) but it would also interest itself in colonial development. Field Marshal Smuts of South Africa has proposed a more limited arrangement which would give to the Dominions a greater share in the administration of colonies. He would decentralize the Empire, taking it away from London and putting it in Pretoria, Canberra, Ottawa and Wellington. The Dominions would administer the colonies nearest to them and "bring their resources and their experience to bear in the development of the colonies." With an eye to American criticism and expansionist tendency, he also publicly expressed the view that the United States should have a say in the West Indies off the American coast, and perhaps elsewhere too.

These proposals for widening responsibility arose from the Pacific war, where it was made amply clear that the British could not protect their possessions when they are attacked by a major power. They were stated when victory hung precariously in the balance. As soon as there was no longer any question about the war's outcome, the more drastic proposals began to fade. Nonetheless, there has been a rebirth of the idea of trusteeship, the idea that colonial territories are held only in trust until the natives can develop far enough to govern themselves. That is the direction future colonial policy may be expected to take. It is, in fact, the basis of the British Empire system, however numerous may be the aberrations to which one can point.

On the whole, the British have nothing to be ashamed of. The citizens of Main Street should know that colonial practices of the past which now seem abhorrent were not so considered at the time, any more than certain things that took place on Main Street a century ago were then viewed as being intolerable. The Empire has developed according to accepted notions of the times and it must continue to do so·or it will crumble.

7

NEAR EAST, FAR EAST

An Englishman walks into a place as if he owns it; an American walks in as if he did not give a damn who owns it. Those attitudes accounted for a good deal of the personal friction between the two in the Near East and the Far East. The farther East one traveled, the more pronounced became mutual suspicion. Americans looked askance at those Englishmen who treated non-British peoples with scorn and condescension, while Englishmen suspiciously watched Americans who exuded a feeling of complete indifference whether the English had priority rights or not. Americans assumed the attitude that Englishmen had no cause for affront just because Americans walked in with that don't-give-a-damn attitude. The feeling was aggravated by the natives and by frequent statements in the United States to the effect that the United States should retain for post-war uses many of the bases and rights obtained to further the war against the common enemy. The natives took a hand by favoring the Americans and whispering into their ears how much they hated the English.

Regardless of what high policy on either side was aimed at being, on lower levels there was a constant tug of war. The Colonial Office in London and its branches in the field have become so traditionalized over the centuries that it takes terrific pressure to shake them loose from narrow conceptions. The Foreign Office, which must be abreast of current conditions, may follow one policy while the Colonial Office follows another. Hence not infrequently the latter sets about to sabotage the work of the Foreign Office. When this happens, nothing will correct it but direct orders from the Prime Minister.

Not dissimilar was the situation created by the multiple agencies war brought to Washington. One agency would go ahead without consulting others, and where more than one was operating in the same field, clashes in practices and policies frequently occurred. This incongruous situation could be rectified only by direct orders from the President. When neither Prime Minister Churchill nor President Roosevelt was sure of what the best interests of his country were, or when one or the other was willing that manœuvring should go on on the side, jockeying for position became a preoccupation. That, generally, was what happened in our relations with the British in the Near and Far East.

Our approach to Asia from the Pacific presented no problems other than military ones. It was exclusively an American show, and there were no British possessions (Australia and New Zealand are not possessions) in the path of size and importance worth troubling much about. Our approach from the land side, however, was quite different. Getting at the Japanese on land meant establishing bases in India, and as soon as possible after Pearl Harbor a skeleton military organization began to appear in India. The military program at that time was quite vague but it was foreseen that eventually an American force might be needed in India. As for the political program, there was none, excepting that China had to be maintained as a going concern; and that at the time was more a military than it was a strictly political consideration.

The United States entered the Near East by way of Lend-Lease before Pearl Harbor. We were assisting in opening the Persian Gulf route for the carrying of supplies to Russia and in supplying the British desert armies in Egypt. By the early part of 1942, we were entering the region from Egypt to Afghanistan in earnest. A big supply base was constructed in Italian Eritrea, a Red Sea colony considered to be far enough off the beaten track should Marshal

Rommel succeed in smashing through to the Suez Canal. That base fortunately never had to be used to the extent forecast.

American assistance in building up the Eighth Army to enable it to make the brilliant campaign that it did under General Montgomery was of great importance. The British had operated throughout the Near East on the barest minimum of equipment and manpower. That was the principal reason for a number of faltering steps and disastrous defeats. A thousand and one American irons were put into the fire. These included: our direct aid to the British armies, the trans-continental air transport route to India and China, and our assumption of responsibility for completing the Persian route to Russia for keeping war material flowing into the U.S.S.R. To accomplish these things meant scattering American service troops over thousands of miles from Africa's Atlantic coastline to India. They manned airfields in darkest Africa and on islands in the seas; they established an elaborate weather reporting system for the protection of the planes flying this extraordinary wartime airline which, at its eastern end, for long was the only connecting link with China. Saudi Arabia was the only country in the Near East where Yanks in uniform were not to be found. In those countries where they were not officially stationed, as in Turkey, they could be seen in the role of sightseers. For that matter, the lifting of a robe in Saudi Arabia not infrequently would reveal an American general in disguise. But not ordinary doughboys.

Modern installations were built of a nature never before seen in those areas. Payne Field, near Cairo, sprang out of desert sand to eclipse anything the British had in that country. Near by, a modern army camp with barracks and buildings of brick was built, while a few miles away British troops lived under canvas. The theater in that American army camp was far better than most cinema houses in large American cities. It boasted of Hollywood premières. A general hospital was connected with the camp and its modernity was equal to that of the camp's other installations. All these installations were to revert to the British or to the Egyptians, whichever got there first. This fact was a source of irritation to some American quarters in Cairo and the British knew it.

We also became interested in raw materials throughout the Near East and in their exploitation and distribution. There was some feeling in the United States that not all sources of primary supplies under British control were being used to their utmost and that something should be done to relieve the burden placed on the United States as the principal supply house of the war. Mr. James M. Landis, who had served the Government in several capacities, was sent to Cairo to represent American interests and to centralize Lend-Lease flowing to and from seventeen different countries. His task was to signal Washington whenever he thought a brake should be applied. He soon was looked upon by the British as an exponent of a policy aimed at interfering with British post-war markets.

Cairo became a center for the propagation of American interests among the Arabs. Traditionally, the Near East has been an Anglo-French domain with the Germans and Italians getting fingers in wherever they could. Our pre-war stake was limited. There were American mission schools and other philanthropic ventures here and there. American Zionists had influenced Washington to continue taking official notice of the Palestine question. Our interference, however gentle, has been a source of concern to the British. The Arab peoples have opposed the creation of a Jewish state in their midst and the British have found it very difficult to satisfy both sides. Britain wished neither to offend the Jews nor to stir up the Arabs, who, in the years preceding the war, were heavily propagandized by both the Italians and Germans. The British need the Arabs in peacetime as well as in wartime. Arab countries of the Near East were sorely disappointed after the last war when they failed to realize ambitions which they were encouraged to believe they would achieve in return for aid to the British. Disappointed, too, was T. E. Lawrence, "Lawrence of Arabia," who was the intermediary in the promises. Creation of a Jewish home in Palestine tended further to weaken the British in Arab eyes. Although the British must manage to get on with the Arabs, powerful Jewish influence in 1917 induced Lord Balfour, then foreign secretary, to issue a statement favoring such a home. That statement became known as the Balfour Declaration and it was subsequently accepted by the principal allies. It said that the British Government "view with favor the establishment in Palestine of a national home for the Jewish people, and will use their best endeavours to facilitate the achievement of that object, it being understood that nothing shall be done which may prejudice the civil and religious rights of existing non-Jewish communities . . ."

After the war, Britain assumed a mandate over Palestine under the League of Nations. Although the national home plan had obtained international support, the British were the principal ones concerned. It was soon discovered that fulfillment of the Balfour Declaration would not be easy. No satisfactory solution has yet been found and with the multiple problems presented by this war, the British were not very grateful for pro-Zionist expressions of opinion and sentiment on the part of Americans, most of whom were neither conversant with the history of the question nor conscious of the responsibility involved.

United States trade with the Near East before the war was not of a nature to make or break anyone, and for this reason some agencies in Washington took the view that after the war we should have a larger share. American oil companies, however, had been operating in the area for years. Oil being the big natural resource of the Near East and the main attraction for Western countries, it was inevitable that it should become involved in some manner in Anglo-American rivalry. Until Mr. Harold L. Ickes took a hand in his capacity as Petroleum Administrator, rivalry in this field had been confined to private companies, although the British oil companies had official diplomatic assistance. Mr. Ickes quoted figures to show that America's domestic wells were fast being exhausted and that it was therefore time for the Government to start assuring the country of a foreign supply. He wanted to associate the Government with oil companies in a project to build a fifteen-hundred-mile pipeline from Saudi Arabia's eastern wells across desert sands to a Mediterranean port. The Saudi Arabian concession is held by an American company. At the time the proposal was made, early in 1944, the need for oil in the Mediterranean had passed and it already appeared that the entire war in Europe might be over before such a pipeline could be completed. Whatever the merits of that specific proposal, it was opposed by the British Government and the American companies as well. It got nowhere, leaving the broad problem of an American government foreign oil policy unsolved. But it gave a fillip to the misunderstanding mutually enjoyed by the British and

Americans in the Near and Far East. It was a feeling which, unhappily, tended to interfere with efficiency.

In Turkey, a country standing on its own feet, no such problems were involved. The United States supported British diplomacy there with Lend-Lease. It was in the interest of both the United States and Britain that Turkey should not join with the Axis. Just before the war started, Britain and France concluded a treaty with the Turks which was aimed at preventing the Turks from joining the Germans as they did in the last war. The Turks were to receive arms and equipment, but when France collapsed, the treaty lost its validity and Britain could not fulfill her side of the agreement. That is where the United States came in. Lend-Lease supplied what Britain was to have provided. Turkey produced products which were badly needed by the Allies and by Germany too. A competition between Germany and the Allies arose with each attempt to monopolize the output. The Turks steered a middle course, with perhaps a slight edge given to the Allies. In sympathy, if not always in acts, the Turks were pro-Ally. They were getting American planes, tanks and other equipment. But their whole policy was to remain neutral. At first that was all the British desired. Turkey was a barrier to German intentions in the Near East. Later, Britain wanted at least to use Turkish bases. Twice Prime Minister Churchill left conferences with the Turkish Foreign Minister believing that soon the Turks would break with Germany and the Allies would get the use of Turkish bases whence to strike at the Germans in the Balkans and the islands of the Aegean Sea. But twice the fish wiggled from his hook.

Eventually, the Turks themselves became concerned. Was the war to end with them still neutral and thus having a weak claim to consideration in the peace settlement? To overcome this they broke diplomatic relations with Germany (but did not declare war) when it was certain beyond the shadow of a doubt that the Axis was beaten.

CENSORSHIP

The British by tradition abhor censorship. Even wartime Britain has been most liberal in spirit and in fact, although there was legitimate reason to impose restrictions of the severest sort. At times stringent supervision of the press and radio was necessary, but invariably it was lifted as soon as the particular danger had passed.

Against that background, the censorship the British have maintained from Cairo eastward becomes most striking. It has been the war's worst, with the possible exception of the Chinese censorship. There is a theoretical wall somewhere in the desert which stops news from flowing either way. What gets behind that wall is just as heavily censored as is what goes out. Newspapers of Egypt and all through the Near and Far East are fed queer reading items. It is difficult to recognize a good democratic debate in the House of Commons. Criticism of the Government is either omitted or, where the subject is of major importance and it cannot be ignored, it is twisted ridiculously. Natives are not supposed to know that differences of opinion exist in the Allied world. As for outgoing news, correspondents who have labored in that vineyard are prematurely gray. Anything indicating even by implication that the British authorities are having difficulty is blue-penciled; anything connected with disturbances or dissatisfaction is forbidden material. Even items on the permissible list are treated with stunning lack of intelligence. And in peacetime censorship practice there is not much better.

There is something about the Near and Far East that warps Western minds. Perhaps it is merely that censorship is a necessary part of imperialism; there is so much about imperialism that needs hiding. But there is more to it than that. American officials out there, although lacking the imperialistic excuse, settle down quickly into much the same state of mind. An American general with an important command fell into the routine of the East with relish. Beyond the regular wartime censorship rules established by the War Department, this general imposed his own whims. His command had the ordinary censors trained in the United States for their jobs. Most American theater commanders require censors to refer to higher levels all news copy involving policy. This general, however, required everything to be sent to him or to the colonel designated by him to be his public promoter. The general's definition of "policy" was all-inclusive: any reflection, however slight, upon the general himself or his command was eliminated. As one of his own censors remarked to me, "If you write that a rock is lying in the driveway of the camp, no matter what you mean by it, the General will cut it out, for he thinks that rock should not be there and hence it is a personal reflection on him." Compare that with the policy General Eisenhower laid down for his much more important command, prior to D-Day: "Write anything you want about the generals and the commanders"—then he paused—"even say they ought to be removed if you think you are justified. On political matters there will be absolutely no censorship." The General was in England when he said that. Prior to that, he had been in Africa where his policy was not as liberal, although it was by no means as petty as was that of the general with the rock.

FAR EAST

Rare it is that man rises above selfish interest even in moments of direst distress. That being so, no base for land operations in Asia could have been found where friction would have been absent. Indo-China excepted, the British have claims staked out in all countries. Indo-China is a French preserve. India was the only location possible for a base, as the Japanese had overrun Indo-China, Burma, Thailand, Malaya and parts of China. Indian nationalists had seized upon Britain's plight to resume agitation for independence. The Japanese were moving toward India, and the frail exponent of non-violence, Mohandas Gandhi, the leader of the Congress Party (nationalist), was exhorting Indians to do nothing to help halt the threatening invader. It was not that Gandhi saw no difference between the Japanese and the British as overlords; he was too well-informed and too intelligent for that. It was chiefly that he believed it was wrong to raise a finger against an aggressor. When the war started in Europe, he advised Britain to permit Hitler to conquer her! Obviously, no such policy could be followed. As much help as possible had to be mustered in India or the Japs would have taken all the Far East, including China. India provided the only access Britain and the United States had to China, and China, after many years of warfare, was in no position to stand alone.

The Indian question is most complicated. The subcontinent is hopelessly cut up politically as a result of its peculiar development. There are 562 states, from one the size of France to others as small as plantations. They have their own rulers who control everything except foreign affairs, which are handled by the Viceroy as the British Emperor's delegate. Besides the states, there is British India proper where British control is more thorough, although there is self-government. The Indian states form two-fifths of the total area. Sixty-eight per cent of the population is Hindu and 22 per cent is Moslem, with the rest scattered among different races. It is a rural country with 89 per cent of the population living on the land. Moslems and Hindus are sharply divided religiously, although critics of British policy maintain that these differences have been exaggerated by the British in order to keep the country disunited. However, if at any time in the past the Indians had come together, nothing on earth could have prevented them from taking independence. At the outset of this war, there were only 57,000 British regular troops in that vast country with a population of 388,800,000.

But Moslems are afraid of the Hindu majority, and within this larger conflict, many others divide the people. Forced by Gandhi's agitation, the British in March, 1942, rushed a mission to India headed by the liberal Sir Stafford Cripps. Post-war independence was offered, with Dominion status, which includes the right to secede from the Empire. The Indians were to draw their own Constitution after the war, but, deferring to the Moslems, the proposal stipulated that any province of British India not desiring to accept the new Constitution could remain aloof. Gandhi, leader of the largest political group, rejected the proposal because it did not grant immediate independence and it paved the way for the Moslems to create a separate state. Gandhi's Congress Party promoted strikes which had to be put down by force. Party leaders were arrested and they went back to jails whose walls have been thoroughly familiar to them for years.

Although a high percentage of the people live on the land, India is one of the eight leading industrial countries of the world. Her factories have increased since the war began and their output has been of great service to the war effort. Her shipyards have been building small warships and her troops have fought with the British in the West as well as the East. The troops for the most part come from princely states on good terms with the British. In spite of this contribution, the country as a whole has remained passive.

Given the importance of India in the United States effort to prevent China from collapsing, some United States officials took the view that Indian politics were a matter of concern to us. It was foreseen at the time that a land attack against Japan proper would have to come from China, and the way to China was through India. So any disturbance that might prevent the use of India was regarded as a vital matter to us. Moreover, some of the United States officials were looking further ahead. They felt India should be prevented from joining an anti-white bloc about which there was a great deal of talk during the early part of the war in the Pacific. It was feared that the Chinese, Indo-Chinese, Burmese, Malayans and the Indonese might fall in with the Japanese slogan of the Orient for the Orientals. There were many differences among the Orientals, but the literates entertained anti-white sentiments strong enough to form a possible ground for unity. Some of these people have since learned not to take stock in Japanese good faith in leading such a movement, but that has not destroyed anti-white sentiment. The Chinese, for example, have amply displayed their intentions in regard to the Japanese, but that has not diminished a whit their dislike of Western imperialism.

Those in the United States Government who were impressed with the anti-white bloc possibility believed that the British should go further in India and grant outright independence at a specific date after the war, with an immediate provisional coalition cabinet of limited powers. They did not believe that the British Government was serious when it made the Cripps proposals in 1942. They believed that a "generous gesture" on the part of the British would dispel bad feelings and lead not only the peoples of India but others throughout the East to pitch in and help defeat Japan. As has since been demonstrated, their fears of an explosion in India that would disrupt Allied war plans were unfounded. Moreover, the value of whatever additional aid could have been realized by a generous British gesture toward India was undoubtedly exaggerated. If the philosophy of Mohandas Gandhi had prevailed after such a gesture was made, the usefulness of India would have been diminished, not augmented.

Hindu nationalists have long had a nimble propaganda service in the United States. They are familiar with the soft spots in the American's heart. They were eager for the United States officially to urge the British to take the final step. When that was not forthcoming, word was spread around India that American troops were there to support British tenure! President Roosevelt took notice of this in a carefully worded statement which he gave to the press in February of 1944. He said, "Nobody in India or anywhere else in Asia will misunderstand the presence there of the American armed forces if they will believe, as we do, that their job is to assure the defeat of Japan without which there can be no opportunity for any of us to enjoy and expand the freedoms for which we fight."

The British and American military commands in Asia did not achieve the same degree of unity that their counterparts in the West enjoyed under General Eisenhower. When the Japanese drove General Joseph W. Stilwell, American commander of the Chinese Fifth and Sixth Armies, out of Burma in May, 1942, they placed the Allies in a most difficult position. From then on, opinions differed widely as to how best to get back at the Japanese with the limited forces available. The appointment in August, 1943, of Admiral Lord Louis Mountbatten as the overall commander-in-chief in Southeast Asia did not end the differences. Generally speaking, the Americans centered their attention on direct relief for China while the British tended to think more in terms of getting the Japanese out of lower Burma, Thailand and Malaya. It was being freely said both in the United States and in India that the British did not want Americans to help chase the Japanese out of those spheres which were distinctly under British influence, as in Malaya, for instance. The reason given was that the British feared the United States either would demand a share in the raw materials produced in those countries or would go to the other extreme and insist that the peoples of those countries be given independence if they so desired. Whatever the reasons behind the lack of unity, British colonial authorities in the Far East were very much on the defensive, with purely military considerations taking a back seat in favor of colonial interests.

This lack of harmony and the loose ends it left floating in the breeze were responsible for a certain concern on the American side lest Britain would not contribute her utmost when the time came to concentrate upon the Japanese. To anyone who did not know what was going on, it must have appeared most unusual that Prime Minister Churchill and Foreign Minister Anthony Eden took occasion so often for more than a year, to say publicly that Britain would put all her might into the fight against Japan. At the Quebec conference in September, 1944, when plans were made for the final phase of the campaign against Japan, Mr. Churchill insisted that the only point of difference at the conference was a United States reluctance to accept as much British aid as was offered.

The phenomenal success of the 1944 campaigns in the Pacific under Admiral Chester W. Nimitz and General Douglas MacArthur altered conceptions held in 1942 as to the importance India would have in the final stages of the effort to defeat the Island Empire. India was no longer an only hope; the American navy was pushing right in toward the heart of the Japanese Empire and the coast of China.

The Chinese have surpassed all other members of the United Nations in their long resistance to aggression. It is amazing that they have done it with such a small amount of equipment and with only a part of the country really heart and soul in the struggle. The small injections of life blood that came from the United States were barely enough to keep the heart beating. There were many alarms during the years of waiting for major Allied help; it was feared the feeble structure of the inflation-ridden country would topple. There were men within Chiang's Government who urged him to yield to the Japanese because the situation seemed hopeless. The more pressure the United States Navy and General MacArthur put on the Japs in the Pacific, the more ardently the Nipponese worked to save themselves by getting control of all China. They used all possible means to attain this end—arms in the field, diplomacy and bribery. From our side, everything that could be done had to be done to support Chiang, for in war plans as well as in post-war plans, China was cast in a big role. If Japan is to be prevented from breaking out as soon as she recovers from this escapade, it will be China's strength almost alone that will accomplish it. The future of Asia and the Southwest Pacific lies largely locked up in the mysticism of India and the struggle for unity in China.

China fell into this major role by default, but she has been accepted, in spite of her need for injections, as being on a par with Russia, Britain and the United States. In the world constellation, she was even placed above France: China was sitting at the world council table while France was not even supposed to exist! It was indescribable optimism to put China on such a level.

China is not united. She has not defeated the curse of warlordism. The dictatorship of General Chiang Kai-shek and the Kuomintang (the only party officially recognized in China) made some headway, but there are mountains still to cross. It is not possible to speak of "a" Chinese army. There are armies in China but the Generalissimo has not been able to dispose of them as he desired. He has had to make deals with the generals commanding the various armies to get them to fight where and how he wanted. With some he has not been able to come to terms. And this nationalist leader of resistance against Japan himself kept large forces tied up fighting communists when they should have been fighting Japan.

Chinese generals are not keen about fighting foreigners, especially better equipped ones. The weapons a general has on hand, he is apt to want for a better purpose—for maintaining himself in power. He does not want to risk losing his equipment for a cause he considers not directly concerned with his personal welfare. The Generalissimo himself is not above such methods. Corruption is another efficiency destroyer. When the full story of the Burma Road is told, it will reveal startling facts. War materials so painfully transported over ocean, mountain and jungle vanished into thin air along the life line, while boxes marked "ammunition," but containing merchandise for private sale, were hauled into the interior. An American colonel told me of going out along the road to get proof of the crookedness which he knew was rife. He stopped a truck, got an axe and hacked open a box labeled "ammunition." Out fell bolts of cloth!

Censorship in China was so strict that true conditions could not be related to the outside world. It was felt better for all concerned that the world should know instead about the intelligence and humanitarianism of the charming Madame Chiang. She was an excellent ambassadress, but her influence at home was extremely limited. And he who had gleaned his information about China only from a visit with her in Chungking, deluded himself.

Some of the facts about the state of affairs in China were allowed to pass censorship, which had been suppressing them in the interest of the war, when President Roosevelt acquiesced in Chiang's demand for the recall of General Stilwell in October 1944. In addition to being commander of the Chinese Fifth and Sixth Armies, "Vinegar Joe" Stilwell was the Generalissimo's chief of staff and commander of the United States Army forces in the China-Burma-India theater. He not only argued with the British over the advisability of opening the Burmese backdoor to China so that supplies could get through, but he argued with Chiang over the latter's failure to throw all of China's weight against the Japs. General Stilwell insisted that a large part of Lend-Lease materials should go to the United States forces which were using them against the enemy. When Washington stepped in more forcefully than it had been accustomed to doing and urged Chiang to stop internal fighting and consolidate all of China's strength against the Japs, the Generalissimo rebelled and asked for General Stilwell's recall.

The Chinese have it in them to do better and if given proper tutelage in the next quarter of a century, they may fulfill the role of being the counterpoise to Japan. They may even do more than that: they may take the lead in booting the Westerner out of Asia. The special treaties which gave extraterritorial rights in China to Western powers have been abolished in recognition of China's services to the United Nations. Britain is holding to Hong Kong on the grounds that the island is British and not Chinese. The Chinese smiled broadly when the Japanese unmercifully humiliated British residents in China during the early part of the Nipponese invasion. British claims to having built Hong Kong are not likely to carry weight for long.

The Chinese already are scattered through Asia. In some colonies they actually outnumber the natives. Chinese immigrants include businessmen as well as workers. They work on plantations in Thailand and in the mines of Thailand, Malaya and the Indies. They are farmers in Indo-China and in the Indies. In the towns and villages they are merchants, jobbers and money lenders. They are bankers, ship-owners, industrialists of many sorts, and they operate rubber, coffee, tea and pepper plantations. They are even civil servants, for in almost every country they form an important minority while in the Straits Settlements and the Federated Malay States they actually are a majority of the population. In Burma, Thailand, Indo-China and the Philippines, Chinese are the principal rice millers and rice traders. All of this in areas where Western imperialism has held sway. The Chinese are resented in these countries as are Westerners, in spite of the fact that they are Orientals.

The groundwork has already been laid for a Chinese Asia and many persons conversant with Asia believe that it will come in due course. But today the question is how to contain the Japanese, not the Chinese. Within that question are several fine points. China, with her size, population and culture far superior to the Japanese, is the white hope of the Western world. The Russians will take care of themselves; they have no love for the Japanese. But neither the United States nor Britain will be able to or willing to remain in or about Japan for a sufficient length of time. United States defenses in the Pacific will be increased against another Pearl Harbor possibility and the British will try to rejuvenate Singapore as a naval base. China, however, will be the cornerstone of Western Japanese policy.

Yet to rely upon the China of today would be equal to laying a cornerstone in a quagmire. Before China can fulfill the role assigned to her, she must have abundant help from the outside and she must find within herself a greater sense of national unity. Part of the help China will need will be naval and air help. It is a paradox that while the Western powers are being called upon to relinquish the special rights, including naval bases, which they have had in China, they are at the same time being obliged to increase their interference in Chinese affairs.

Unless the war leaves Japan so helpless that it will take at least a generation to recover, China will hardly have time enough to rise to the standards set for her. Even that space of time may not be sufficient.

8

CAN WE GET ALONG?

Can the good citizens of the United States and the equally good citizens of Great Britain get along in the post-war world?

Well, rah-*ther!*

If "Well, rah-*ther!*" is not the answer, then there is no hope whatever for the ideal of international collaboration. If two countries whose cultural foundations rest upon the same rock cannot compose their national differences in a mutually helpful spirit, what hope is there for coöperation among countries with radically different cultures?

Anglo-American coöperation does not presuppose a union or even formal ties of lesser nature. Indeed, to be forced to make such ties would be admission of weakness as well as a danger signal to other peoples. A counter-bloc would form as surely as night follows day. That which exists between the United States on one hand and Great Britain and the Commonwealth on the other is of value only if it flows with the ease of an artesian well.

Historical development is bringing at once greater understanding to Anglo-Americans intellectually and greater misunderstanding to them economically. In theory, the intellect should govern the stomach, but in fact, the stomach is master. Men of great intellect can die of starvation, and some do. Lofty ideas and intentions never halted death. On the other hand, man guided by his stomach alone is destined to premature death. The secret of the dilemma lies somewhere between theory and fact.

The coming of age of the United States is gradually attracting more and more Englishmen to inquire into the intellectual accomplishments of the forty-eight states. The rawness of the American branch and the Englishman's slowness to realize that a monopoly of Anglo-Saxon culture might not always remain within the mother country, long prevented him from giving a thought to what was taking place in American literature, art, architecture, science and scholarship in general. That was quite natural during the time that America had no backlog of her own accomplishments. That time has passed. Today it would be difficult to name a single field in which the United States is not a leader or at least abreast of Britain. World War I started an awakening of recognition in Britain and this war has continued it.

Conditions are proper now for great strides to be made, and unless either side of the Atlantic slips once again into deep slumber, the coming years should mark tremendous advancement in mutual appreciation.

The attitude English universities have held toward American scholarship was pointedly illustrated by an episode that took place a few years before the outbreak of World War II. An American foundation offered to send an American professor for one term to each of six British universities. The foundation was willing to bear all expenses, but mindful of a queer kink in human nature, it thought that the professor would be more appreciated if each university should pay something. A token payment of fifty pounds was decided upon. The Vice-Chancellors of the six universities selected met with a foundation representative. Two of the Vice-Chancellors arrived with the fifty pounds in pocket. They thought the idea excellent. Two others were not certain the scheme would work; they said that perhaps they could scrape together a little money but fifty pounds was too much. Anyway, they were interested in hearing what the other Vice-Chancellors had to say. The remaining two insisted on paying nothing, if indeed they should deign to receive an American professor at all. This was how they reasoned: "If we take an American on our staff, we give him access to our library and laboratories and give him the benefit of meeting with our professors and pupils. That is a great privilege to extend to an American and we do not understand why we should be called upon to pay in addition. Moreover, if we had fifty pounds to spend either on books for the library or on an American professor, we should not hesitate in making a choice; we should buy books."

Any American who has attended Oxford or Cambridge has encountered that state of mind. An American at Cambridge reported this choice bit as having come from the lips of a lecturer who was recommending a book: "This is a product of trans-Atlantic scholarship, so you must not expect profundity or thoroughness." If their Excellencies, the Four University Vice-Chancellors, and his Highness, the Cambridge Lecturer, had been as learned as their poses implied, they would have been conversant with some of the things Continental text books have to say about the English. As a result, perhaps, they would have been more humble. In this connection it is interesting to note that history books in Spanish secondary schools until the last ten years taught young Spaniards that "The cause of the brutal nature of the English is their love of whisky and rum."

Close working relationships during the current war have done more to bring each side nearer to the truth than decades of patient work by foundations and societies could have done. Professors and scientists were knee-deep in this war; they were forced to crawl out of their normal shells and look about for inspiration wherever they could find it. It has been my experience that this has brought about an appreciation of mutual accomplishments much wider than existed before the war. This appreciation extends down through less exalted levels. The sum total of the many months thousands upon thousands of American soldiers of all gradations spent in Britain was a boon rather than a detriment to the cause of Anglo-American relations. The American boys, for the most part, learned that the Englishmen he met were not very dissimilar to the folks back home and that they labored day in and day out with much the same problems as did father and mother. Few Englishmen managed to escape contact with the American boys who swarmed over the Isles and they, too, found that while the lads from across the sea had perhaps a different spirit, essentially they were cut from the same cloth.

Appreciation of intellectual and human qualities create the necessary atmosphere in which desire to be reasonable about economic and political matters can grow. Economic problems far surpassing the boundaries of our two countries are staring at us. I have already described the British preoccupation with respect to their own bread and butter and their fears of being crushed between the United States and Russia. The British are wondering whether the United States is going to be reasonable in this matter.

For the United States, given the absence of an effective world organization, the overall question to be decided is whether or not, with the power now in its hands, it wants to push the British Empire to the wall. The isolationist mind reasons that our participation in the past two wars has been solely for the purpose of underwriting the Empire; it reasons that we are foolish to waste our patrimony on others and argues that instead we should gird ourselves sufficiently and let come what may. This presupposes, falsely, that such a policy would keep us out of conflicts. It is true, especially in this war, that United States action saved Britain. It is equally true that Britain saved the United States, for what would have happened if Britain had not taken the stubborn stand that she did? It is also true that Russia had a big hand in the "saving" process, for what would have happened to Britain and the United States if Russia had stopped the fight and Hitler had gained control of the raw materials of the Ukraine? No claim to priority can be lodged by any one of the United Nations. However far-fetched it may seem, the fact is that the United States has been dependent upon the British for partial protection and that protection long was enjoyed without cost to us. What the past two wars cost therefore could be regarded as delayed payment. The fallacy in the United States' position was that it relied on the British fleet in the Atlantic while at the same time it refused to take a hand in the political and economic affairs of the world which governed the ultimate effectiveness of that protective arm. We are supposed to be a nation of great business people, but no businessman would conduct himself in such a manner.

The fact is that in the two world wars we have been fighting first of all for our own protection. If the British Empire were to go down by whatever means, we should be obliged to find a substitute for the large measure of protection which the Empire has given us. No suitable substitute could be found entirely within our own borders. A responsible general staff would not erect a defense which would necessitate action entirely on our own soil. The object of enlightened defense is to keep the enemy as far away from our home soil as possible. The isolationist argument that we should gird ourselves sufficiently could only in the end mean that we should be obliged to acquire bases in Asia, South America and Africa and maintain a tremendous military establishment. It would force us into an imperialistic policy far beyond anything ever dreamed of in this country and beyond anything foreign countries ever feared that we might do.

The last war has been fought in which United States' continental territory has remained inviolate; and even in this one Japanese submarines managed to fire a few shells into our Pacific coast. The next time, in one degree or another, our homes and gardens, our skyscrapers and forests will most certainly suffer. Even some America-Firsters may get killed while sitting on their front porches, placidly knitting. This is foreshadowed by aerial developments. What then becomes of the Atlantic protective arm, the British fleet? That arm will not be able to offer protection in the air, but its usefulness will by no means be reduced to nil. Moreover, the fleet is not alone today. Beside it, apace with developments, is the R.A.F., and as far as United States strategy is concerned, it, like the fleet, is in the front line where it has bases on home soil whence the United States air force could operate as it did in this war. The United States today has a navy for the Atlantic as well as the Pacific. Our navy now is the largest any nation ever possessed. But no one should think that the people will be willing to continue paying for such a navy in peacetime. Furthermore, the navy's effectiveness, regardless of size, depends upon bases. Our Atlantic fleet would be purely a coastal defense force if it could not use the British Isles.

This war brought to the people of Main Street their first consciousness of what other nations meant when they talked about their national security. Only a few people on Main Street had had any conception of the British fleet's relationship to our security. More understand it now, but still not enough do. For unless the old system is to be discarded consciously, or it is to drag along to an untimely end with no plan for its replacement, serious thought must be given as to how to keep it vitalized. Keeping it vital under present conditions will require broad conceptions of economic as well as political policy. Britain has been dragged down by two wars to such an extent that if her foreign trade is not prosperous, she will be unable to stand the strain of an adequate navy and air force. She lives by her dealings abroad. Britain and the United States are the two major trading countries. For them to engage in vicious practices against each other would be to cut each other's throats.

Both countries face the future with trepidation. The British hope to increase their living standard in the years to come but first they must find a way back to their old pre-war standard. In the United States, there is genuine fear that there will not be enough jobs to go around when war production ceases. This fear has stimulated more interest in the possibilities of exporting surplus products than ever existed before and it has moreover created a strange belief that foreign markets will solve domestic problems.

Obviously, here is a field of conflict between Britain and the United States. Delegations from the two countries have met head-on in the international conferences concerned with economic matters. Each country has adopted a position which it feels is the most likely to bring it the greatest amount of foreign business. This divergence in views was immediately apparent, for example, at the Bretton Woods monetary conference, the Chicago civil aviation conference and the Rye businessmen's conference. The basic differences between the two countries were these: the United States favored the widest possible latitude for businessmen the world over, while the British advocated restrictions, cartels and pools. The reasons behind these respective stands were that the United States will be in a strong financial and trading position after the war and it believes it will be able to out-trade any other country in a free market, while the British, being in an unfavorable position, believe they will not be able to meet competition and therefore they will need restrictions and a fencing off of markets and opportunities. The Americans found themselves using arguments which the British employed when they were the dominant trading nation. The British have been forced so far from their traditional laisser-faire stand that they even became suspicious of the campaign started in the United States for a free exchange of information throughout the world. The resolution Congress passed favoring a free press as a necessary element in any foundation looking toward the prevention or curbing of future wars, was regarded by some sections of British opinion as nothing more than an effort to place American news agencies in position to dominate world dissemination of news!

War-ravaged countries are supporting Britain's advocacy of controls, not because they desire to channelize trade but because circumstances make it imperative that these governments for many years to come will have to exercise a high degree of direction. The governments in countries where Nazis juggled business and industry have fallen heir to large chunks of industry and raw materials sources. Moreover, as in Britain, it is feared that the lowering of all bars would prevent a balanced recovery and unless there is a balance from which all segments of the population will benefit, there will be social disturbances which will change the face of Europe far more than is now anticipated. What rationing and multiple governmental controls did in wartime to make the living standards of the high and the low more nearly equal, are cited as guides for what must be undertaken in the post-war years, at least during the immediate recovery period.

American espousal of untrammeled private enterprise therefore runs counter to conditions existing in all continental countries thrown out of gear by the war, as well as in Britain. The United States, however, has not been entirely consistent in its stand. Industry and business as a whole have led the fight for free enterprise, but the Government has not always followed. Government delegates at the international civil aviation conference in Chicago were adamant in their fight to prevent curbs being placed on the tremendous expansion in the air that is bound to come; the United States is far ahead of other nations in aviation and the Government listened to industry's plea for freedom to expand as business and technological conditions permitted. But in the field of raw materials, where the United States has deficiencies, the Government has favored international regulation.

The United States needs a strong British Empire and Great Britain badly needs the United States. In the rush for post-war markets, therefore, the only common-sense thing to do is to keep the principle of give and take, the law of decent return, close at hand.

FRANCE, FRICTION AND FUMBLING

*Errors like straws upon the surface flow,
He who would search for pearls must dive below.*
—DRYDEN

9

FRANCE ISN'T FINISHED

President Franklin D. Roosevelt will go down in history as a man who grasped the meaning of high strategy at a critical period in world history. He will go down also as the author of one of the most baffling episodes of modern diplomacy. The President always bristled with pride over his knowledge of the French language, French history, French character, and all things French. Yet his handling of the French after France fell was so incomprehensible that it made one pause to wonder upon what he had based his conceit.

The President broadcast to the French people as the Allied armies were landing on the soil of French Africa in November, 1942, saying: "I have held all my life the deepest friendship for the French people—for the entire French people. I retain and cherish the friendship of hundreds of French people in France and outside France. I know your farms, your villages and your cities. I know your soldiers, professors and workmen. I know what a precious heritage of the French people are your homes, your culture and the principles of democracy in France. I salute you again and reiterate my faith in liberty, equality and fraternity. No two nations exist which are more united by historic and mutually friendly ties than the people of France and the United States."

In spite of his fine words, the President proved by his subsequent actions that he knew little of the "culture and the principles of democracy in France"; else why did he make such a colossal mistake as to ignore and hinder General de Gaulle in every way he could and also stubbornly refuse to accept him as the real leader of Free France even after he must have known that he was beaten?

Excepting in those colonies which had declared for the Free French (later called the Fighting French, then the Committee for National Liberation and finally The Provisional Government of France), some of which we needed for Pacific bases, the President elected first to ignore the Gaullists and later to try to block them. Continuous friction resulted, for the Gaullists represented a force far more profound than the President recognized. The friction did not abate until the second phase of our relationship with defeated France came to an end with the visit to Washington of General de Gaulle in July, 1944. That meeting marked the defeat of the President's policy which was based on the fiction that there is no France today. The expression, "There is no France today" is the President's, although there is some evidence that it originated with the backers of General Henri Giraud. It is true that the President was given a generous amount of misinformation about men and conditions in France and elsewhere by his agents in the field, but he bears responsibility for the evaluation of such information and the policy followed, for he deliberately assumed full control, with the State Department playing only a minor role. In fact, Secretary Cordell Hull apparently did not know it when the President, through Mr. Robert Murphy, concluded an agreement with General Giraud.

When M. Jacques Lemaigre-Dubreuil, General Girard's representative, returned to Algiers from Washington in January, 1943, he gave his colleagues a startling report. When a certain agreement was mentioned, he said that Secretary Hull knew nothing whatever about it; in fact, in M. Lemaigre-Dubreuil's presence, Secretary Hull telephoned the President to find out what it was all about. M. Lemaigre-Dubreuil stated that the President confirmed the existence of the accord and told Secretary Hull he would tell him about it when he next saw him!

From the very beginning, inconsistencies manifested themselves between the public utterances of the State Department and its subsequent actions. Publicly it was stated that the United States was bent upon reëstablishing France as a strong power. In the negotiations which were to bring General Giraud into the North African invasion scheme, the President's personal representative, Mr. Murphy, in the name of the President, gave the General a letter on November 2, 1942, assuring him that France would be restored to her former size and greatness. The first three paragraphs of this letter * read as follows:

> Referring to declarations made on several occasions by President Roosevelt and to engagements already made by the American Government as well as by the British Government, I am in position to assure you that the restoration of France to full independence, in the same extent and greatness possessed before the war in Europe as well as overseas, is one of the aims of the United Nations.
>
> It is understood that French sovereignty shall be reëstablished as soon as possible over all of the metropolitan and colonial territory over which the French flag waved in 1939.
>
> The Government of the United States considers the French Nation as an ally and will treat it as such.

All too soon thereafter the folly of trying to proceed with such a man as General Giraud became apparent and the Administration began to act as if it neither expected nor desired France to rise again. The French, whether Gaullists or Giraudists—the only media of expression the "French Nation" had—were not treated as an ally. They were barred from international meetings and committees considering the post-war world, excepting a few toward which they could contribute something. If it was sincerely desired that France should resume her former place and not be so weak that she could not speak, was it not shortsighted to expect her to fit unprotestingly into a new Europe, in the creation of which she had no say whatever? Did this method not risk making of France a disgruntled power, conditioned to take the lead as Germany did after the last war, in upsetting the entire peace settlement? The distinct impression was given that the United States and Britain intended to dictate the exact size of the cubicle into which France was to be

---

* The translation of all French documents is the author's.

squeezed. Was Mr. Roosevelt aiming at getting control of Dakar, the important port in the Senegal, and of French possessions in the Western Hemisphere and in the Pacific? The President had spoken of the importance of Dakar, facing Brazil, to the defense of the Western Hemisphere. It looked as if the plan, at least, was to eliminate France as a possible peace-table trouble maker. Remember the tussle Mr. Lloyd George and President Wilson had with M. Clemenceau after the last war? And the long struggle between the two wars when the British and French could not reconcile their views regarding Germany, a fact which gave Germany her chance? In this war, if France were eliminated from the peace table entirely, it would mean one less voice of possible discord and would thus make it easier for Britain and the United States to get the kind of Europe they want.

There was, furthermore, a contradiction between the President's statement that there is no France today and his pledge to General Giraud to treat the "French Nation" as an ally. If no France existed, how could it be treated as an ally? The pledge was given before the non-existence of France was proclaimed. This meant to the Gaullists that the President would recognize that France existed only if it existed in a form that pleased him. The Gaullists did not please him. So France did not "exist today"; but it might have "existed" if Giraud had not proved to be such a dud.

A high-sounding principle was announced in Washington as a basis for this government's policy. To Americans, it was an appealing principle. It said that we would not allow anyone to return to the motherland and impose himself upon the French people. The people alone must be permitted to determine their own regime. Yet, General Giraud informed the State Department on December 28, 1942, that he had an "explicit" agreement with Mr. Murphy that he would be recognized as the "chief of a French Government" to act until France was liberated. Whether General Giraud had an "explicit" or "implicit" agreement will be discussed later, but had everything worked out as was originally foreseen, he would have been in position to influence the choice of a regime in France. This matter of being able to influence, if not manipulate, the wishes of the French people was one of the cardinal points in Washington's refusal to recognize the Gaullists. What was correct for Giraud was considered dangerous and against our principles when applied to de Gaulle.

Frenchmen, regardless of faction (despite appearances, there are many Frenchmen who are just Frenchmen in love with their country), these past two years have had more than one heart pang over Anglo-American policy. Were the American and British armies really liberators? Doubt hovered annoyingly about for many months in Africa; even after the invasion of France itself, by which time both the Allied political and military branches had had time to correct many of the glaring errors made in North Africa, the question was posed. The French, outside of the handful who at the end remained with Vichy, wanted a part in their own liberation. It was not merely a matter of the organized Gaullists in Algiers; it was not a matter of a group of power-thirsty men, as Washington regarded the Gaullists for so long, who wanted to wedge their way into a noble undertaking; it was a most natural feeling for anyone who loved his country to have. Whether the individual participated directly in the liberation or not, he wanted to feel that the expulsion of the Germans and of the Vichy crowd was a French achievement made possible by France's allies. They did not particularly care to have a United States and a Britain defeat the Germans singlehanded and then patronizingly turn France back to them and await French applause. They wanted a common undertaking; it would have been shrewd statesmanship to foresee the tremendous spiritual boost it would have given the French for them to be associated more intimately with every move, especially in Metropolitan France. French self-confidence had suffered tremendously and it needed just such a stimulant. Therefore, there were heart pangs when our attitude frequently appeared to be that of a conqueror rather than that of a co-liberator. Even General Giraud, our own creation, through his emissary, M. Lemaigre-Dubreuil, complained to Secretary Hull on January 9, 1943, two months after our forces had landed, that the impression was growing that North Africa was being treated as occupied rather than as Allied territory. M. Lemaigre-Dubreuil said he felt obliged to remind the American Government that the intervention of American troops had been requested, prepared and facilitated by Frenchmen. He further told Mr. Hull that the American Government, and not the British, was responsible for the odor of occupation. When the Allied armies went into France in June, 1944, stress was placed on the notion of liberation. By that time there were more Frenchmen participating on the military side and the Algiers Committee, or Provisional Government, tagged along to take over civil affairs. The French Forces of the Interior had received some but not much encouragement from the Allies. This added increment of participation had had to be fought for at every turn. The Committee had been obliged to take the bull by the horns and proceed as if the White House, whence came the obstruction, were a shack on a barren island.

For sound military reasons, the United States, after Pearl Harbor, led the way in formulating Anglo-American policy toward the French. The Churchill Government at first embraced General de Gaulle as a gift from heaven. Coolness set in after the Dakar and Mers-el-Kebir fiascos, for which the British should bear as much responsibility as General de Gaulle, and thereafter British policy followed along in the wake of Washington's lead. Eventually, with D-Day approaching and the hard fact that General de Gaulle was the accepted French leader staring them in the face, the British decided to risk a fissure in the Anglo-American front by composing differences with the General. This was done only after trying in vain to convince the President that self-interest demanded that he climb down from his high horse. The British foresaw that we were heading straight into a muddle far worse than anything experienced in North Africa and they reluctantly decided to hedge at the last moment as best they could to protect themselves. This unilateral action by the British was part of the secret behind General de Gaulle's visit to the President in July—after the invasion—and the studied cordiality of which he was the object. That marked the end of the second phase of our relations with defeated France. The first phase ended when our Embassy left Vichy, upon our entrance into North Africa. This first phase was a successful one from an Anglo-American viewpoint, but it was the breeding ground for the defeat of the President's policy in the second phase. The third act started to unfold in a void.

If Washington desired France to be restored to her former position in the comity of nations and if, as was the case, that could only come about through Allied effort, a basic question arose. What sort of France? Republican and democratic, certainly. Decomposed as she was when she went down? What good would it do the cause of peace in general, to have a new France unable to stand on her own feet? Obviously, the value of France to Britain and the United States would be in proportion to her internal strength. The next question therefore involved the type of Frenchman with whom we were to work.

When Admiral William D. Leahy was sent to Vichy as Ambassador a few months after France's fall in 1940, he went for the specific purposes of trying to prevent the French fleet from falling into German hands and of keeping his government informed about what the Germans as well as the French were doing. Later, the Embassy had the new task of doing what it could to prepare the way for the North African invasion. The French fleet did not fall into German hands, and Mr. Sumner Welles, in his book *The Time for Decision*, credits the Admiral with having frustrated such an eventuality on at least one occasion. The prime consideration, from the fall of France to the North African invasion, was military. It was therefore considered necessary to deal with certain men in and about the Vichy Government regardless of their past actions or their current views. The General Staff considers only strategic aspects of the problem involved, ignoring future effect. It is a question whether rigid adherence to such a rule is advisable, for in the end neat execution of a military problem may prove to be a Pyrrhic victory. Fundamentally, however, it is a sound dictum, as the Germans have shown on several occasions during this war, when Adolf Hitler injected political and prestige considerations into what should have been purely military problems. But when the fighting aim is wrapped in idealism, real or unreal, and the assistance of men opposed to the announced aims is accepted and even solicited, no one should be surprised when cynicism results and the long range aims are threatened. "It is difficult," says Mr. Welles, who was Under-Secretary of State at the time, "to see how our occupation of North Africa, the keystone in the strategic design for the defeat of Germany, could have been successfully carried out if the United States Government had based its plans at the time of the landing operations on questions of ideology rather than of military and naval strategy."

This is the usual defense offered for our entire policy toward the

French. Mr. Welles, however, limits his statement to the period of the North African landing operations. It was precisely after the landings in North Africa that our policy became so difficult to understand. Once conditions demanding close attention to military needs ended, the general policy did not switch to one in line with our announced war aims. French civilians in North Africa who played a role in our landings, for which they have not been given credit (Frenchmen who were sincerely anti-German, anti-fascist and anti-everything that Hitler's New Order in Europe stood for), condoned the military expediency line we followed right up to and through the acceptance of the notorious Admiral Darlan in order to obtain what it was thought he could give the Allies in a military way. But they were completely disillusioned when it appeared that we were not only prepared but delighted to have him stay on. An assassin's hand eliminated the Admiral, but the bullet did not kill the policy we had been following. With the dangerous military period at an end, we went right on backing the reactionary elements with which contact had been made during the first phase of our relationship with the Vichy Government. These elements either bore heavy responsibility for the fall of France or were not far removed from the pitiful feudalistic National Renovation plans of Marshal Henri Philippe Pétain, the Vichy Chief of State. General Giraud himself stubbornly refused to renounce his allegiance to the Marshal. In short, our policy of military expediency began to appear in a different light. Was it expediency pure and simple or had we deliberately chosen conservative and highly compromised men because we thought they would create a post-war France free of social upheaval? This was the beginning of the impression, which subsequently spread over most of the world, that the United States is the champion of reaction.

A strong and healthy France could not be built by the men who gloried in the opportunity to surrender to Hitler. The men of Vichy reveled in France's defeat. To them it meant the downfall of leftism and a golden opportunity to kill democracy and establish a fascist state.

Marshal Pétain, three months after the Armistice, set forth his beliefs very clearly in an article he wrote for the September 15, 1940, issue of the sedate magazine *Revue des Deux Mondes*. The Marshal said, "Liberalism, capitalism, collectivism are imported products which France, restored to herself, naturally rejects. She understands today that she was misguided in trying to transplant to her country institutions and methods which were not made for her soil and her climate." Then he went on to say that when France comes to "examine the principles which have brought victory to her adversaries, she will be surprised to recognize everywhere her own, her purest and her most authentic tradition." The French, he said, "have less trouble in accepting the National-Socialist idea . . . for it is part of our classic heritage." A search for the National-Socialist idea in French life "would lead us by every road to the truths which were ours, which we have forgotten, which we can take up once more without borrowing them from anyone and without ignoring the merit of those who were able to profit from them better than we . . . And thus, we will see how, without sacrificing ourselves in any way, but, on the contrary, by finding ourselves again, we can articulate our thought and action with those who will preside tomorrow in the reorganization of the world."

That was the Marshal's philosophy. Nothing that the French Revolution stood for and accomplished was French. The ideal of liberty and freedom was foreign to French nature; real French nature was expressed by Hitler's National Socialism! The Marshal intended to lead the way back to the faith of the forefathers, but in doing so he would be most careful to give Hitler credit for carrying on where the French had faltered. The Marshal's "National Renovation" program was designed to do just that, but his own people showed him how wrong he was before he had hardly started.

At the time Allied armies were marching toward Paris and the Marshal disappeared from Vichy, a letter was circulated in France which was supposed to be the Chief of State's last sad word to "his people." He had always acted, he said, in their best interests although it may at times have seemed to them otherwise. The impression created by the letter was that he had been driven to embrace the Nazis. Now that Marshal Pétain is again before the bar of public opinion, it is well to recall what he wrote in September, 1940. Surely he was not obliged to write that *Revue des Deux Mondes* article. Moreover, it is known that what he then wrote accurately expressed views he had held for years preceding 1939.

Not all the men in Vichy, however, belonged to the military caste or to the trusts. Some of them were leftists of a brand that never was far distant from fascism. M. Marcel Déat, the editor, who in 1939 proclaimed he would not fight for Danzig and who became the most rabid of collaborationists, was an example. Of the two hundred Socialist former deputies and senators, thirty plumped for the Pétain fascist state. No impartial observer of pre-war France would be so rash as to lay the blame for the collapse of the country at the feet of a few groups. Decay ran all through the national life. The Left, the Center and the Right, to use terms common to the country, all were afflicted. There was good and there was bad in each group. The French communists gave themselves a black record by their shiftiness and failure to understand the national interest. Their leaders did not come to their senses until it was too late. On their behalf, let it be said that they did not await the German attack against Russia before they became anti-German. A clandestine communist party began operations in France immediately after the Armistice. The first leaflet it distributed ended with these words: "We have profound faith in the people's strength and in their future, the future of France. Our people will not perish. Their will to liberty, their love of liberty, will not be destroyed by the evil forces of traitors, exploiters, plunderers and conquerors." This leaflet was distributed at a time when the German had just come in and when he was bending over backward to win the people to collaboration for his bright "new" Europe. The people who read the leaflet were eating at German soup kitchens and listening to excellent Wehrmacht band concerts. The quick rebound of the communists underground was frightening to some of our policy-makers. Together with socialists, trade unionists and other leftist groupings, they were the first to hit the patriotic trail. It took moderates and conservatives considerably longer to disentangle their thoughts amid the confusion. A feeling that, in spite of everything, the Marshal in Vichy was doing what he could for the best interests of France, lingered on among moderates and conservatives for about two years.

From 1942, however, Marshal Pétain's prestige waned. Those of the middle and upper classes who were supporting him began to have a little hope that the Germans would be defeated. Vichy was bogged down administratively and was getting worse. More and more, Vichy revealed itself as a mere tool of the Germans. The Riom trials in February, 1942, where former Premiers Edward Daladier and Leon Blum made such brilliant defenses of themselves and turned the spotlight on the Marshal himself as a co-bearer of the responsibility for military unpreparedness, helped enormously in swaying large bodies of Pétain's original supporters. Because of this, Marshal Pétain had to end the trial abruptly without conclusion; but the men on trial were not liberated. The final blow to Vichy's prestige was the wholesale delivery of French manpower to Germany. Surely a government that would lend even a feeble hand to such an odious enterprise was not French.

The working classes reacted more quickly to this state of affairs, for Pétain's National Renovation hit them first. His Labor Charter took them back to another era, involving abolition of the trade unions. It shocked into reason even the Teachers' Union which, before the war, wrote one of the darkest chapters in the history of French trade unions. The Left came along first, but abreast was a staunch conservative and intensely patriotic group called the Republican Conservative Party headed by a Lorrainer with handlebar mustaches, M. Louis Marin. Throughout the Aristide Briand peace era, Louis Marin was the bitterest critic of Briand's Geneva peace policy. He lived to see come to pass what he feared. Instead of sulking and crying "good riddance" along with the Vichy band of corruptibles, M. Marin rose to the occasion and fought with the underground.

Of a certainty France is not finished. It would not be surprising if she came back with despatch. On the Fourth of July, 1944, towns and villages in liberated Normandy joined with American soldiers in celebrating the occasion. In the square before the Mairie of the fishing village of Grand-Camp-les-Bains, I stood beside a mother whose teen-age son had recited a touching composition addressed to American boys and girls. After that mother and the women around her, young and old, had vibrantly sung the call to action contained in the words and tune of the "Marseillaise," I wondered who could doubt that France would rise again. They threw themselves into the fighting words as if they themselves were actually on the march to the barricades. The women of France are far more influential than their counterparts elsewhere, although they have not had the same legal rights. Identical displays of rebirth were later witnessed all over France, as cities, towns and villages were liberated. It must not be forgotten that it is the vanquished and not the victors who inherit spiritual regeneration from war. France has had the tremendous shock of ignominious defeat; at the same time she has the advantage of coming out of this war with her material possessions more or less intact. Hers is the world's second largest Empire. French economy is more nearly balanced than is that of any other European country save Russia. She has always been able to come back financially and economically, when she set her mind to it. She amazed and frightened Bismarck with her recuperation after the Franco-Prussian War of 1870. Following the more devastating World War I, she had a difficult time but eventually made it, and she was the very last major country to feel the effect of the 1929 depression. She has now had time to search her soul, mull over what went wrong and rediscover the meaning of the stirring words in the "Marseillaise." The French have a great heritage descending from ancient Greece. But unlike the Greece of today, France's experience is more modern, more alive and more in tune with current aspirations. France's foundations are solid. Within the country are men of probity and virtue capable of pruning the rotten limbs—if they are afforded the opportunity. The spirit of Jeanne d'Arc still lives. While there is a vast difference between the Frenchman's logic and the Englishman's ability to change his course regardless of theories or past practices, there was not a great gulf between the state of mind in France and in Britain during the years preceding the war. The Englishman by nature is more apt to cast prejudices aside in the national interest than is the Frenchman. The French at home tend to be doctrinaire, so intolerant of opposing ideas that they cling to their own, come hell or high water. Professor André Philip has justly called this trait an attempt "to practice both a democratic policy and an authoritarian type of morality." Nevertheless, it is by no means certain that Britain would not have succumbed as did France, if their geographical positions vis-à-vis the German blitz had been reversed. We might today be praising France for a heroic stand instead of Britain.

A strong hand will be needed in the immediate future. It is not primarily a question of dealing with the Comité des Forges or the so-called "Hundred Families," both of which have been popularized as sinister factors in the undermining of the country. No matter what is done to current occult forces, others will replace them unless there is a renovation in private as well as national life. The trilogy—Liberty, Equality, Fraternity—while still as noble as ever, had been perverted by 1939. Fraternity had gained the upper hand over Liberty and Equality. A spirit of "camaraderie" existed among national and provincial politicians who remained pretty much the same men over two decades. A French critic called it the "Republic of Comrades." The purpose of this "camaraderie" was not social; indeed, it was anti-social. The purpose was mutual protection for shady deals. The French Constitution left judges subject to political influence. Courts faced with cases wherein the Government had an interest almost invariably handed down decisions that would please the cabinet of the time. Judges could not be removed, but they were appointed by the minister of justice and their advancement depended upon the ministry. Cabinets and ministers changed so often that a judge more mindful of his personal position than he was of justice did not dare refuse favors to a deputy or a senator. Tomorrow the deputy or senator might be minister of justice, and frequently was. Likewise, public prosecutors were appointed and removed by the minister of justice. Thus it was easy to manipulate equality before the law. A large percentage of parliamentarians were attorneys. They sat in the seats of law-makers and practiced law at one and the same time. The result was that every crook in the land engaged a deputy or senator as his attorney.

Many holes will have to be plugged in governmental practice, but one root of the malfeasance was embedded in private morals. The pourboire to the casual visitor in France meant merely a tip for some personal service. In actual fact, it was a business principle that made honest dealings a rarity. Retail stores even gave anyone who would bring in a customer ten per cent of the amount the customer purchased. This system replaced advertising. "Mon Dieu, mon Dieu, my customers would think I was going bankrupt if I had to advertise," was the way one merchant expressed himself. It was difficult to carry on legitimate business without having to pay someone on the side. It was not uncommon to discover that that "someone" was the president or the vice-president or the general manager of a firm. Few deals went through without a percentage for some private pocket. I recall an occasion when a friend of mine had to make up his mind whether he wanted to play the game or stand on principle. He was interested in an investment which the board of directors of a certain Parisian bank had under consideration. An expert was called in by the board to give his opinion as to the soundness of the investment. The expert tore the proposal to bits so completely and thoroughly that he left the board feeling foolish for ever having given a thought to such a shaky venture. But as the meeting broke up, the "expert" quite calmly sidled up to my friend and made it plain that his opinions were flexible and there could be reconsideration!

Blackmail was notorious and seldom prosecuted. Fly-by-night newspapers specialized in it. There were hundreds of organizations with appealing names whose sole purpose was to extract money from some person or industry which had something to protect. There were Chicago-sounding names such as the "Association for the Protection of Milk Producers," "The Republican Association for Industry and Agriculture," and "Association for the Protection of Widows and Orphans."

A purging was absolutely necessary. "Liberty, Equality, Fraternity" are still sound. That trilogy is far better than Pétain's fascistic "Work, Family, Country," if the privileges granted by Liberty, Equality and Fraternity are used and not abused, as they were. The purpose of reform is to proceed, not recede. The venerable Pétain, in his dotage, tried to take the country back to some period before the great Revolution.

Strong and sometimes bitter medicine is called for if the patient is to recover. Yet it is this sort of medicine that we sought to spare the sick man. The movement headed by General de Gaulle stood on two pillars: first, liberation of France from both the Germans and the Vichy crowd, and second, the cleansing of vicious practices that frittered away the country's vitality. The difference between the men of Free France and the men Washington chose to support is the difference between the fresh, crisp air of a spring morning and the air in a foul, smoke-filled room. Mr. Welles in his book, *The Time for Decision,* says that President Roosevelt had tried to get certain French leaders to leave France in the belief that they could do more to hasten the day of liberation outside the country than they could inside. Mr. Welles did not say which leaders were approached, but he added that the majority of them were jailed when the Germans took over all of France subsequent to the Allied landing in North Africa. Were the men Flandins and Bonnets or were they Mandels, Herriots and Jeannenys? I know that an expedition of secret agents was sent to the elder statesman M. Edouard Herriot. An English officer whom I know made the journey to M. Herriot's retreat outside Lyon, prepared to remove from France the ex-Premier and President of the last Chamber of Deputies. He described for me his experiences with the "sympathique" leader and how he declined to leave France. M. Herriot morally was absolutely above reproach, but he was not a torch-carrier of the type the hour demanded. He was more apt to weep with his beloved Beethoven at his side than he was to sharpen a knife and cut for blood. He could be counted on to do nothing shocking.

In spite of the dismaying collapse, it was a certainty that with an Allied victory restoring her material possessions, France would come back. How strong and healthy she would be was another matter. The United States and Britain were in a position greatly to influence that by the choice of the men they encouraged. The dictum that the French people and only they would determine the sort of future regime they wanted was, in practice, impossible to realize. Someone had to take over the functions of governing before it would be possible for the people to have a means of deciding what they wanted. It was neither advisable nor practicable for the United States and Britain to assume civil control over a great people such as the French. Irreparable harm would have been caused if they had tried. Frenchmen had to do that themselves. The Frenchmen chosen to do it were General Giraud and the dubious clique at his feeble elbow. Heaven and earth were turned unsuccessfully to keep General de Gaulle from being the man. That is what made it the most baffling episode of the diplomatic side of the war.

10

THAT DANGEROUS FRENCHMAN CHARLES DE GAULLE

That "dangerous" Frenchman, Charles de Gaulle, is the General who left Bordeaux for London on June 17, 1940, in an R.A.F. plane, and the next day over the B.B.C. said: "France has lost a battle! But France has not lost the war!" He was the General who felt that the Armistice with Germany was a crime and who proposed to do something about it for the sake of France, and the rest of us, too. Out of 42,014,594 Frenchmen (as of 1936 census), he was the only one to come forward in the hour of defeat and say to the British: "I'm single-handed, but I'll do my best to gather the remnants of my countrymen together and fight on with you." He was the only one who did what all anti-Axis sympathizers were praying that the entire French Government would do: move out and fight on. Yet, in subsequent years he was to be knocked about by the United States, and not all blows landed above the belt. He was pushed against the ropes on several occasions, but eventually his staying powers proved too strong for his redoubtable adversary, and he came out a graceful winner.

The tall, slender, cold-looking, fifty-four-year-old General has had a unique but disappointing military experience: he conceived of the blitzkrieg, had his own general staff turn it down with scorn and then saw the Germans adopt it and prove its value by crushing his own France. The only happy touch to the story is that in their turn the Allies took the weapon from the Germans and used it to blitz the blitzers out of the General's homeland. But General de Gaulle has personally never had a chance to develop his own notions in the field. The Nazis never hid the fact that they took his theories of modern warfare and put them to fateful use. I recall that during the years when the Germans were building their devastating war machine (I was in Berlin at the time), they used to talk about a French Colonel named de Gaulle who had written a magnificent book about tank warfare. I had never heard of the Colonel. His book was called

The Army of the Future, and it was published in 1934, a year after Hitler took power. That book, the Germans said, taught them everything. In it he wrote: "Tomorrow the professional army will move entirely on caterpillar wheels. Every element of troops and services will make its way across mountains and valleys on appropriate vehicles. . . . Six divisions of the line completely motorized and 'caterpillarized' and partly armored will constitute an army suitable for carrying through a campaign. . . . Aerial units . . . always supporting the same comrades in battle and lengthening the range of familiar artillery, will be the eyes of the main unit. . . . A battle of this sort immediately increases the importance of the role of aircraft. . . . For troops who proceed by surprise and speed, aeroplanes will be in everything, not only auxiliaries but indispensable comrades in arms. . . . Each manœuvre consists essentially of turns made by the attacker in order to attack from behind, while the artillery covers the operation by means of fire distributed all round the area where the action is taking place and by sending out smoke-screens to conceal those tanks which have to stay in one place.

"At the same time, measures must be taken to ensure that progress is not unduly hindered by slow mopping-up. The leading elements must therefore be used to break through and to push on towards the final objective as promptly as possible. Their supporting units will finish off what they have begun . . . if the enemy puts up a determined resistance, the attacker will soon appear in the form of groups of tanks figuring in great depth, while the first wave will have continued its advance and the artillery will have taken within its field of fire not only the outer edge of this whole field of combat, but also certain blocks of territory in the back areas which have already been by-passed."

That sounds almost like an actual account of battles that have taken place since 1939. The General was on active service all the while that he was formulating his ideas about modern warfare. While he was preparing his book he was General Secretary of the Higher Council of National Defense. He had ample opportunity to expound his theories in the highest quarters. He did expound them and as a result he became something of an outcast; the French General Staff was still lost in the Argonne—it could not shake off the idea that the next war, like the last one, would be fought from trenches. Obviously, traces of personal bitterness between some of the top-ranking officers and General de Gaulle were bound to remain. They were so terribly wrong; the outcast was so terribly right. History may have to record that the outcast rendered a tremendous service to the army. There was much suspicion of the army before the war and even during its course, for so many of the officers were believed willing to sacrifice their country for political reasons. At best, they were suspected of being unwilling to fight to the limit of their capacities lest victory bring social changes abhorrent to them, or they were just plain defeatists. This suspicion was chiefly responsible for the selection of General Maurice Gamelin to be commander-in-chief. There were other generals far better than he, but they were not considered "safe." General de Gaulle, a devout Catholic and a conservative, by his courageous action, helped to reëstablish the army's prestige. Very few outside of the military knew about de Gaulle. His book was a technical one and so its circulation was extremely limited. But a few of the more alert members of Parliament read it. Among them was Paul Reynaud, who was to become Premier during the last fateful days of unconquered France. Long before he became Premier, M. Reynaud had advocated military changes in speeches in the Chamber of Deputies; he had mentioned de Gaulle's ideas, but no ears heard him. So when he took over the Government, as things were falling apart, he sent for de Gaulle and made him Under Secretary of State for National Defense. But the Premier did not do this until June 6, 1940, just eleven days before Germany was asked for an armistice. Even if the Premier had called de Gaulle as soon as he entered office in March, it would have been far too late. What de Gaulle wanted, demanded years of preparation. De Gaulle went to the Reynaud Ministry from the field. He was promoted to the rank of general in May and given command of the Fourth Armored Division. His task then was to turn his brain around and try to devise means to stop his own monster now being used by the Germans. He fought in the battle at Abbeville where General Weygand, the commander-in-chief, made his last desperate attempt to seal off German armored units which had pushed through to the Channel. After that battle, General Weygand cited de Gaulle for bravery with these words: "Admirable leader, full of pluck and energy. Attacked with his division the Abbeville bridgehead, very firmly held the enemy. Broke the German resistance and progressed fourteen kilometers through the enemy lines, taking hundreds of prisoners and capturing considerable matériel." That was General de Gaulle's last major action in the field. Paradoxically, the Germans, by so successfully using his ideas of modern warfare, established him as a great military strategist, and he established himself as a leader in the field by his actions in May and June 1940.

After he went to the War Ministry, most of his time was consumed trying to persuade the powers-that-be not to give up the fight. Those were the days when Prime Minister Churchill was striving to keep the French fighting. One proposal after another was made, and there were flying visits to and fro between France and Britain. General de Gaulle had been sent to London on several missions by Premier Reynaud. He had returned to Bordeaux from London on one of those missions on June 17th to find that everything was lost. He climbed back into the Royal Air Force plane and flew off again to London disgusted with his colleagues in the Cabinet and declining to have anything to do with their defeatism.

This austere, unsympathetic-looking, stiff General may give the impression that if he has any of the milk of human kindness in him, it has curdled. Yet he has passion, feeling and warmth within him. He amply revealed that in the radio appeal he made the day after he washed his hands of the Bordeaux capitulation.

"The chiefs who have been at the head of the Army for many years have formed a Government," he said.

"This government, alleging the defeat of our armies, has made contact with the enemy to put an end to the fight.

"There is no question that we have been, that we are swamped by the mechanical strength of the enemy on the ground and in the air.

"Far more than by their numbers, we are thrown back by the tanks, the airplanes, and the strategy of the Germans. It is the tanks, the airplanes, the strategy of the Germans which surprised our Chiefs and brought them to the point where they are today."

In this preamble he got in some licks at his former chiefs who turned down his ideas. Then he gave the signal for the future.

"But has the last word been said? Is all hope gone? Is the defeat final? NO!

"Believe me, for I speak to you with full knowledge of what I say. I tell you that nothing is lost for France. The very same means that conquered us can be used to give us one day the victory.

"For France is not alone. She is not alone. She is not alone. She has a vast empire behind her. She can form a coalition with the British Empire, which holds the seas and is continuing the struggle. She can, like England, have limitless access to the immense industrial powers of the United States.

"This war is not limited to the territory of our unhappy land. This war has not been decided by the Battle of France. This war is a world war. All our mistakes, all our delays, all our suffering do not alter the fact that there exist in the world all the means needed to crush our enemies some day. Although we are today crushed by mechanized force, we can in the future conquer through superior mechanized force. Therein lies the destiny of the world."

After that prophecy, which has been fulfilled, he invited all Frenchmen able to do so to join him in London.

"Whatever may come, the flame of French resistance must never be extinguished; and it will not be extinguished."

That was mighty high talk for a man whose only material resources were the uniform on his back and a few odds and ends in a traveling bag. Nonetheless, Free France was born with that radio speech made before the Pétain Government, which succeeded the Reynaud Cabinet, had signed the Armistice with Germany. Two days later, Free France consisted of de Gaulle and a Lieutenant de Courcel. Five months later it consisted of 35,000 men under arms, twenty warships in service, a thousand aviators, sixty merchant vessels, armament workers, territories in Africa, India and the Pacific; committees working all over the world, financial resources, newspapers, radio stations and, as the General put it, "above all, the knowledge that we are present every minute in the hearts and minds of all the French of France." This had come about through an agreement on August 7, 1940, with the British who furnished finances, arms, equipment and hospitality. "General de Gaulle," the agreement read, "is engaged in raising a French force composed of volunteers. This force which includes naval, land and air units and scientific and technical personnel, will be organized and employed against the common enemies. This force will never be required to take up arms against France. This force will, as far as possible, retain the character of a French force in respect to personnel, particularly as regards discipline, language, promotion and duties. His Majesty's Government will, as soon as practicable, supply the French force with the additional equipment which may be essential to equip its units on a scale equivalent to that of British units of the same type . . . All vessels concerned will remain French property . . . Any expenditure incurred for the purpose of constitution and maintenance of the French force under the provisions of this agreement will be met, in the first instance, by the appropriate Departments of His Majesty's Government in the United Kingdom, which will be entitled to exercise any necessary examination and audit."

By the time a fusion was effected between the forces under General de Gaulle and those under General Giraud in June of 1943, de Gaulle had more than 100,000 men under arms in his land army, 5,000 naval officers and sailors, and 50 warships, with 281 vessels in the merchant fleet. Of the French Empire, he had Equatorial Africa, Madagascar, Somaliland, Reunion Island, New Caledonia, Tahiti, other dependencies in the Pacific and Indian oceans, French India, the Cameroons and Syria and Lebanon. He did not, however, have the bulk of the Empire, for the concentrated part of it fell to the authority of General Giraud when the United States put him in command of the territories conquered by Allied arms in Africa.

Singly and in groups, Frenchmen outside France flocked to answer de Gaulle's radio call of June 18th. Some of them had been evacuated by the British at Dunkirk. Others came from ships or the colonies. Soon they began to trickle in from France. In October, 1940, he organized a Council of Empire Defense. From among diplomats who were outside France when the end came and from men who were arriving direct from France by devious routes and means, de Gaulle was able to gather an administrative body. Fifteen months after his first radio appeal, he set up what he called a French National Committee. Up to that time, his principal occupation had been concerned with colonial administration and the functioning of the armed forces under him. Now, however, Free France began to take the attitude that it represented more than just a fighting force and a holding body for those parts of the Empire which had rallied to it. The ordinance of September 24, 1941, creating the National

Committee set forth the new development and the reasons for it. It said:

"Considering that the situation resulting from war conditions continues to prevent any meeting and any free expression of the representatives of the nation;

"Considering that the Constitution and the laws of the French Republic have been and remain violated on all the metropolitan territory and in the Empire, as well by the action of the enemy as by infringement by the authorities who collaborate with him;

"Considering that proofs substantiate the fact that the immense majority of the French Nation, far from accepting a regime imposed by violence and treason, recognizes in the authority of Free France the expression of its wishes and of its will;

"Considering that, by reason of the growing importance of the territory of the French Empire and of the territory under French jurisdiction, as also of the armed French Forces who have joined us to continue the war by the side of the Allies against the invader of our country, it is of great importance that the Free French authorities be enabled to exercise, in fact and provisionally the normal attributions of government control; we prescribe,

"Article 1.—Owing to the circumstances of war and until a representation of the people of France can be constituted which can express, in a manner independent of the enemy, the national will, the management of public affairs will be provisionally carried out under the conditions determined in the present ordinance.

"Article 2.—A National Committee, composed of Commissioners named by decree, is constituted. General de Gaulle, Chief of the Free French, is the President of the National Committee."

This attempt to "exercise in fact and provisionally the normal attributions of government control" was made ten weeks before the United States became legally involved in the war by way of Pearl Harbor. At that time we still recognized Vichy as the legal government of France. Not long after Pearl Harbor, and about the time that President Roosevelt began to plan the North African landing, an abundance of "apprehensions" about this new self-accorded power of de Gaulle's was apparent. The man who was generously applauded in June of 1940 as a great patriot, was put under suspicion. An anti-Gaullist feeling was spread throughout the United States. The Committee in London fought back and on May 27, 1942, the General held a press conference in London in which he tried to defend his actions. He said:

"I read recently in American newspapers, in American despatches and in declarations of certain American personalities the following appraisal of Fighting France: 'It is fitting that Fighting France remain exclusively a military movement.' To reinforce this idea, these newspapers and these personalities say: 'The Fighting French themselves do not wish to be involved in politics.' And since these newspapers and these personalities say that the Fighting French themselves do not wish to be involved in politics, they conclude that the Fighting French are not qualified to represent in a national aspect the general interests of France among the democracies and must remain exclusively a military organization. . . .

"To restrict Fighting France to an exclusively military organization amounts to asking General de Gaulle to supply the dead and the wounded on the battlefields, as well as those who die before the firing squads, without France deriving any national advantage among the democracies. Fighting France fights for the general interest of France, which it claims to represent. Moreover, it wishes to enlist the French people in the war. How can the French people be included in the war if Fighting France has only an exclusively military character? And lastly, it is a fact that Fighting France has the responsibility of governing important territories, that it exercises in the name of France a French mandate over the Middle Eastern States and that it is, therefore, obliged not to stop at an exclusively military role." He said, however, that he did not head a political party, for the "Fighting French and the great majority of Frenchmen in France do not at present wish to be at odds over internal politics. . . . The Fighting French are of no one party. They include men of all parties, of all opinions who are agreed on one question: the liberation of France." Then he explained that he and those about him knew that "the representation of the French people, the true representation of the French people, is naturally in the French people. We, a handful of men, cannot lay claim to constitute the political representation of the French people. This representation will begin again only with the liberation when the French people can themselves build anew their sovereignty and political representation. This is a primary fact which must be understood. But, in the meantime, there remain general national interests of France which must be upheld and represented by Frenchmen."

The logic of this concept of his job moved no one in Washington, at least no one with authority to accept it as just and logical. The General from Bordeaux had accomplished the first aim of his task: the rallying of the spirit of France to resistance and the continuation of the fight against the common enemy. The time had now come when concrete French national interests had to be defended in the councils of the world. There was no one else to look after Marianne; Vichy, of course, was out of the question as a defender of French interests either before the Germans or the rest of the world. In September, 1941, when the National Committee was created to "manage" French public affairs until the French people could speak, there was, from a French viewpoint, valid need for some such direction. At the time General de Gaulle took this step, the British appeared to be in full agreement with him. It was not until after the United States became a belligerent that this question of de Gaulle's "managing" French affairs became acute. The General's defense at the May 27, 1942, press conference was as water off a duck's back. Forty-seven days later, the British Foreign Office announced that another change had been made in the French arrangement. It was a change that jerked the National Committee back to where it was prior to September, 1941. It was to have nothing to do with "managing" French affairs. It was to fight and nothing else. The wording of the Foreign Office announcement was clear and precise:

"Fighting France: A union of French nationals, wherever they may be, and of the French territories who joined together in order to collaborate with the United Nations in the war against the common enemies. It will be the symbol of all French nationals who do not accept the capitulation and who by all means at their disposal contribute, wherever they are, to the liberation of France by a common victory of the United Nations.

"French National Committee: The directing organ of Fighting France; it organizes the participation in the war of the French nations and territories who join in collaboration with the United

Nations in the war against common enemies, and it represents their interests with the United Kingdom."

Thus Free France became "Fighting France" and the National Committee became, by definition at least, a steering committee for Fighting France. Actually, the National Committee never sank quite that far back. For, as General de Gaulle pointed out in his press conference, Fighting France was in fact governing territories and exercising in the name of France a mandate over Syria and Lebanon. Hence, Fighting France was obliged to perform functions in the name of France which were not exclusively concerned with the prosecution of the war.

In truth, both the British and the United States governments had recognized this either tacitly or in fact by agreements made with the Committee, and the efforts made from time to time to dodge this recognition constitute one of the main inconsistencies in the dealings with the Gaullists. As early as November 11, 1941, just short of a month before Pearl Harbor, the Free French were permitted to receive Lend-Lease inasmuch as "the defense of any French territory under the control of the French Volunteer Forces (Free French) is vital to the defense of the United States," as President Roosevelt put it in a letter to Mr. Edward R. Stettinius, then Lend-Lease Administrator. In March and April of 1942, when our Pacific forces were coming to life in the struggle against the Japanese, and when the African Atlantic coast was looming up in importance, the United States recognized the Committee as the "authority" governing French possessions in the Pacific and also in Equatorial Africa and the Cameroons. The United States further established a Consulate General in Equatorial Africa. When the Committee's authority over the Pacific island possessions was recognized, the State Department said: "With the French authorities in effective control of French territories in the Pacific this government has treated and will continue to treat on the basis of their actual administration of the territories involved. This government recognizes in particular that French island possessions in that area are under the effective control of the French National Committee established in London and the United States authorities are coöperating for the defense of these islands with the authorities established by the French National Committee and with no other French authority. This government appreciates the importance of New Caledonia in the defense of the Pacific area." Before this statement was issued, however, the Committee in London had had to ask Washington what was going on, for the American authorities started out to deal directly with French officials on the spot, ignoring the London Committee.

The Committee, therefore, was in several ways recognized officially as being more than a hollow shell. Territory governed by the Committee was furnishing war materials for the Allies and on October 6, 1942, a reciprocal aid agreement was signed with the Committee. That agreement said in part: "The fundamental principle to be followed in providing such aid is that the war production and war resources of Fighting France and of the United States of America should be used by the armed forces of each in the ways which most effectively utilize available materials, manpower, production facilities and shipping space." Manifestly, the Committee was a government or at least an "authority" acting as a government. But in spite of this de facto recognition of the Committee as a government, a running fight was carried on by Washington to prevent the Committee from exercising authority other than that which would be useful to the prosecution of the war. Washington did not want the Committee to defend and protect the general interests of France. It did not want the Committee to speak for France even in the provisional role in which the Committee saw its duty. The reciprocal aid agreement from which the foregoing quotation was taken was signed on October 6, 1942.

Just one month later, a Lend-Lease accord was signed with General Giraud, a Frenchman with no territory and no authority whatever behind him. Furthermore, General Giraud later said he understood from his dealings with us that he was to become the head of a government which was to be made possible by arms of the United States.

DE GAULLE AND THE FRENCH UNDERGROUND

When the London Committee set itself up on September 24, 1941, as something more than a mere fighting unit, it said that "the immense majority of the French Nation, far from accepting a regime imposed by violence and treason, recognizes in the authority of Free France the expression of its wishes and of its will."

How much truth was there in that September 1941 pretension?

The Germans came close to getting everything the French had, but they failed to get what de Gaulle took with him from Bordeaux on that June 17, 1940. Material possessions the Germans got, but the flame of France that eluded them was richly endowed with spiritual possessions, the flame he rescued set one little bonfire after another until in time the people within France were warmed by the glow. Considerable scorn at one time swept through American Government quarters, and through them crept into the press, over a reference made to de Gaulle as "another Jeanne d'Arc." The remark was made by one of his supporters who had in mind the analogy between the spark Jeanne kept alive and the one de Gaulle had rescued. The comparison in this sense was not ridiculous, but the remark was interpreted as meaning that the General was listening to queer voices à la Jeanne and that he was scheming to become a dictator! Had not the General himself dared to mention the name of the girl from Domremy? In a speech in London in July, 1942, he said: "We have chosen the hardest road, but also the most intelligent, the right road. . . . For in the extremity to which France has fallen, there are no possible compromises or half-way measures. What would have become of our country if Jeanne d'Arc, Danton and Clemenceau had wished to make concessions?" He threw in Danton and Clemenceau, to boot! A dangerous man, indeed!

The collapse of the country in 1940 created great moral confusion. It struck deep into the hearts of a proud people. How could it have happened? What to think? Who was responsible, who was right? Moorings were knocked loose. Some thought the Pétain Armistice perhaps was a good thing under the circumstances; others warmly welcomed it. Some thought it was treason; others were completely befuddled. Some thought de Gaulle's action in going off to London and setting up the Free French was treason and they agreed when Marshal Pétain condemned de Gaulle to death. Others took heart when they tuned in to the Free French broadcasts from London and heard that the fight still went on. Before many months had passed, more and more faces within France were turning toward the Free French across the Channel. So near, and yet so far off, a tiny flame was still burning. It gave hope.

While General de Gaulle was bringing about the rebirth of a French army, navy and air force outside France so as to be able to show that France had never ceased fighting, changes of consequence were taking place inside France. Resistance groups were springing up cautiously but surely. Clandestine news sheets were appearing by the dozens. Where the precious paper came from, who printed the sheets, remained a mystery to all but a few. The first class to react to the defeat was the workers. Communists, socialists and trade unions as groups began to breathe through bits of what was left of their former organizations, now outlawed. The workers were the first to feel the combined German-Vichy blow and that is one reason that they stood out already in 1940 as Resistance leaders. They were not able to do much, but they were groping. Eventually, through 1941 and 1942, other classes came out of the fog. British agents were working in France from the very collapse in 1940. These agents were fostering Resistance; they were organizing and keeping in function one of the best underground railways that ever existed. R.A.F. flyers, and in time, United States airmen, were reaching their English bases after having bailed out over France. Many of them knew not how they got back. They returned to England with tales of having had fabulous luck, when, in fact, they were all the while in the hands of an organized group, working so smoothly and quietly that the flyers did not guess the nature of their "fabulous luck"!

There were in the beginning two branches to French Resistance, the one outside the country headed by de Gaulle and the one inside the country. The one inside France was not organized by de Gaulle. It consisted of many groups, mostly with political backgrounds, and was a single movement only in the sense that the groupings sought a common aim: liberation from both the Germans and Vichy. They did not, in the beginning, work with one another. And even at the end when France was finally freed, they were none too closely knit. When Resistance within became conscious of itself, it naturally looked abroad and there found one man and only one carrying on. This is an important detail of the Gaullist controversy, overlooked by those American officials and Vichy-inclined Frenchmen abroad, who tried very hard to find that the General was scheming to get a stranglehold so he could ride down the Champs-Elysées on a beautiful white horse, or at least in one of his beloved tanks, and install himself in Madame de Pompadour's boudoir as the dictator of all the French! De Gaulle did not send agents from England into France to set up an underground network for his personal benefit. The underground, spontaneously organized, went to de Gaulle. Contacts between them during 1940 were few and precarious. In 1941, they increased as the two movements gained strength. It became apparent to all concerned that there ought to be some unison among the many groups in France. This was effected in mid-1942 after the various underground groups had thrashed over principles with representatives of the National Committee in London. Up to the beginning of 1942, Resistance in France had looked upon de Gaulle almost exclusively as a military leader, as a symbol of the spirit of Resistance. The idea that he might become a political leader had not impressed itself upon the underground. This was testified to by underground leaders themselves and was added proof that de Gaulle had not been manipulating the strings. Perhaps he did have dark designs but the underground, was it being duped? Anyone who knows the French understands that they are not easily duped. He also knows that ever since the Napoleonic period, every time anyone tried to impose authoritarian government, short shrift was made of the experiment. In the case of de Gaulle, the guard was up. On April 22, 1942, the underground paper *Coq Enchaîné* wrote:

"France will need a Government—other than that of Laval. Do you at once say de Gaulle? Certainly. But de Gaulle together with whom? The General who saved the honor of the French army will march at its head under the Arc de Triomphe on the day of victory. That will be simple justice. But in 1918 when Foch, Joffre—and unfortunately Pétain—passed through there, Clemenceau was Prime Minister and Poincaré the constitutional President of the Republic. Who will be the Clemenceau, who the Poincaré of 1942? We do not know, but the people of France must watch henceforth that those who surround de Gaulle are faithful friends of the French people. Reliable and strong. From what the people know of officers, this cannot be affirmed of any one of them. We call to you to think of this. For on it will depend your destiny for many years to come."

Previously, the underground paper *Franc-Tireur* had written: "We have written and we repeat: we are entirely with General de Gaulle in his fight for the liberation of the country, but we shall be against him if, when victory is won, contrary to what he has always affirmed, he should envisage a dictatorship no more tolerable to us if imposed by a General than the dictatorship we do not accept when imposed by a Marshal."

The underground was looking out for dictatorial tendencies that might crop up in the actions of General de Gaulle. The fact that the underground was on the alert was available to our official gatherers of information. The London Committee's claim in September, 1941, to having the majority of the French nation behind it for *all* matters was slightly premature. It did have for everything concerning the struggle for liberation, but for broader affairs of the nation, it did not. Full backing, however, was to come a few months later. It had that authority as definitely as it was possible to get it, under the circumstances, by July, 1942, when the Committee was obliged by pressure from the United States to recede from its pretension of the preceding September and return to a purely military basis.

The most active of the Resistance groups—communists, socialists, trade unionists, certain Catholic groups and moderate republicans—in June unified their work within France with that of the Committee without. This was accomplished on the basis of a declaration made by General de Gaulle. The Resistance press published the General's views and from then on the London Committee had a firmer foundation within France, although much against American official wishes.

In that unifying statement, General de Gaulle made it clear what his intentions were toward his country after victory: "The last veils behind which the enemy and the traitors have been working against France have now been torn down. The issue at stake in this war is clear to all Frenchmen: freedom or slavery. It is the sacred duty of every man to contribute with all his might to the liberation of our country by crushing the invader. There can be no solution and no future for us except through victory."

This spirit of refusal to accept defeat or compromise was later to be stated in the Roosevelt-Churchill "unconditional surrender" formula.

"This tremendous ordeal, however, has revealed to the nation that the danger threatening its existence came not only from outside, and that victory without courageous and far-reaching internal reconstruction could not be real victory."

This phrase probably scared numerous persons in Washington, but anyone familiar with pre-war France knew that what the General said was a fact.

"One moral, social, political and economic regime," de Gaulle continued, "has abdicated in defeat, after having become paralyzed by corruption. Another, arising from a criminal capitulation, glories in personal power. Both are condemned by the French people who, even as they unite for victory, gather for revolution."

Phew, revolution!

". . . We want France to recover everything that belongs to her. For us, the end of the war means the restoration both of complete integrity to our home country and the Empire; the restoration of our French heritage and the nation's absolute control over its own destinies. Any attempt at usurpation, whether from inside or outside, must be crushed and wiped out. As we mean to make France once again sole mistress in her own house, so shall we see to it that the French people are their own and sole masters. When they have been freed from enemy oppression, all their liberties must be restored to them. Once the enemy is driven from their land, all French men and women will elect a National Assembly which will decide, in the full exercise of its sovereignty, what course the future of the country shall take."

Puzzle: search for the dictator in that paragraph!

"We want retribution," the General continued, "for every menace which has been or may be aimed at French rights, interests and honor and such threats must cease completely. This means first, that the enemy leaders who violate the laws of war to the detriment of the person and property of Frenchmen, together with the traitors who coöperate with them, must be punished. It also means that the totalitarian system which aroused, armed and incited our enemies against us, as well as the systematic coalition of private interests, which in France has acted in opposition to the national interest, must once and for all be overthrown."

Aha, that settles it. The General is a communist!

"We want all Frenchmen to be able to live in security. In the sphere of foreign policy, we must obtain material guarantees which will render France's traditional invader incapable of further aggression and oppression. At home, practical guarantees must be worked out to put an end to the tyranny constituted by the perpetual infringement of rights and to ensure liberty and dignity in the work and life of every citizen. For us, national and social security are imperative and inseparable aims.

"We want to destroy for ever the mechanical organization of mankind such as the enemy has achieved in contempt for all religion, morals and human kindness, simply because he thought he was strong enough to override others. And moreover, in a vigorous renaissance of the Nation and the Empire under planned technique, we want the age-old French ideal of Liberty, Equality and Fraternity to be henceforth applied in our land, in order that every individual may be free in thought, belief and action; that, from the outset, all may have equal opportunities in their social life and that every man may be respected by his fellows and helped as needed."

Some of that sounds akin to what the majority of Americans want for themselves; but that "vigorous renaissance" is suspicious!

"We want this war," the declaration went on, "which affects the destiny of all peoples alike and unites the Democracies in one and the same effort, to result in a world organization establishing lasting solidarity and mutual help between nations in every sphere. And we intend that in this international organization France shall take the prominent position to which her genius and achievements entitle her."

Going to push France forward, make demands and be a trouble-maker, is he?

"France and the world struggle and suffer for freedom, justice and the right of the individual to self-determination. This right of the individual to self-determination, this justice and freedom, must win this war; it must be established, actually and legally, to the benefit of every man and every state."

My, my! Sounds like Henry Wallace speaking.

The declaration ended with this:

"Only such a victory for France and humanity can compensate our country for the unparalleled trials she is undergoing and once again open for her the road to greatness. Such a victory is worth every effort and every sacrifice. We shall win."

Such were the thoughts and the ambition of that "dangerous

Frenchman Charles de Gaulle" as expressed in June, 1942. At that time, the North African landing plans of President Roosevelt were coming into shape. From July on, men and equipment were gathered together and trained for the expedition in the United States and Britain. Our consular agents, ostensibly doing quite another job, had been quietly preparing the way in Africa. Under Mr. Robert Murphy, they were gathering information about the military men and the civilian rulers and forwarding it to Washington. The prejudice in Washington against General de Gaulle had already been abundantly manifested. The information the agents sent to Washington from Africa merely deepened that prejudice. The General from Bordeaux, the acknowledged leader of the French, fighting for the same thing that we were, was to learn of the Anglo-American landing in North Africa for the first time, after it was already under way, and he learned of it in a most humiliating fashion. He was at a Russian Embassy reception in London on the night of the seventh to eighth of November, 1942. An attaché of the Czech Embassy, who had received a telephone call, announced the news to the General. De Gaulle had lunched that day with Prime Minister Churchill, but nothing was revealed to the Frenchman about the impending big event. North African Resistance leaders tried to inform the General just before the landing of what was in the offing. A Polish officer was despatched by them to London for that purpose. He went by ship with the full knowledge of the British Secret Service. When the Pole arrived at an English port, he was taken into custody—or more politely "detained"—until twenty-four hours after the landings in Africa had been made. Then, and not until then, was he allowed to see General de Gaulle.

11

AFRICAN EPISODE EXTRAORDINARY

General de Gaulle and the French Committee bitterly resented being kept in complete ignorance of the President's plan to attack French Africa in November, 1942. Not only were they not given a chance to help, they were not even told of the strategy involved, or of the reasons why they were not being asked to participate in the largest blow aimed at liberation of France since its defeat in 1940. The General's forces had been fighting with the English and Americans all over the world. These Frenchmen were giving all that they had toward the common end. Therefore, when ignored in a matter directly concerning their country, it was human that they should resent their treatment, especially in view of the increasing manifestations of support for the Committee coming from within France. General Staffs like to limit the knowledge of future operations to as few persons as possible. That is common sense. But our military men do not look at political aspects. It is the duty of politicians to point out possible political or other repercussions which might result if military considerations alone are followed. In this instance, the London Committee was not to be used at all, so the military men reasoned it would be dangerous to share the secret with the Committee. The political branch of our government, having no love whatever for the Gaullists, acted unconcerned about what de Gaulle and his Committee might think or do, or what the effect would be on Frenchmen within France.

There were excellent military reasons for not working with de Gaulle in the landing operations. French North Africa had been a stronghold of Vichy and collaboration. All of the top military leaders and all of the top political leaders held their jobs because Vichy put them there. Quasi-military shock troops of Marshal Pétain's imitation fascist National Renovation were well entrenched. In Algiers alone there were 20,000 armed members of the Pétain Legion, all civilians, while 30,000 anti-Vichy residents were in concentration camps and prisons. Moreover, Marshal Pétain had sentenced de Gaulle to death for treason, and those officers who held by their oath of loyalty to the Marshal did not think further than that. In addition, the association of de Gaulle with the British in the attempt to seize Dakar in September, 1940, had been used by the Vichyites to inflame opinion in the army against him. He had, it was said, fought against Frenchmen and thus confirmed himself as a traitor. Even after the amalgamation of the forces of Generals Giraud and de Gaulle later on, there was disunity in the army—one section being pro-Ally, another pro-Vichy.

Men, who behaved at the time of the Armistice like a certain captain at Gafsa, remained pro-Ally, and, as time went on, won many converts. This captain was ill with double pneumonia when de Gaulle's June 18, 1940, broadcast from London was read to him. He got out of bed, walked with a cane to the hospital courtyard and harangued the patients. "Nothing is finished," he said, "we are going to fight the Boche!" Many company commanders in Africa posted de Gaulle's speech. But a contrary attitude was more prevalent. After the amalgamation, some generals in the privacy of barracks spoke this way: "Listen, my men, the Allies are here and we've got to be nice to them. That's what we must do. But we know who the real enemy is and the day is coming when we shall get at England." One general was so bold about his feelings that a friend of mine, dressed in a French uniform, although he was not a Frenchman, attended one of the general's harangues in order to make a wax record of it.

There were Gaullists among the population and in the armed forces. They were Gaullists in exactly the same way that Resistance groups in France from inception were Gaullists: they regarded de Gaulle as the symbol of all those Frenchmen determined to get rid of the Germans and the Vichy collaborationists. They listened to the London radio for guidance, but there never had been direct contact with the General. Means of communication with the outside were practically nil. They tried to reach de Gaulle through the British Intelligence Service, but they did not succeed. At this time, the whole British Intelligence Service was far below its usual level. However, numerous groups came into being very quietly in Algeria, Tunisia and Morocco. They were composed of men of all political beliefs who did not quite know what they were going to do or what they wanted beyond freedom from the double yoke of Berlin and Vichy. Scarcely two months after the Armistice of 1940, a few bold spirits sent to London, by way of the British Intelligence Service, a plan for an English attack against North Africa. The British Government replied that it was in no position to undertake such a task. A few weeks later, an attack was made against the German general commanding the Armistice Commissions in Africa. The instigator of this attack was none other than the Chief of Counter-Espionage sent by Vichy to track down Resistants! He later became an important cog in the underground network that facilitated the Allied landing in Algeria. This attack served as an announcement to all who were thinking about resisting that somewhere underground an active cell was already in business.

By the early part of 1941, the groups in Algiers and Oran were getting together. In them were officers and police as well as civilians. Unification was effected largely through the untiring efforts of an escaped aristocrat from Paris who was living in Oran. His name was Henri d'Astier de la Vigerie. He was to become one of the key men with whom Mr. Murphy dealt in preparing for the landings; he was at the hazardous secret meeting with General Mark Clark when final arrangements were made at Cherchell two weeks before the event. The d'Astier family has a remarkable record since the fall of France. There are three brothers and each, without the others knowing it, jumped into the fight against the Germans and Vichy upon conclusion of the Armistice. François, a general, resigned from the army in 1940 and went to London where he became de Gaulle's principal military adviser. Emmanuel followed Henri to Africa and in February, 1944, became the Interior Minister on de Gaulle's Algiers Committee, a post he held when the Provisional Government moved to France. Beyond having labored tirelessly for the American landing, Henri can claim another achievement: he was eight months and five days in prison after our troops landed! Unfortunately for America's honor, Henri d'Astier, who was known by our underground network as "Mr. Five O'Clock," was not the only one arrested after our landing had been made. Others who helped us were arrested, too, when they became known to the Vichyites. "Mr. Five O'Clock," the civilian coördinator of the pre-landing network for all of French Africa, the civilian leaders in Oran and Algiers, an elderly Algiers doctor who risked his neck and his home for us, and numerous friends of ours in Morocco, were arrested at one time or another on differing charges, none of which was ever proved or presented any hope of being proved. Vichy's officials were left in command in Africa because of our "military expediency" policy and they were getting even with the "traitors" who had conspired with us. A few police officers were taken into custody but they were soon released. No military men were touched, but Admiral Darlan tried to drive them from the army. If he had lived, he probably would have succeeded.

The repression of the men who had saved countless lives of American soldiers began while Mr. Murphy was still threatening Admiral Darlan and General Juin with arrest if they did not submit and give the order not to oppose our landing which was to begin within a few hours. They were at the Villa des Oliviers in Algiers. The only force behind Mr. Murphy's threat of arrest was the armed civilians who had isolated the Villa and surrounded it. During the argument, the Admiral asked permission to send a letter to the Admiralty. He gave his word of honor that in it would be no order to fight. On this assurance, Mr. Murphy granted him permission. An American consular officer was despatched with the letter to make sure that it would arrive safely. The American, however, on his way stopped at the underground headquarters. Henri d'Astier happened to be there. He was not so impressed with Admiral Darlan's word of honor as was Mr. Murphy. The letter was opened and in Darlan's handwriting was a formal order to the Admiralty to respect the terms of the French Armistice with Germany, that is, to fight our men when they landed. This letter, naturally, never went further, and it is preserved today as a piece of evidence bearing on the character and intentions of Admiral Jean Darlan.

One letter was not sufficient for the Admiral. A little later he sent a second one and this time the courier, who again was a member of the American Consulate, did not halt on the way at the underground headquarters. He went straight to the Admiralty with this letter. It arrived about a half-hour after General Mast, who was our chief military accomplice in Algeria, had informed the Colonel commanding the Mobile Guard in writing, that General Giraud had taken command of all troops in French Africa which would again take up the fight on the side of the Allies. An officer of General Juin's staff (General Juin was the army commander in Algeria) happened to be with the Admiral who received Admiral Darlan's letter containing, as did the first letter, instructions to fight. When the Mobile Guard received the notification from General Mast, who was second in command to General Juin, they shouted with joy and sang the "Marseillaise." But not for long. Juin's staff officer went immediately to the Mobile Guard's barracks and announced that General Mast's order was false. Thereupon the Colonel commanding the Guard took a detachment of men and headed for the Villa des

Oliviers, where they took over from the civilian volunteers. From then on the repression of our friends continued for months until outraged public opinion in the United States and Britain and the growing influence of the Gaullists gradually brought it to a halt.

Henri d'Astier, "Mr. Five O'Clock," was labeled a Royalist. When Admiral Darlan was assassinated, it was said that Royalists, wishing to put the Comte de Paris on France's long empty "throne" (the Count was then in Algiers), had committed the crime. French Royalists are a joke as far as influence goes, but there is a noisy, nervy band of Royalist youth known as the "Camelots du Roi." However, there was never any substantial evidence to show that Royalists had anything to do with Darlan's assassination. The behind-the-scenes author of Darlan's elimination is not much of a mystery today. Some time after his release from prison, I questioned M. d'Astier about the alleged Royalist plot and why the Comte de Paris had come to Algiers. He said he saw no chance of a restoration in France and that there had been no plot. The pretender had come to Algiers to see Darlan. The extreme conservatives in Africa were disgusted with the Admiral's behavior in not breaking with Vichy, and the Royalists among them induced the Count to come to tell the Admiral that he ought to resign his post, which the Americans had given him, for he would not get the backing of the extreme conservatives. Beyond this, M. d'Astier said there was no "plot." The police investigation after the assassination bore this out in that it uncovered none. But M. d'Astier languished eight months in prison just the same and our American officials lifted not a finger to get him out.

The trumped-up charge that followed the "Royalist plot" was the "discovery" on December 29th of a plot to kill General Giraud and Mr. Murphy. Who was involved? General Giraud stated that twelve persons were arrested and that they included Axis sympathizers. He said only two of them had given any aid in the Allied landing while four of them were policemen who knew about the plot to kill Admiral Darlan, but did not report it to their superiors. He expressed himself as satisfied that the plotters had intended to kill him and Mr. Murphy, as well as Admiral Darlan. In truth, every last one of those arrested had been active in our behalf; all had been in favor of bringing General Giraud to Africa and some of them had worked intimately with Mr. Murphy throughout the months of scheming.

The General, as I have mentioned before, was not very quick to catch on, and he was constantly manœuvred by the crowd around him. I have no doubt but that he really believed what he said. Mr. Murphy, however, knew who those arrested men were. Among those arrested in this round-up were the chief of the Oran underground, Roger Carcassone, a miller who furnished all of the finances for the entire Algerian Resistance; the chief in Algiers, José Aboulker, who did a remarkable job for our soldiers during the night of November 7th and 8th, after having efficiently organized the Algiers region; and Bernard Karsenty, likewise an indefatigable worker for our cause. Like Henri d'Astier, Karsenty was at the Cherchell meeting on a farm west of Algiers and along the coast. He went out to General Clark's submarine, lying in the Mediterranean, with the General and was in the ferryboat when it turned over, after which, in the scramble, General Eisenhower's emissary lost his pants. Karsenty returned to joke about having seen the untrousered rear of an American general.

Arrested also was José's father, Dr. Henri Aboulker, a venerable and respected professor of the Faculty of Medicine. Dr. Aboulker and his married daughter, Madame Colette Danan, made dangerous contributions to the American cause. The Doctor's home and office at 26 Rue Michelet, in the heart of Algiers, became the headquarters, under the noses of the police and military, for the organization built to neutralize Algiers while our troops landed. It was in Dr. Aboulker's bathroom that Mr. Murphy set up the radio sending and receiving outfit, manned by an American, by means of which contact was kept with Gibraltar and the fleet in the Mediterranean. It was to Dr. Aboulker's home that Mr. Murphy and other members of the American Consulate frequently went to confer with the underground chiefs. Yet, the sixty-five-year-old doctor was arrested and taken to an unhealthy spot in the desert on a charge of participating in a plan to kill Mr. Murphy!

Another among the arrested was a young man named Pierre Alexandre. He was from Oran. One of the missions he carried out for Mr. Murphy was the cutting of cables connecting Oran with Metropolitan France. With a friend, he worked nights under water until two cables were cut at the proper time. Unfortunately, there was a third cable, but its existence was unknown to the underground. All these Frenchmen retain the feeling today that the Americans delivered them to the enemy. During the short-lived Darlan regime and the subsequent Giraud experiment, the Vichyites taunted the pro-Americans with this: "You helped the Americans and then you found how they took care of you!"

The Vichy and anti-American crowd themselves were said to have hatched a plot as late as June 1943. It was their last stand. General de Gaulle had just arrived and the amalgamation between his forces and those of General Giraud had just been announced. It was certain that General de Gaulle would insist on a housecleaning that would eliminate the last vestiges of Vichy. A putsch was planned for June and one of the leading spirits of it was Vice-Admiral Emile Muselier, the man who seized St. Pierre et Miquelon islands off the American coast on Christmas eve, 1941, when he was naval chief under General de Gaulle. That seizure got the Free French into trouble with Washington and in the aftermath, Admiral Muselier and General de Gaulle parted company. The Admiral joined the group around General Giraud when it appeared in Africa a little later, and in April, 1943, he became prefect of Algiers. Some of the investigators of the planned putsch believe that he was given that job for the sole purpose of executing the putsch. The British Intelligence Service picked up the scent of the plan. The Intelligence Service was especially active in June, 1943, because King George VI was making an African tour. When the Monarch's warship put into Algiers harbor (the ship was the King's abode while in Algiers), the Admiral commanding it was advised of what was in the wind. He went to Admiral Muselier and asked if the information he had was true and if there was likely to be trouble. The Frenchman was said to have admitted the veracity of the report and to have added that there might be some shooting. The King's Admiral then warned that if anything like that happened while the King was there, he would be obliged to level Algiers with the ship's guns. That ended the matter and soon thereafter Admiral Muselier was swept out by the de Gaulle broom.

The underground would not have been able to function so smoothly had it not possessed a guardian angel. During the critical period of the preparations in 1942, that guardian was the well-placed Military Intelligence Branch (Bureau Central de la Sécurité Militaire pour l'Afrique du Nord) of the North African army. The chief of that service was a Lieutenant-Colonel Chrétien. His second in command was a professorial-looking commandant named Dullin. In our underground were brothers by the name of Calvet, Guy and Eli. They maintained a lady's apparel shop in the Rue d'Isly, the main shopping street of Algiers. When the conspirators were not at headquarters in Dr. Aboulker's apartment, they were sitting around an octagonal table in a mirrored room in the rear of Elysée Couture, the Calvet shop. There was very little to sell in that store: the motive was not profit, it was conspiracy, and when the storm broke, the Calvet glass broke with it. An Axis bomb fixed up the front of the shop quite nicely. Boards replaced the window glass and conspiracy went on even after the French Committee moved to Algiers and matters settled down by comparison to what they had been. Mysterious figures still came and went.

The Calvet brothers knew Commandant Dullin, and in May they told this intelligence officer from Vichy about the underground. The Commandant had well-founded suspicions that something of that nature existed. Anyway, Dullin, sure of his chief, approached Lieutenant-Colonel Chrétien and the two of them threw in their lot. In subsequent months their task was to protect the underground, a job they fulfilled with skill. All messages sent to Vichy about the underground were either stopped cold or circumvented. The Germans and Vichy constantly were inquiring about bits of information they had acquired concerning persons and events. They asked about d'Astier, Carcassone and others. The Chrétien-Dullin combination ostensibly made an investigation and reported back that these were ordinary persons going about their business. From time to time Vichy officials went to Algiers with specific information. Each was assured by the chief of the military bureau which occupied itself with such matters, that Vichy's suspicions were ill-founded: North Africa was a model of obedience to Pétain and loyalty to Germany.

Nine weeks before the landing, an Algiers police official took to

Colonel Chrétien a detailed written account of an underground movement which had been discovered. This was getting hot. A copy of the report was forwarded to Vichy. An official from Vichy arrived in great haste to investigate. But Colonel Chrétien's straight face convinced the gentleman from Vichy that he had been misled. At the time that he was throwing this police officer off the trail, the Intelligence Chief was in the midst of his first interviews with Mr. Murphy. The Colonel was active for us until after the landing; he went with Mr. Murphy to the critical Darlan conference at the Villa des Oliviers the night of December 7th and 8th. He and Commandant Dullin managed to hold their jobs after our troops arrived in spite of their previous actions. Our government later on awarded decorations to Frenchmen for aiding the landing. This was further cause for bewilderment inasmuch as decorations were given to some officers who had worked tooth and nail against us while civilians who had sacrificed everything for us were ignored. Colonel Chrétien was one of the few recipients who richly deserved it.

After the Algerian underground had reached an intra-mural understanding early in 1941, it made contact with groups functioning in Morocco and Tunisia. The Tunisian one never developed, but in Morocco very active American agents were at work. There was never the same degree of unity in Morocco as there was in Algeria, where army officers and civilians were intertwined in the same organization. In Morocco, army officers and civilians worked separately and even the various civilian groups had little or no knowledge of what other civilian groups were doing. The connecting thread was provided by American agents who gave orders and received reports. In Algeria, great reliance was placed on civilians. They seized buildings on the night of November 7th-8th, arrested generals and held them and tied up the city during the critical hours. They did it with pure bluff and intelligence, for they had no arms beyond a few relics and one Sten gun which had come to Algiers in the United States diplomatic pouch. Mr. Murphy had promised arms; the types and the amount had been decided and they were to be brought over at night from Gibraltar. Four times a rendezvous was given by signal to Gibraltar, and four times, for unexplained reasons, the boat failed to put in an appearance. On the invasion night, when the underground was manning its posts, Mr. Murphy gave M. José Aboulker cigarettes to distribute—instead of guns!

In Morocco, specific tasks such as arresting military and Vichy leaders, cutting telephone wires, and sabotage were assigned to civilians, but these were never called upon to fulfill them. General Emile Béthouart, commander of a brigade in Casablanca, who was our main military stand-by there, was scornful of the value of civilian help. Furthermore, he was so certain that he alone could handle the matter of preventing French troops from firing on our boys that at the last minute he forbade any form of sabotage as being useless destruction. He planned to kidnap General Noguès and he actually went to the General's residence in Rabat for that purpose on the night of the invasion. Everything had been arranged in Casablanca for General Béthouart to announce the coup by radio and to issue orders to troops and civilian authorities not to resist the landing Americans. However, instead of going about his business of kidnapping, General Béthouart tried to reason with his superior. He told him about the promises Mr. Murphy had made to General Giraud and included the statement that American troops as well as French would come under French command within forty-eight hours after the landing. It did not take General Noguès long to consider the matter. The reply he gave was this: "Your affair is not in earnest. You've probably been mystified by Allied propaganda. If there are landings they can only be Commandos destined to be destroyed." Whereupon the would-be kidnapper was arrested and held until after the Armistice. So in Morocco, where no civilian aid was used at the hour of delivery, although civilians had been furnished with American arms, our forces experienced their worst fighting. It went on for three days, while in Algiers it lasted but one day.

Moroccan civilians, however, did a man-sized job during the months preceding the invasion. Their spy work was invaluable; they harbored our radio sending and receiving sets, reported on the disposition of ships in Casablanca Harbor, and stole papers from under German noses. M. Malvergne, the chief pilot of Port Lyautey, was in league with our agents. He was taken to Gibraltar and thence to the United States to come back with the invasion fleet as an expert on the Moroccan coastline. About a month before the landing was made, General Vogel, of the German Armistice Commission, went to Morocco and sent a report to Berlin stating that four divisions of German troops were needed immediately, as Morocco was open to the Atlantic and thus might be tempting to the Allies. This report found its way into the hands of our agents. Evidently as a result of the Vogel report, General von Wuelich, another member of the Wiesbaden Armistice Commission, went to Casablanca to prepare for a German landing. The Germans were to arrive some time in December, 1942. Von Wuelich scented that the Allies were planning something and he so advised Berlin, suggesting that the Germans beat us to the punch. His reports likewise found their way to our High Command. Our landing was made on November 7th-8th.

The Moroccan underground really had blood in its eye. Von Wuelich was to be shot down on his way back to Germany. His plane was to be attacked by R.A.F. fighters as it passed the Balearic Islands, but the clandestine radio message giving instructions to the R.A.F. was garbled, and the British missed their prey. Another surprise party was set for the German-Italian Armistice Commission, resident in Casablanca. On D-Day, a group of Frenchmen were to corral the thirty to forty members and indecently slit their throats. This was frustrated by General Noguès, the French Resident General of Morocco, who took the Germans and Italians out of Morocco. He provided automobiles for their escape into Spanish Morocco a few hours after he learned about our landing. The flight was being prepared when the throat-slitters turned up at Anfa to give them a ride of a different nature. The would-be killers were arrested on general principles: the police had no knowledge of their real mission. The men General Noguès saved eventually became a further thorn in the Allied side. In Spanish Morocco they established radio stations and reported on ship movements at Gibraltar and along the Atlantic coast as a guide to U-Boats. They also carried on extensive anti-Allied propaganda in French Morocco which culminated in a native uprising early in 1944.

The same disillusionment that seized our collaborators in Algeria, when they saw that Vichy went right on controlling matters, gripped our friends in Morocco, although none of the Moroccan leaders was arrested. The American landing did not bring the immediate release of arrested anti-Vichyites; on the contrary, American sympathizers continued to be arrested, and it took a special order from General Patton staying all executions, to prevent General Noguès from liquidating a number of the pro-Allies! Pétain's Legionnaires continued to roam the streets for days after the "liberation." Even after his submission, General Noguès passed out word that the Americans were to be considered as invaders. He assigned a French Military Mission of thirty men to United States Army Headquarters in Morocco. Their duty was to slow down our military progress, not to aid it. Anti-aircraft batteries manned by French crews were ordered not to fire on German or Italian planes. Mobilization of the French Army (to aid us, of course) was used as an excuse to send officers who were known to be pro-Ally into the Moroccan interior where they would not come in contact with our army. Civil servants caught being too friendly with our officials were reprimanded. Certain French naval officers at Casablanca openly said they would sabotage American activities and some railway officials said the same thing, yet they were not removed from their posts. General Noguès, who next to Admiral Darlan was perhaps the smartest man of any nationality in Africa, undoubtedly believed that the Germans would return to Africa and he was playing it safe. How long after the events of November and December, 1942, he continued to believe that, I do not know. The Germans had no illusions about him. Dr. Theodore Auer, the Gestapo agent in Morocco, who was disguised as a consul general, called General Noguès "an eel coated with vaseline." All the while that he was working underhandedly against us, the General was dining with our generals and filling his newspapers with accounts of cordial interviews and receptions with American commanders. These accounts plus the remark that General George S. Patton made upon the cease-fire order, added to the dismay of those who thought that by aiding us they were getting rid of the French collaborationists as well as the Germans. General Patton was our Moroccan commander and when he met General Noguès at Fedhala, where the Armistice was signed, he said he admired the courage, ability and loyalty of Noguès's troops. General Patton may have thought that was a chivalrous thing to say, but all of those, including Americans, who had worked for months to prevent Noguès's troops from fighting at all, those who had argued that real courage and real loyalty lay in joining in and helping

General Patton to get his troops ashore without having to fight his way, all these held a decidedly different view of it. This is one of many incidents in the war which led to the conclusion that our military commanders should be made more conscious of any possible repercussions of their acts outside the strictly military field.

ENTER GENERAL GIRAUD

Although comparatively small in numbers, Resistance in North Africa was a going concern by the time President Roosevelt asked Consul Murphy in January, 1942, for information about a possible landing. Mr. Murphy, his consular and other American agents, had been working there for many months, but up to that time their action had been chiefly aimed at preventing Vichy from succumbing completely to Hitler. The projected invasion gave new point to the existence of the Americans there and it gave a definite objective to the Resisting elements. Thenceforth, Resistance was to bind itself closely to the Americans. Through the Americans they hoped to get rid of the Germans and Vichy in North Africa and then carry the fight to the homeland. Resistance was not interested per se in seeing an American victory unless it contributed to the liberation of France. That was a natural feeling. As for ourselves, the attack in North Africa was not made purely and simply to liberate the French; it was made there because it was deemed the best spot to get at the enemy at that time. Our agents (diplomats, consuls and some non-careerists), however, were not always enlightened in this matter. It proved difficult for some of them to grasp the fact that the French were willing to help us only in so far as that help meant self-help. The French did not want us to go into Africa as conquerors; they wanted us only as friends coming to help their liberation. That, moreover, was the spirit of the public statements that had come from Washington. The attitude of many of our agents and of the Resistants can be illustrated by a conversation between an American colonel and the head of one of the Moroccan groups. The colonel was asked for some assurances as to United States intentions in Africa. The colonel replied rather impatiently that he was not authorized to sign international treaties. All the colonel was interested in was knowing how many bridges the French could blow up. To this the Frenchman replied that he was not going to blow up any bridges—or cross any either—until he knew why he was doing it. The colonel's attitude was that of a conqueror seeking aid from the intended victims; that is, seeking the aid of traitors rather than patriots.

In January, Mr. Murphy asked Resistance leaders if they could suggest a French general who could assume command in North Africa. It is significant that the reply was General Weygand and not General de Gaulle. General Weygand, the former commander-in-chief of the French army, and after the Armistice, Marshal Pétain's viceroy in Africa, had been recalled to France upon demand of the Germans. The Germans became suspicious of him when he made economic agreements with us that enabled our consular agents to enter North Africa. They were unduly alarmed, however, for General Weygand was not the man to go against the Marshal, or any other constituted authority, for that matter. After General Weygand's departure from Africa, Vichy cleaned house and put strong collaborationist generals and civilians into office.

Resistance sent an embassy to the General, who was then living near Antibes, to sound him out. He turned down the proposal. Resistance then suggested General Béthouart, who had a command at Casablanca. Mr. Murphy rejected him as being too young and too unknown to carry influence. A third suggestion was the head of the "Chantiers de la Jeunesse," a Vichy organization modeled after the Nazi labor corps. The head of it, however, was a member of the underground. He was turned down because he was not a military man. After several months elapsed, following this first sounding period, Mr. Murphy went back to say he had heard General Giraud had escaped from the German prison at Koenigstein. If he could be persuaded to take command, United States troops would land in Africa. A messenger was thereupon despatched to the General, who was living near Lyon. He immediately said he was willing but he would have to have a written understanding with Mr. Murphy beforehand. That started a long series of negotiations, with the underground as the intermediary, between the General and Mr. Murphy. The negotiations culminated in the submarine visit of General Clark to Cherchell in October and an exchange of letters between Mr. Murphy and General Giraud on November 2nd, six days before the landing. Resistance, therefore, was agreed that General Giraud should take over the military command; it recognized the inadvisability of associating General de Gaulle with the first phase. However, its leaders anticipated that once the military situation had been mastered, General de Gaulle would come down from London and assume charge of civilian affairs. The French underground leaders, as well as the Americans, were to learn a great deal during the following months about the personality of this General Giraud who had escaped from the Germans in two wars, and who had established himself as a patriot.

Apart from Henri d'Astier, the civilians in the Algerian underground with whom Mr. Murphy had been negotiating were not what might be called "substantial" persons. With the entrance of General Giraud into the scheme came persons who could be classified as "substantial." In the Oran underground was a Paris ex-editor named Jean Rigaud. He had been editor of *L'Echo de Paris*, a blatantly conservative paper. The owner of that paper, as well as of *Le Jour*, in the years immediately preceding the fall of France, was an industrialist named Jacques Lemaigre-Dubreuil. He was the proprietor of the well-known vegetable oil concern, Usines Lesieur. M. Lemaigre-Dubreuil had tarried in Vichy for some time after the fall and was tarred with the Vichy brush. There was suspicion that he had been sent to Africa to orient affairs in a manner favorable to Vichy. This was not proved, but he did show himself to be Vichy-minded. He had good reason to go to Africa. In 1939, he transferred most of his business to Casablanca and French Equatorial Africa. He had visions of developing his vegetable oil business more widely in the colonies. M. Lemaigre-Dubreuil associated himself with the underground where his former editor already was working, becoming the important cog in the negotiations with General Giraud. Another name entered into the picture, that of Tarbe de Saint-Hardouin, a career diplomat who had been with General Weygand in North Africa and had remained behind. M. de Saint-Hardouin was to become director of foreign affairs for Admiral Darlan and was to remain in the same capacity under General Giraud. M. Lemaigre-Dubreuil was to become General Giraud's backbone during the early part of the General's attempt to run affairs, but he was to fade out when his Vichy past and his suspected present became an easy target of Gaullists, Americans, and English, interested in knowing the sort of government we had created in North Africa. The underground, including the extreme Rightist d'Astier, broke with him as it did with General Giraud as soon as the pair made their policy clear.

President Roosevelt's formal commitments with General Giraud rested upon three letters to the General written by Mr. Murphy in the President's name on November 2, 1942. They embodied the results of the long conversations that had taken place. The first three paragraphs of the first letter were quoted in chapter IX. They were assurances that France would be restored to its former greatness, that French sovereignty would be reëstablished as quickly as possible wherever it existed in 1939, and that the United States would consider and treat the French Nation as an ally. From there the letter read:

"I add [wrote Mr. Murphy] that in case of military operations on French territory (either in Metropolitan France or in the colonies) in every case where French collaboration is forthcoming, the American authorities will not interfere in the slightest [n'interviendront en rien] with affairs which belong uniquely to the authority of the national administration, or which arise from the exercise of French sovereignty.

"Concerning the command, the Government of the United States has no thought or desire other than to place the military command of this region in the hands of Frenchmen as soon as possible. Nevertheless, during the periods of operation which include debarking, the establishing of security in French North Africa, and the furnishing of the necessary base, it is considered essential that the American command and organization which has been set afoot with such great effort and difficulty especially for this operation, should remain unchanged. (The above clause was drawn after the recent conference between the American and French representatives. It was written before the receipt of your note of October 27, which read as follows:

" 'It is normal, and it is understood, that all debarking operations shall be regulated by the E.M. of the American army.

" 'The interallied command will come into play after the debarkment, that is, for each debarkment point, 48 hours after the hour fixed for the beginning of the initial landing operations of the first convoy. In regard to later operations, the American troops will pass under interallied command as soon as they have landed.'

"I am sending your suggestion to the General Staff of the American Army and I am certain that an acceptable formula will be found.) During this period, the Government of the United States will expend every effort with a view to furnishing French forces with modern arms and equipment. While the French forces are being thus organized and equipped, the details concerning the command can be completed in order that the French will be in position to assume the supreme command at the desired time. In order to facilitate the direction of operations, it would be desirable that a General of the French Army be associated with the Commander-in-Chief immediately after the landing."

The second letter was in reply to General Giraud's concern lest General de Gaulle creep somehow into the projected invasion and also in reply to a desire to keep the English out of it. Mr. Murphy wrote:

"I have received your letter of October 28 which read as follows:

"'I attach the greatest importance to the fact that, in case of combined military operations on French territory (whether Metropole or overseas) which is not occupied by the Axis Powers according to the terms of the Armistice Convention, the United Nations expeditionary corps which will come to collaborate with local French troops, should be an expedition essentially American and placed under American command.

"'It should not have any French dissident elements whatever.

"'In case of need, it is not until later and after an understanding between local French authorities and the American authorities that non-American formations, Allied or French dissidents, would be allowed on this French territory.'

"I am happy to assure you that your views are completely in harmony with those of my Government."

The third letter promised the extension of Lend-Lease for "the purpose of giving the French Army the means of participating in the common struggle," and also promised that the American Government would facilitate the delivery of such arms and food supplies needed by the civil populations of whatever territories were liberated. General Giraud was an individual without resources of any nature

and even without a command. He had far less authority than did
General de Gaulle. General Giraud had to hypothecate the future
and he would have no future unless we made it for him. Deliveries
of food and merchandise to territories eventually to be under the
General were to be considered as "official French purchases" and
were to be charged at world prices. Payment was to be made by
compensation. General Giraud was to open credits in North Africa
in favor of the American Government and to the amount of the
purchases made. These credits would be used by the American
Treasury to pay for eventual military expenses or for the purchase
of North African products to be sent to the United States. In that
way, General Giraud would not be obliged to pay cash, and he
would get a reëquipped army and food and goods for the civilian
population.

With these understandings, signed and exchanged a week before
the invasion, General Giraud consented to take the leap. The invasion fleet was already under way at the time. British troops and the
Royal Navy were a part of the expedition at the time that Mr.
Murphy, on November 2nd, was "happy to assure" General Giraud
that no non-American formations would be used until some time
later, and then only if agreed to by the French authorities. It was
planned that the General should arrive by air in Algeria simultaneously with the landing of the American troops, that he should proclaim himself the leader and call upon all of North Africa to join
the war again on the Allied side. A hitch developed that kept him
away until after a head-on collision had been made with Admiral
Darlan who, by design or by chance, happened to be in Algiers on
November 7th. That hitch came at Gibraltar. A British submarine
had taken General Giraud there from France to make last-minute
arrangements with General Eisenhower, whose headquarters were
then deep in the Rock. The hitch arose over General Giraud's understanding of the meaning of words and intentions. The General
thought he was to become the supreme Allied commander. The
agreement he had made with Mr. Murphy said: "Concerning the
command, the Government of the United States has no thought or
desire other than to place the military command of this region in
the hands of Frenchmen as soon as possible," and "While the
French forces are being thus organized and equipped, the details

concerning the command can be completed in order that the French will be in position to assume the supreme command at the desired time." Those appeared to General Giraud to be unambiguous words, but General Eisenhower would not accept them. He explained that it was politically impossible for American forces to be placed under French command at any time. Had the Americans deliberately tried to trick General Giraud, or had there been a lamentable lack of coordination between the President's civil representatives and his military representative? Did one hand not know what the other was doing? Whatever the origin of the discrepancy, General Giraud felt he had been tricked and it took many hours of arguing before the Frenchman agreed to proceed to Africa. By the time he got there, "his" Proclamation assuming command had been read over the radio. It was written by someone else and read by someone impersonating the General. The underground felt it was absolutely necessary that the impression be given that the General was in Africa and that the insurrectionists had a firm grip.

In the next three months, General Giraud was to complain on several occasions about the discrepancy between the treatment promised him and that which he actually received. He was always prompted by M. Lemaigre-Dubreuil. The "military expediency" deal with Admiral Darlan placed the Admiral at the head of civil affairs while General Giraud became commander-in-chief of French forces. But the Americans had to threaten to arrest the Admiral and the Vichy officers around him before he would agree to accept General Giraud. The Admiral was assassinated on Christmas Eve, and General Giraud was then appointed by the Imperial Council (all Vichyites) to the functions of civil as well as military chief. Three days after the assassination, M. Lemaigre-Dubreuil arrived in Washington on behalf of General Giraud. He had left Algiers before General Giraud knew he was to take Admiral Darlan's place. From what M. Lemaigre-Dubreuil had to say to Secretary Hull, it appeared that he had set out from Algiers for the purpose of building a fire under Admiral Darlan. As it turned out, when M. Lemaigre-Dubreuil spoke his piece the Admiral was already out of the way. Among the points made in his conversation with Mr. Hull and two other members of the State Department, M. Lemaigre-Dubreuil said that it was upon the invitation of a group of Frenchmen who had never accepted the

German victory, that discussions pertaining to the entrance of American troops into Africa had been conducted. These conversations were carried on with the object of bringing about the reëntry of France and of French North Africa into the war as a French entity (entité) rather than as a consequence of the American occupation. He said General Giraud had agreed to reappear and direct this movement on the basis of an explicit accord with Mr. Murphy which recognized him as the chief of a French government, and that the constitution of such a government should not be delayed inasmuch as delay gave the French National Committee in London opportunity to assert itself as being the provisional French government. Such delay only weakened the position of General Giraud. He added that the necessity for a single command under the supreme direction of General Giraud was inherent in the military situation. He further stated that General Giraud considered that General de Gaulle should be included in the general French organization, first, by association with the Imperial Council (which Admiral Darlan had created) and second, as military chief.

That General Giraud was to become the chief of a provisional government may have been mentioned during the negotiations with Mr. Murphy, but it did not appear in words in the basic documents sealing the agreement. It could be considered as having been implied, however, in the economic and financial accord. Participants in the negotiations told me that the General did not go to Africa in the belief that he would become the civil head, but he did expect to be the supreme commander. The underground, obviously with the exception of M. Lemaigre-Dubreuil, expected General de Gaulle to take over the civil function eventually. General Giraud, however, fell in with the idea of being the top man in all things when M. Lemaigre-Dubreuil and the men with whom he associated (not from the underground) developed big ideas. As M. Lemaigre-Dubreuil explained it, they wanted General de Gaulle to become the commander of the French armed forces while General Giraud was to become chief of the government and supreme Allied commander. He took this line in two subsequent interviews at the State Department, and he wrote it in a letter addressed to Admiral William D. Leahy, ex-ambassador to Vichy, who by that time had become the President's personal Chief of Staff. M. Lemaigre-Dubreuil hoped the Admiral might help him, but instead he side-stepped the matter, pleading incompetence. This letter was also interesting in view of a charge it made that the United States had violated the original agreement with General Giraud in another way: "From an internal point of view, different measures have been adopted since the arrival of American troops in Africa which infringe upon French sovereignty. They are contrary to the Giraud-Murphy accords."

In a second interview with Secretary Hull on January 9, 1943, General Giraud's representative said that unless the United States took steps to create certain "material and moral" conditions in Africa, it would be impossible to counter allegations made by the English, Gaullists, and the Axis and French stations under German control to the effect that North Africa had been "occupied" by the United States. He recalled again that the "intervention of American troops had been demanded, prepared and facilitated by the French" to whom assurances were given at the time that necessary material would be furnished them and that they would be treated as allies in full possession of sovereignty. Nonetheless, "two months have passed since the promises were made to furnish arms and equipment to the French forces, and the Mission [General Giraud's Military Mission in Washington] still does not know the date when this equipment will start to arrive or the quantity of material that will be furnished the French troops." He esteemed it essential that some "concrete manifestation of America's good intentions" should be soon forthcoming. The impression was growing, he said, that the United States was treating North Africa as an occupied country rather than as an ally, and in order to dispel this impression, it was necessary to alter the Darlan-Clark agreement especially to recognize French Africa formally as an ally. He wanted French Africa to have civil as well as military representatives in various countries. Such civil representation was necessary, he felt, inasmuch as General de Gaulle had diplomatic emissaries in several countries. These gave de Gaulle an advantage over General Giraud, for he could discuss matters directly with the British and American governments, thus giving the impression that he, de Gaulle, was the chief of French Resistance. As one corrective measure, M. Lemaigre-Dubreuil suggested that General Giraud make a declaration, to be drawn up in accord with General Eisenhower, which would clearly indicate to General de Gaulle that the real problem to be solved until France was free, was military and not political, and that General Giraud was to be considered as the "depositary" of French interests until the end of the war.

Two days later, on January 11th, M. Lemaigre-Dubreuil went back to the State Department to review the points he had made in his previous interview with Secretary Hull. This time he did not see Mr. Hull but spoke to the two State Department officials who had been present with Mr. Hull during the previous conversations—Mr. Ray Atherton and Mr. Samuel Reber. To what he had said before, he added that General Giraud's proposed declaration should be followed by a statement from President Roosevelt to confirm that, in the opinion of the American Government, no French Government exists, and that the American Government recognize General Giraud as an ally having charge of the military defense and protection of French interests, this to constitute a trusteeship until the French people can take charge in their own name. He also desired reaffirmation of the spirit contained in the exchange of letters between General Giraud and Mr. Murphy.

When the Frenchman left, it was understood that he would discuss the matter with General Eisenhower upon his return to Africa and the State Department would await a report from the American General before deciding what to do. This procedure was not necessary, for the Roosevelt-Churchill Casablanca conference was to come upon the heels of this visit. There the whole matter was thrashed over again with, as we shall see, various results.

At the close of the Casablanca conference, General Giraud sent an enthusiastic résumé of what he had obtained (or thought he had obtained) from the two chiefs of state, to his French Mission in Washington. He said France had been recognized as an ally of the United Nations; that the letters exchanged between him and Mr. Murphy before the landing remained in force, with the exception of the stipulation about the interallied command; that it was understood that France no longer had a government, but that the United States and Great Britain recognized that the commander-in-chief with headquarters in Algiers had the right and the duty to preserve all French military, economic, financial and moral interests; that French forces would receive priority for the promised materials, and that with General de Gaulle (who attended a part of the conference) an accord had been reached that should soon result in a union of the two groups. He repeated: "I am recognized as the trustee of all French interests" and added that these "results constitute a success for us."

What made General Giraud think he had won victory all down the line, with the exception of the fact that he did not get his coveted, formally promised, Supreme Allied Command? He had in his possession memoranda signed by both President Roosevelt and Prime Minister Churchill with the contents of the various points of the accord that had been reached. There were two American memoranda and one British memorandum. One of them was not formally signed by the President but it had his marginal annotations denoting acceptance. "Yes" was written beside the following paragraph:

"In the political field: It has been understood by the President of the United States, the British Prime Minister and General Giraud that it was in the common interest of all that the French fighting against Germany should be united under one single authority and that every facility should be given to General Giraud to realize this union."

On this same memorandum were the details of the military supplies which the United States was to furnish and later did furnish to equip the French army which fought in Italy and France. The other memorandum, which the President signed, contained other points which General Giraud mentioned in his telegram to his Mission in Washington. The third section said:

"Inasmuch as the Nation and the French people have the sole right to name their representatives and designate their government, and inasmuch as the French Metropole finds itself at the present time in a state of impossibility to freely make a choice, France therefore does not possess a government.

"In the interest of the French people, for the safeguarding of their past, present and future, the Government of the United States and the government of Great Britain recognize that the Commander-in-Chief, with headquarters in Algiers, has the right and the duty to preserve all French interests, military, economic, financial and moral. They engage themselves to aid the Commander-in-Chief by all means in their power until the day when, having recovered liberty, the people and the French Nation shall be able to designate their regular government."

The Anfa conference ended on January 24th. M. Lemaigre-Dubreuil had returned from the United States to find his position as General Giraud's backbone seriously compromised by the compaign against him, emanating from various quarters disillusioned by the fact that a clean break had not been made with the pro-Vichy elements. M. Lemaigre-Dubreuil was blamed as the man largely responsible. Two weeks after the conference, he wrote a letter to the General which testified at once to his fall from favor and also to General Giraud's need for someone to tell him what to do. The letter was dated February 6, 1943. He said that quite "by chance," while in the General's office that morning, he had learned about certain American proposals which in his opinion "annihilated" all that he had accomplished during his Washington trip and a part of what the General had obtained at Anfa. In order to forestall such an eventuality, he urged General Giraud to have Mr. Murphy write a letter in the President's name, in which everything that was favorable to General Giraud in the Anfa convention be restated. Four days later, the General timidly followed M. Lemaigre-Dubreuil's advice. He recalled that when he gave his consent to the memorandum of the Anfa accord, he had made one objection. It concerned but one paragraph: "I should like to know in what manner President Roosevelt intends to confirm that he recognizes the Commander-in-Chief, with headquarters in Algiers, as the 'trustee' of French interests, either in the United States or in the countries influenced by America." He said he would be very much obliged if Mr. Murphy would inform the President by telegram of his viewpoint. Nine days later General Giraud had his answer. This is what an astonished pair of eyes that had seen the inside of a German prison fortress read:

"Monsieur le General: I did not fail to communicate immediately the contents of your letter of February 9, 1943, to the President of the United States who has authorized me to reply that the Government of the United States considers you as the trustee in the United States of French military, economic and financial interests which are connected, or will be connected, with the liberation movement actually existing in North Africa and in French West Africa.

"Considering the relations existing between the Government of the United States and the French Committee, it is not possible to recognize you as trustee in the United States for French interests which are not connected with your movement.

"As was agreed in Article III of the common Memorandum, the French Nation and the French people alone can decide who their representatives are to be and designate their government. As the question of a future government of France cannot at present receive a final solution, there can be no question of the recognition of a French government until the French people are free to express their will. Consequently, there can be no question of a diplomatic and consular service.

"My Government, nevertheless, will welcome a civil representation as a part of the French Military Mission now in the United States.

"The question of a representation in other countries, including those of Central and South America, similar to the one herein envisaged, should be discussed between the interested countries and the French High Command. Should any of these countries ask the advice of my Government, the reply will be in the sense of the preceding paragraphs.

"I have received instructions to inform you that on this basis you may rest assured of the most cordial coöperation of the United States.

"Je vous prie d'agréer, Monsieur le Général, l'assurance de ma haute considération." (signed) *Murphy*.

The difference between that letter and the Anfa memorandum was so striking that it took the wind out of the Giraudists. At Anfa, the President agreed that the commander-in-chief in Algiers, who was General Giraud, had the right and the duty to preserve all French interests without limitation of any sort and he engaged himself to support General Giraud to that end. In the letter, written three weeks after the Anfa conference, the President limited the General's sphere to military, economic and financial interests connected with North Africa and French West Africa. The Anfa memorandum did not specifically recognize General Giraud as the head of a provisional government, but how could "all French interests" be "preserved" excepting by a government? Moreover, the validity of the Murphy-Giraud agreements was confirmed and they recognized the "French Nation" as an ally. Was that recognition a mere expression of sentiment? The purpose for which the agreements were made was anything but sentimental. The only way that a "nation" effectively can be an ally is through a government.

Prime Minister Churchill affixed his name to a memorandum at Anfa just as did President Roosevelt. The critical political parts of the Churchill memorandum read as follows:

"The French nation and the French people have the sole right to fix their representation and to designate their government. Because of the impossibility of the Mother Country to freely make its will known, France does not now possess a government that can be recognized and the question of a future government of France is not now susceptible to receiving a definite solution.

"In the interest of the French people and with the aim of safeguarding the past, present and future of France, the President of the United States and the British Prime Minister attribute to the French Commander-in-Chief whose Headquarters is in Algiers, the right and the duty to act as trustee of French military, economic and financial interests which are associated or will be associated with the movement of liberation now established in North Africa and French West Africa. They engage themselves to aid him in this task by all of the means in their power . . .

"In the political field, it has been understood between the President of the United States, the British Prime Minister and General Giraud that it was in the common interest of all that all Frenchmen fighting against Germany should be united under a single authority and that all facilities should be given to General Giraud and to the French National Committee under the direction of General de Gaulle to realize this union."

Thus Mr. Churchill limited General Giraud's action to French North Africa and to French West Africa; he said nothing about France's "moral" interests and he pledged as much help to General de Gaulle in the matter of union as he did to General Giraud.

If the United States had followed the Roosevelt memorandum, and Great Britain the Churchill one, obviously there would have been two policies toward the French instead of a single Anglo-

American one. All through this French affair there was a tendency toward two distinct policies, but that was avoided chiefly because Mr. Churchill on most occasions permitted the President to take the lead while he sat back in passive resistance. Given the close Anglo-American working conditions, it would have been disastrous for the two to have taken opposing courses. As it was, it came close enough to that, all too frequently. Oddly, the Roosevelt memorandum included the Prime Minister in its pledges and the Churchill memorandum included the President. Why did General Giraud accept such a contradiction? A more astute person would not have done so. M. Lemaigre-Dubreuil was not at his elbow at Anfa to stiffen him, but the vegetable-oil merchant did "utter a cry of alarm" when he found out accidentally what was going on, and this cry brought forth the letter from the General to Mr. Murphy in which clarification was asked. The General in that letter indicated that he had accepted the contradiction because he appreciated that the Prime Minister could not be as favorable to him as was the President; he was aware that British public opinion was for General de Gaulle, the Prime Minister therefore being restrained from giving such full support to General Giraud. The General in the letter also expressed his appreciation that the President had been willing to support him so completely. However, when General Giraud received the President's reply, he found to his stupefaction that the President had used the terms of the Churchill memorandum and not those of his own. Whether there had been deliberate deception or whether the wording of the memorandum at Anfa was slipshod or whether Washington had afterward abruptly changed its mind, was all the same to the Giraudists; they naturally felt that they had been deceived again.

The President's reply put an end to the high aspirations of the Giraudists to get top position in all French affairs. Thereafter, General Giraud received some support from the President's representatives, military as well as civil, for the General's struggle to hold on in the face of the much smarter Gaullists. But in reality that reply closed the Giraud chapter which began when he was sought out in France and asked to come to Africa and help put France back into the war. Although the President gave no sign of realizing it, it also ended his fight to prevent General de Gaulle from assuming political leadership. From then on, the United States lagged far behind the procession.

From the Anfa conference in January until the following June, Generals Giraud and de Gaulle sparred with one another over the unity of action which had been discussed at the conference. Formulae by the ream passed between London and Algiers. As Frenchmen are wont to do, they argued over "texts" and the precise meaning of words, with each side aiming for predominant position. Finally, through the mediation of level-headed General Georges Catroux, a Gaullist, General de Gaulle went to Algiers and on June 1st, a double-headed French Committee of National Liberation was formed. Being double-headed, it was a monster; it could not live long with two Generals having equal power. General de Gaulle began immediately to insist upon relieving the Vichy hold-overs. M. Marcel Peyrouton was removed as Governor General of Algeria. M. Peyrouton had been virtually lifted by Washington from Buenos Aires, where he had been Vichy's ambassador, and set down in Algiers to help General Giraud. M. Peyrouton was a former Vichy Minister of the Interior and as such had a hand in repressive measures against French patriots and in measures favoring the Germans. Although M. Peyrouton had technical ability, the length to which the United States Government went to hand-pick a man so despised in France was evidence to the patriots that "chance" and short-range "military necessity" were not the sole guiding principles of Washington. M. Peyrouton was arrested a short time later by the "Commission of Purification," which investigated alleged treasonable activities of numerous ex-Vichyites, and he was still in jail at the time France was liberated a year later.

Another one to go was the "eel" General Noguès who had been kept on as Resident General of Morocco. One by one the outstanding ones were relieved of their duties: General Jean Bergeret, former Vichy Air Minister; M. Pierre Boisson, Governor General of West Africa, both of whom had been members of Admiral Darlan's Imperial Council, and several others. General de Gaulle also insisted that the army be purged of those officers who had taken a prominent part in favor of Vichy and collaboration. In most of these demands,

General Giraud or his backers opposed General de Gaulle. During the months between January and June, when General de Gaulle arrived on the scene, General Giraud had been pushed into making some reforms in Vichy-made laws and into making speeches that gave the impression he was wholeheartedly a democrat laboring against great odds. He did not, however, satisfy the Gaullists who were urged on always by the Resistance within France. Between June and October the Gaullists steadily pushed General Giraud, now shorn of all the men who used to guide his actions, into a corner. On August 4th, a decree was published making General Giraud Commander-in-Chief of all French armed forces (heretofore, he had been commander of all excepting those outside North and Equatorial Africa which were under General de Gaulle), but he was to cease his functions as co-president of the Committee whenever he took the field with his army. A National Defense Committee was created under the presidency of General de Gaulle. That gave him added power, for the National Defense Committee would determine where French forces were to fight—in other words, where General Giraud was to fight. This change still was not satisfying. For one thing, it did not completely subordinate the military apparatus to the civil, according to French law and to the law in all democratic countries. Further changes were made on October 2nd which completed this reform, making the military fully subordinate to the civil, placing General de Gaulle as the sole president of the National Committee of Liberation and General Giraud as the Commander-in-Chief when there was fighting to do; between times, he was just inspector general of the armed forces. That put an end to the two-headed committee monster. General Giraud held on in this subordinate position until April of 1944 when he was eliminated altogether, passing quietly out of the story to take up residence near Oran where he looked on from afar while France was being liberated in the summer of 1944.

The series of manœuvres that culminated in General Giraud's disappearance was regarded in official Washington as confirmation of one of the objections that had been made to General de Gaulle; he was a dictatorial man bent on fastening his organization on France. Yet while these manœuvres were taking place, steps were being taken by de Gaulle to create a National Consultative Assembly, an instrument which would have been in his way had he entertained the designs attributed to him by our officials. Two weeks before General Giraud's eclipse, a Consultative Assembly was created. It was composed of forty-nine representatives of Resistance from within France, twenty-one representatives of Resistance outside France, twenty members of the former Senate and Chamber of Deputies and twelve representatives from the General Councils (regional governing bodies in the Republic). None of the members of the body was nominated by the National Committee of Liberation. The representatives from within France were named by the National Council of Resistance, which was composed of eight members from the larger Resistance movements, six from the principal political parties and two from the trade unions. These delegates hitch-hiked to Algiers as best they could. They, in turn, chose the twenty-one representatives from Resistance outside France from a list submitted by Resistance outside the Metropole. The twenty representatives from the former Senate and Chamber of Deputies were chosen by those senators and deputies who were outside the country, while the General Councils' representation was named from the Councils in North and West Africa and the colonies. The only intervention in the matter that the National Committee made was to assure that none of the members chosen had been compromised by association with Vichy. Otherwise, the National Consultative Assembly was an independent body and it soon showed that it meant to exercise its independence. It could not legislate—the National Committee was not bound to do what the Assembly directed. Its purpose was what the name implied, consultative. In practice, the Committee did heed the Assembly and even relied on it. The Assembly became a valuable part of the governing apparatus. It was as representative as was possible under the circumstances.

The important thing was that General de Gaulle brought such a body together. No would-be dictator would have done that. The fact was that from early 1942, the General had been following the wishes of the underground within France in his general policy. Many of his acts, which were labeled by his detractors in Washington as those of an authoritarian schemer, were made upon the express wishes of the underground. The men who came from France were of all shades of political opinion and some had no politics at all. They were united, however, in their desire to free France from Vichy as well as the Germans. I found the members I knew to be honest, sincere patriots sorely troubled by the state of affairs at home and determined that there should be democratic reforms. When I asked them about General de Gaulle and how he was regarded at home, unanimously they said that the General would take orders from the people or he would be displaced. There was no hero-worship among them. To them, the General was merely the man who had carried on the fight when others failed and if he attempted to act in any other spirit, he would be blocked. Some members of the Assembly and of the National Committee favored making Gaullism a political party to be taken back to France as such. The matter was at one time discussed freely in the Assembly lobbies. This brought immediate reaction. As far as I could determine, there was no evidence that the General himself favored such an idea. If he ever did, he soon relinquished it.

The French Committee of National Liberation thus was developing in as democratic a manner as was possible. Repeated pledges had been given by General de Gaulle to the effect that he desired only to act until the people of his country had an opportunity to say what they wanted. The exact steps in the transitional period between liberation and the election of a national assembly to decide a future regime for France were delineated. Various plans were prepared to meet needs during this interim period. The Committee, advised and even goaded by the Consultative Assembly, was acting like a provisional government in defiance of Washington. In the spring of 1944, it decided to change its name again, this time to "The Provisional Government of France." Washington fussed and fumed, said the presumptive General could not do a thing like that and continued on in the old groove. General de Gaulle also continued on: he called the Committee the Provisional Government when he felt like it and at all times proceeded as if he no longer cared what President Roosevelt felt, said or did. It was as the unchallenged chief of a Provisional Government that he entered France behind the Allied armies.

12

WHY WE HAD TO BOW

French North Africa was a bulwark to the men who knuckled down and made the Armistice with Germany. Marshal Pétain and his followers promised to defend that territory against all comers in return for a German pledge not to occupy all of Metropolitan France. The Marshal thought he was outsmarting the Germans when they made that pledge. He was obsessed with the idea of remaining on home soil, rather than with trying to carry on the fight from abroad. He would never, he said, desert his people. Anything was better than yielding all of France. With even a small corner he could bring into motion his long-held notions of how France should be reorganized and governed. Hence, North Africa became his trump in dealing with the Germans. "Safe" officers were put in command there and the civilian governing apparatus was welded to the Vichy policy by the same means. This meant inevitably that the leaders there hated General de Gaulle, who had taken a diametrically opposed line to that of the Marshal. This meant also that when it came time for preparations for the Allied landings, General de Gaulle had to be passed over in favor of someone who might have a better chance to win the aid of the North African leaders. Thus it came about that General Giraud was chosen as the likely man and that the "temporary military expediency" policy came into being.

This, however, does not tell the whole story. It was with pleasure that Washington found it militarily desirable to work with someone other than General de Gaulle. An idea was hatched some time before the invasion that a middle group should be built up in France, one that would stand between Vichy and the Free French. Such a group would have to be built from the bottom. This "middle" notion seems to have been shared by both the President and the State Department; it may have originated in the United States Embassy in Vichy. The advantages of such a group sponsored by the President would be these: it would tend to take the sting out of criticism that our policy favored fascist Vichy and it might, if strongly enough built, eliminate the Free French altogether. The Embassy in Vichy was reporting that Free French backers in France were chiefly communists and that others were of radical tinge. General Giraud was a military hero and had not been compromised by either Vichy or the Free French. He was, it was reasoned, a natural choice to rally middle-of-the-roaders.

Two things were wrong with this idea. The first one was that by the time we were ready to act, only a handful of Frenchmen had not already taken sides either for Vichy or the Free French, and the second one was that while General Giraud was a hero, he did not have the capacity to carry out such an assignment.

The conception of this proposed middle group was that it would be composed of persons who economically and politically were of what would be called in the United States the middle class. In other words, it would not have the "radical" tendency attributed to the followers of the Free French. It would be safe and sound. It was a mistake to think of the French middle class in this way. France is a land of the "petit," small people as well as things. The upper bourgeoisie, which include the remnants of the old aristocracy, is a small group and what lies between it and the "small people" is not much more important. Furthermore, during the war the patriotic urge cut across group lines, still further diminishing the number of persons who otherwise would think and act with their groups; it was patriotic to oppose the Germans and hence also collaborationist Vichy. People who would be classified as middle class in the United States are among the "petit" in France and they veer to the Left, not the Center. Even farmers, who, wherever in the world they own their own land, are considered as ultra-conservative, tend to be Leftists. Their land was given to them by the Revolution of 1789 and they have never forgotten it. No middle group, however it might be viewed, existed in France which might have been capable of bringing about the end the dreamers desired.

The forces and meaning of Resistance were constantly misjudged by Washington. Until the very end, Resistance was regarded as not responding to the majority will of the people; rather it was looked upon as animated by radicals who were going to tear the country asunder if given half a chance. The following quotation, taken from *La Défense de la France*, if it was ever read in Washington, was ignored: "Resistance is truly turned towards the future. By the energy it has managed to generate in itself, it becomes a promise of vitality and force for our nation; not brute force, but of the force which creates greatness, the greatness of the individual. French Resistance proves to the world that France is alive. When the enemy has been driven out of French territory, when the world has found peace again, France must not forget and turn away from those who will have been her saviors. The men of outstanding quality who sought and found each other during the struggle must not be scattered afterwards. They must remain united, protecting the unblemished purity of their mission. . . . She (France) has meditated about the past and has understood that the Third Republic was truly dead since it had accepted defeat and surrender, that the old political parties have no longer any meaning and that their leaders must be put aside for good. France no longer wants to have dealings with creatures like Chautemps, of whom our colleague 'Resistance' has said so aptly that he was the 'manifestation of all the inherent baseness of a worn-out ruling system.' She has no use for wretches who still have enough unfortunate cleverness to stir up Frenchmen against each other and to deceive America about the real France. France demands new men who have never made any compromise, men who have proved themselves under German occupation. . . . It is imperative that the world should know that de Gaulle has all the weight of France behind him." *La Défense de la France* was an underground paper started in 1941 and the quotation was taken from its issue of April 20, 1943. *La Défense* had a large circulation. It was not a radical sheet. Its birthplace was a room in the cellars of the Sorbonne and its writers came from what we would call the middle class. Yet note the emphasis on the necessity to purge the political roosters of a "worn-out ruling system" and the imperativeness that "the world should know that de Gaulle has all the weight of France behind him."

As for General Giraud, at the time he was selected, he appeared to have dropped from heaven instead of from just over the walls of Germany's Koenigstein fortress. Not much was known about him except that he had been captured by the Germans in World Wars I and II and that on both occasions he had escaped. Between his two escapes he was not an outstanding figure; he was a run-of-the-mine general. After he had been taken to Algiers, he soon became a disappointment to both the Allies who had to deal with him and to his countrymen who had looked with favor upon his connection with the invasion. He had very little knowledge beyond his military duties, and no feeling for the role in which he was cast. He was easily manœuvred and quite unfit for grand scale leadership. He had too much respect for constituted authority to be a good rebel. It was not displeasing to the Americans but it was disillusioning to all anti-Vichy French when it became evident that General Giraud considered himself still in Marshal Pétain's hands. One of the pledges he made when the Imperial Council named him to assume full leadership after the assassination of Admiral Darlan was that he would rule in the name of the Marshal. He was obliged by pressure later to deviate from this pledge, but even then he never formally renounced allegiance to the Marshal. Each step he took away from the Vichy regime by abolishing its laws was made under pressure and then he did not appear to be fully aware of what he was doing or why. During the first few months of his High Commissionership, he was a complete tool of the Vichy people in Africa. It took Admiral Darlan but a few minutes to talk him into believing that he could not rally French African forces to his command. That was when the Admiral took over and began his eventful but short Commissionership. One opinion of him in France was expressed in February, 1943, by the leftist clandestine paper *Combat*. After recalling that when the General escaped from the German prison in March, 1942, it devoted an entire page to him in which it said: "In our opinion, Giraud is a fine soldier without a stain on his record. He has kept his sword immaculate in order to use it in France's service." *Combat* continued: "Today, after having applauded the French North Africa army's reëntry into the war under the command of General Giraud, France stands amazed and indignant to see that this great man is surrounded at Algiers, Casablanca and Dakar by Vichy men, Hitler's lackeys. Giraud! Fate has called you, a soldier, to assume a crushing load of political responsibility. It is not enough for you to fight against the Germans, you will have to drive out all the men who have been in his service and who are now seeking to save their positions, their regime and their own skins; you will have to succeed in this third and most difficult bid for freedom. Break free from these associates who are exploiting your prestige, escape from these men whom France will never forget!"

His lack of political astuteness made the General an easy person to influence. He needed someone at his elbow—the right someone.

As soon as the Vichy crowd became less and less numerous in Algiers, the General became more and more ill at ease. He was no match at all for General de Gaulle. General de Gaulle was once asked what he was going to do to counter a move General Giraud was about to make against him. "Nothing at all," replied de Gaulle, "nothing at all. Giraud will do it for me!" A story was told in Algiers about a remark General Giraud was supposed to have made after he had signed the decree as co-President of the Committee of National Liberation, which abolished his status as co-President with General de Gaulle. Someone mentioned that he had signed away his job. "What," he exclaimed, "nobody explained that to me!" The story may be apocryphal but its foundations are real.

There was apprehension among some of our diplomats in Algiers when General Giraud decided to visit the United States in July 1943. They feared that he would expose himself and the American public would discover it had been led to believe he was something that he was not.

The fanciful dream of creating a middle French bloc was destroyed when the General showed that he could not measure up to expectations. It would have been difficult to discard him, for agreements had been made with him bearing on future military operations. From then on, Washington's policy bordered onto the negative; it neither supported General Giraud to the extent promised in the Giraud-Murphy agreements nor did it do anything to encourage General de Gaulle. Washington drifted along, content to snipe at the Gaullists who were growing stronger month by month and to barricade itself behind the "France must choose for herself" dictum. Just how it was expected France would be governed until the French people could freely make their choice, not only of men but of the type of regime, was never clarified. Hard practical problems were involved which never seemed to have been given consideration. The experience of AMGOT (Allied Military Government of Occupied Territory) in Sicily and Italy was a warning against trying to take over all of the functions of civil government in France. The

French would not stand for an Allied military government and General de Gaulle so informed Britain and the United States. Such a government was bound to fall into serious trouble, no matter how many experts in government were included. The anti-Gaullists in Washington scoffed at de Gaulle, declaring he would only bungle matters. The answer to that criticism was simple: if Frenchmen bungled, that would be their affair and they would have themselves to blame. Allied blunders would be in a far different category.

Eventually, AMGOT was abolished for Northern Europe: it was not to participate in the western invasion. The army had to have a civil affairs section to take over while given territory was a zone of operations and immediately thereafter. Accordingly, a branch was added to the army and called G5, or the civil affairs section. Men who had been trained for AMGOT were put into this section. There was to be no Allied military government in any country except in enemy territory. The French Committee of National Liberation was informally assured of this and was also told that United States Army authorities would not use the services of the Vichy Government or of anyone who had ever been connected with it when our armies entered France. Well and good, but how could strangers in uniform, hurriedly moving in, know who was who? The army makes use of the man who seems capable to perform a task at the moment. It does not have time to investigate thoroughly. In Sicily and Italy many of the old fascists became our chief helpers, to the disgust of those who had been oppressed. That made liberation farcical. And who was to take over after G5 had performed its temporary task? There was to be no repetition of the Italian experience, but what was to take its place? This was a question that hung ominously over Supreme Allied Headquarters in London for several months. The British were ready to make it clear that the French Committee in Algiers should assume all civil governing as soon as a given area was no longer a combat zone. Washington sat tight, stubbornly refusing to see the trend. General Eisenhower had learned bitter lessons in North Africa and he had no desire to go through them again. Two weeks before D-Day it was frankly made clear at his headquarters that he was disturbed over the lack of direction he had received. The civil affairs section was handicapped in its preparations; it did not know exactly what duties, in the end, it would have to perform, for it looked as if Washington was going to throw the political aspects of the invasion into the lap of the military. This would mean nothing more or less than a great additional burden which could not but hamper military operations. The Supreme Commander realized that the majority of Frenchmen expected General de Gaulle to take over and in accordance with the military expediency policy which had been so much vaunted by Washington in North Africa, he favored giving as free a hand as possible to the Algiers Committee. In France, it would be in the best position to give the Allies the greatest assistance, whereas in North Africa, it was not. General Eisenhower began patching up differences with General de Gaulle at the time he left Africa to assume the Supreme Command of the western invasion. The difference in General Eisenhower's tone in his conversations with General de Gaulle was noted in Algiers. Thereafter, they had no difficulty getting on together. General Eisenhower, however, was in a ticklish position. He was a servant of the British as well as of the Americans and the British in the weeks before D-Day were doing everything possible to persuade President Roosevelt to drop his anti-Gaullist prejudice and recognize the French Committee as an urgent matter. By this time only a few of our diplomatic representatives abroad still clung to the old policy. One emissary after another, both military and diplomatic, flew from England to Washington to try to persuade the President to change his mind. In despair, the British went ahead and started negotiations with General de Gaulle looking toward turning over all civil affairs to the Committee.

D-Day came and went with the President still adamant. Fortunately, the Algiers Committee had proceeded to prepare itself for the governing task. General Eisenhower's desire (backed by the British) that it should do so, made it possible for the Committee's representatives to go into Normandy immediately and take charge. The men General de Gaulle designated for the task were coolheaded men who functioned smoothly with the Anglo-American armies. These men knew in advance who was who in the towns and villages, for they were in touch with the Resistance people who had lived there throughout. Some local officials were removed, others were kept on and numerous arrests were made. General Eisenhower's G5 officers kept a "hands off" policy as much as possible. When

Normandy was thus opened up, all doubt about General de Gaulle's strength was dispelled. I traveled from town to town, from village to village and from farm to farm, questioning inhabitants. Without exception, I found amazement that anyone should have thought the French inside France might not want the Algiers Committee to form the governing nucleus during the interim period. The General was to them the heart and soul of all they had been fighting for and they assumed that he was the same thing for all that we had been fighting for. I discovered that apart from the top Resistance leaders, the people were unaware of the way Washington had treated the General. That was indeed fortunate. Subsequently, throughout France it was found that the people felt about General de Gaulle as did the Normans. He was given tremendous receptions wherever he went. It would have been disastrous if he had not gone into France in association with the Allied armies. Yet, if the President had had his way, he would not have been there at all.

D-Day was June 6th. In July, General de Gaulle was invited to Washington. In order to keep up the fiction that the President had been right all along, it was made to appear that the General had come to the White House a much chastened man. The truth was the exact contrary: General de Gaulle was firmly in the saddle and was not to be unhorsed by the President no matter how long the latter chose to keep his eyes closed to the facts.

The "result" of that visit was announced in August. Still the President did not give in completely, but he was forced to extend himself to find phraseology which would make possible clearing up some of the practical difficulties in France, without appearing to have acknowledged the defeat of his entire French policy. General Eisenhower, accordingly, was "authorized to deal with the French authorities at Algiers as the de facto authority in France so long as they continue to receive the support of the majority of Frenchmen."

Grudgingly, another step had been taken: recognition of the Algiers authorities as the "de facto authority in France" denoted progress, but it still fell short of reality. Moreover, the President admitted for the first time that de Gaulle did have the support of the majority of Frenchmen.

Obviously, this type of recognition was not satisfactory to the French. Within France, Washington's attitude had not greatly hampered the de Gaulle Government; the General's prestige grew, and there never was any doubt that he was the man to hold the reins for the time being. But in the problems of peace, especially in what was to be done about Germany, the non-recognition of the de Gaulle Government as a Provisional Government barred France from having her just and proper say at international council tables. Although she was one of the principal powers concerned with what was going to happen to Germany and with the sort of peace that was to issue from the war, she was being held off at arm's length. This situation troubled not only the de Gaulle Government but every thinking Frenchman; they were pained and puzzled by the superior attitude toward them manifested in Washington.

Finally, on October 23rd, recognition as a Provisional Government was granted by the United States, Britain and Russia (and by several lesser powers). All but the United States had been ready to take this step many months earlier. The State Department's announcement said, "The Government of the United States has today recognized the French de facto authority established in Paris under the leadership of General de Gaulle as the Provisional Government of the French Republic." The occasion seized upon as a time to take this action was the formal transferring of a large part of France from the authority of the Supreme Allied Commander to the civil authorities. In practice, however, the French already had been administering their civil affairs wherever the Germans had been driven out and the Allied armies had moved on.

The State Department's announcement said further that, "Pending the expression of the will of the French people through the action of their duly elected representatives, the Provisional Government of the French Republic, in its efforts to prosecute the war until final victory and to lay the foundation for the rehabilitation of France, can count on the continued, full and friendly coöperation of the Government of the United States."

That was all General de Gaulle had ever asked for. But once again he got more words than he got action. It soon became apparent that the "full and friendly coöperation of the Government of the United States" was not going to mean that France would be immediately accepted and given a full voice in the conduct of European affairs. France was still kept on the outside while major decisions were made.

This question remains: What effect will the long period of friction and fumbling have on the future relations of the United States and France?

The President made one mistake after another, but the basic one was his failure to realize that de Gaulle was the true soul of France and not just a general; that in hounding de Gaulle from pillar to post he was also hounding the French nation. The French have been humiliated not only by an Ally but by a country which they had considered to be among their best friends. The French now put little stock in the explanation that the United States Government's attitude was dictated by a personal dislike on the part of the President for General de Gaulle; they believe, rather, that it was an attempt to hold France back from a speedy return to her former place in the concert of nations. They believe the latter explanation because they cannot understand how the head of a great nation could allow a purely personal matter to influence national policy over so long a period.

The men to whom we have given direct affront are the men who will create the future France. Until France was liberated, the French people as a whole knew very little about the way General de Gaulle had been treated. After liberation, they learned the whole story and kept abreast of new developments. It is difficult to see how the dragging of the French over a needlessly long and rocky trail can fail to bedevil future Franco-American relations.

RUSSIA, WORLD'S NEIGHBOR

When desperate ills demand a speedy cure,
Distrust is cowardice, and prudence folly.
—Dr. Johnson, *Irene*

13

HOW WAR HAS AFFECTED COMMUNISM

Future historians of the Soviet Union may record that the Communist Revolution reached its end during the "Patriotic War." Some may argue that pure communism died when Josef Stalin won out over Leon Trotsky in 1927, but all may agree that the books of the revolutionary "movement" which were opened by the collapse of Czarist Russia in 1917, were closed by Adolf Hitler in World War II.

The U.S.S.R. today is just another country trying to get along on a nationalist basis. Its motives and actions in the foreign field are as orthodox, for example, as are those of the United States and Great Britain. There are no indications that communist ideology any longer dictates Russia's foreign policy. There are, on the contrary, indications that abolition of the Comintern in May, 1943, was not a subterfuge. That act did not abolish Russian official sympathy with the working classes the world over, but wherever the Kremlin the past two years has supported avowed communists in foreign countries, it has done so with an eye to the needs of nationalist Russia rather than to foster world communist revolution.

The past two years have been war years and many things are tolerated in wartime that are not condoned in peacetime. What of the future? If the nationalistic trend had originated in the war, it could hardly be called a trend this early in its development: in fact, it would scarcely be noticeable. A clear trend does, however, exist and it has been evolving for more than a decade. With the impetus given to it by the war, it can be expected to continue after the war.

The most pronounced support of an avowed communist went to Marshal Tito of Jugoslavia. He was the leader of many who were not communists but who represented a progressive element willing to give their lives fighting Germans. The one thing the Russians were interested in more than anything else after June 22, 1941, was the killing of Germans in any manner that could be accomplished. Russia's prime interest in Marshal Tito was his activity in this respect.

In the Polish question, two things were involved from a Russian viewpoint and neither had to do with communism as an ideology. The first thing of interest was the killing of Germans and the second was to have a future Poland friendly to the U.S.S.R. The Polish Government-in-Exile in London was given ample opportunity to fulfill this role before a serious effort was made to bring together another government that would. An army representing the Government-in-Exile was organized and equipped in the Soviet Union and formal agreements were made with that Government in 1941. General Sikorski, a far-sighted man, was then the head of the Polish Government, but although he managed to obtain acceptance of his arrangements, there was wide opposition to what he had done. When the General was later killed in an airplane crash near Gibraltar the true feelings of the Poles in London began to appear. The army formed to fight on Soviet soil was withdrawn by the Polish Government through Iran into the Near East. One incident led to another until Russia again broke relations with the Exiles in April, 1943. After the Polish troops had been taken out of Russia and the Exile Government had shown its intentions to follow the anti-Russian policy the country had employed between the two wars, a Polish committee was formed in Moscow, as a possible nucleus for something different. Thousands of Poles were still stranded in the U.S.S.R., and some of them proposed to the Russians that a new army be formed upon a basis acceptable to the Russians. Thus it was that Polish divisions went back to their homeland with the Red Army and that a Russian-sponsored government came into being in Lublin as soon as eastern Poland was liberated. Only a small percentage of believing communists were among the Poles who associated themselves with this enterprise. Nor was there an energetic attempt at indoctrination on the part of the Russians or of the Poles who were communists. As Polish officers explained their action to me, they were convinced that the policy their country had followed between the two wars of trying to be a first-class power when it lacked the resources and at the same time defying both the Germans and the Russians, was stupid. They believed that in order to exist, Poland would have to remain on friendly terms with the big neighbor to the East. As for the territorial demands made by the Russians, they were willing that Russia should have those portions of White Russia and the Ukraine east of the Curzon line which Russia had regained through the treaty with the Germans in 1939. That area had been taken by the Poles from Russia by force of arms and against the wishes of the major powers at the end of the last war. The majority of the inhabitants were not Poles. The eastern frontier question was used by the Exile Government as the main obstacle to its willingness to come to terms with Moscow. The Polish group in Russia was willing to fight with the Red Army and to return home, pledged to establish a more liberal Poland not antagonistic to the U.S.S.R. The Exile Government in London could have been the one to begin functioning in Lublin if it had been able to cast off the country's impossible between-wars policy.

Russian behavior in Rumania, the Baltic States and Finland was of the same nature; it was nationalistic and not communistic. In other parts of Europe not directly affecting Soviet security, no more support was given to communists than Britain and the United States gave to political and economic groups which interested them. In Italy, for example, Moscow recognized the government of Marshal Badoglio, which rested upon the Italian monarchy, and did it at a time when Italian communists were making headway by preaching the simple needs of the people while other political parties were talking in theoretical terms. The Marshal was the choice of the United States and Britain as against all others, yet neither had gone so far as to recognize his government. As for the French, Moscow consistently went further in accepting General de Gaulle as the representative of France than did the United States. He was not a communist nor were a majority of his followers communists, but he was the undisputed popular leader who was at the same time throwing his full weight against the Germans.

The feud between Stalin and Trotsky revolved around the question of world revolution. It was the latter's view that Russia could not exist as a communist state in a world of capitalism. The only valid policy to follow, therefore, was that of world revolution. Stalin held that the first thing to do was to set an example within Russia. This question was decided when Stalin in 1927 managed to get the upper hand and sent Trotsky into exile. Since that time, the trend toward nationalism has been constant, although the Comintern, the instrument of world revolution, functioned until 1943. It was only in looking back after the Hitler war had brought many changes that the full extent of the trend was realized. While it was developing, manœuvres of the Comintern created uncertainty as to which way the cat was jumping.

It can now be seen that the purges of 1934 and 1937 were a part of this settling-down process, however bizarre the trials in those purges may have appeared from the outside. Practices prevalent in the beginning of the revolution began to change soon after Stalin took over the direction. In the nineteen thirties the divorce laws were tightened, making a second divorce more costly than the first and a third more costly than a second—like a graduated income tax. But it still remained possible for a couple to become divorced by the mere appearance of the two at a certain window in the government recording office, or the appearance of one with a written consent from the other. This procedure was drastically changed in July, 1944, when the Supreme Soviet issued a decree for the purpose of consolidating the family as a fundamental unit of Soviet society. Now divorces can be obtained only through court action in much the same way that they are obtained in western countries. A petition is submitted to the People's Court by one of the parties in which the reasons for the desired action are stated. The court then summons the defendant and proceeds to try to reconcile the parties. If the court fails, then another petition can be filed in a higher court. The case is heard in open court with witnesses testifying to the accuracy or inaccuracy of the charges. An announcement that a divorce petition has been filed must be published in the local newspaper at the expense of the petitioner.

The alteration making divorce more difficult was just the final part of the 1944 decree. The other parts increased state aid to mothers of large families and to unmarried mothers; increased the privileges for mothers and expectant mothers, and extended the institutions for protecting mother and child; created medals for mothers who have reared upwards of five children; increased the tax on childless men and women; instructed state prosecuting organs to enforce vigorously criminal laws already in existence against those guilty of performing illegal abortions or forcing women to undergo abortions, and those guilty of "insulting and humiliating the dignity of mothers and of refusing to pay alimony for the upkeep of children."

In the very midst of the war to defend the fatherland, when women were performing the tasks of men, the government took another step that ran counter to the old practice of encouraging women to get into the professions and trades. It abolished the co-educational system in the "ten year" schools (ages seven to seventeen) in order to be able to give girls more training in the art of keeping a home and a family. Prior to this decision, all pupils in these schools had started to carry small blue-backed identity cards in the rear of which were twenty do's and don't's for the children to follow. A more acceptable guide to conduct could not have been drawn by a school superintendent on Main Street. The twenty rules are quoted exactly:

Every pupil is obliged:
1. To be stubbornly insistent to acquire knowledge and become an educated, cultured citizen, and be of as much use to the Soviet motherland as possible;
2. To attend school regularly and not be late;
3. To submit freely to the orders of the director and teachers;
4. To come to school with all necessary textbooks, pencils, paper, copybooks, and prepare everything necessary for his lessons beforehand;
5. To be clean, with hair well combed, and correctly dressed;
6. To keep his classroom seat neat and orderly;
7. To enter the classroom immediately after the bell and take his seat, and not leave the room unless permitted to do so by the teacher;

8. During lessons, to sit straight, not lean against anything, listen attentively to the teacher's explanations and answers, and not talk or cause other distractions;

9. When the teacher or director enters or leaves the room, they shall be greeted by rising;

10. When answering questions, rise from the seat, stand straight, sit down only when permission is granted by the teacher, and raise the hand when desirous of answering or asking a question;

11. To write in the copybook all assignments, and show them to parents, although homework must be done alone;

12. To be respectful to the director and teachers; to greet the teachers and directors in the street by a polite bow, with boys doffing their caps;

13. To be polite to adults, and behave modestly and decently in the school, and in the street and public places;

14. To avoid the use of bad language and rough expressions; not to smoke or gamble;

15. To be careful of personal belongings and those of comrades;

16. To be courteous and attentive to elders; small children to give their seat or right of way to the sick or weak, and assist them in every way possible;

17. To be obedient to parents and help them to care for younger brothers and sisters;

18. To keep the home clean, clothing and bed in order;

19. To keep the pupil's card and produce it when requested by the director or teachers;

20. To esteem and honor one's school and class as one's own honor.

For violation of this discipline code, a pupil can be expelled.

Revolutions come to an end eventually. By the very nature of things, what is new today is conservative tomorrow. Moreover, a people has not yet been found who enjoys going right on blazing a path, without sitting back and plucking some of the fruits of its labor. The necessity to defend the fatherland against a ruthless invader opened a way for the Soviet State to consolidate and fit itself into Russian history. Russian patriotism was called forth in a holy war of defense; all Russians, Great and Little, from the Baltic Sea to the Pacific Ocean and from the Arctic Ocean to the Black Sea, found themselves to be of one mind. Bygones were found to be bygones; animosity created by the regime's liquidations proved not troublesome. The appeal was to patriotism, to all lovers of the home soil, to Russians; at no time was the defensive war called a war of the workers to defend their rights won by revolution. This was the meaning of the fact that officially the war has always been called the "Patriotic War."

The tendency to reach back into the past for heroes, noticeable before Hitler started his mad race to the East, surged forward as a result of the Patriotic War. Changes had already been made in the slant history books gave to what had taken place in Russia prior to 1917. By 1944, when I visited a Russian school, there was no exaggerated emphasis on communist doctrine in the curriculum. The history and constitution of the U.S.S.R. were taught as American history and government are taught in the schools on Main Street. There was one course in the constitution given to the seventh grade. The walls of the school were filled with pictures not of revolutionary leaders but of Russia's great men of the past. On the walls in the lower grades were pictures depicting well-known Russian fairy tales. In the rooms and hallways of the upper grades were photographs of Russian scientists, musicians and writers.

Alexei Tolstoy's historical novel about Peter the Great broke a revolutionary tradition. The novel was started before, but was completed after the German invasion. Before Tolstoy's work appeared, Soviet writers had rigidly considered life prior to 1917 as bad beyond contemplation. The appearance of Tolstoy's book seemed to set off a careful search for heroes, customs and ideas of another age that might be suitable for the new state. At times imaginations were stretched a bit and a round peg has been fitted into a square hole, but generally speaking, the sifting process has turned up a remarkable number of heroes who accord perfectly with the conception of the Patriotic War. Ivan the Terrible has been reinterpreted. He is still a terribly cruel man, but nonetheless he is seen as having been a progressive Russian leader. As a purely wartime feature, the opera "William Tell" was sung in the Bolshoi theater for the first time. The relationship of that story of Swiss defiance toward the Austrian intruder to the defiance of the Russians toward the Germans was obvious.

With this lowering of the bars in regard to the past, lectures on various phases of history became popular in Moscow, and stories of the lives of Marshal Suvorov, Marshal Kutuzov, Prince Alexander Nevsky, Bogdan Khmelnitzky and Peter the Great were made into films. New military orders were named after these and several other heroes of czarist days. Suvorov was a marshal of Catherine the Great who fought Napoleon in Italy; Kutuzov was the marshal in charge when Napoleon made his disastrous march to Moscow; Nevsky was the Prince of Novgorod who in the thirteenth century defeated the Swedes and Teutonic Knights at Lake Ladoga; Khmelnitzky was a Ukrainian hetman in the seventeenth century who fought off Poles. Military orders were also named after Prince Dmitri Donskoy, a fourteenth-century victor over the Tartars; Admiral Nakhimov, who fought in the Crimean War; and Admiral Ushakov, who fought against the Turks in 1787-91 and in the Napoleonic wars.

In line with this fusion of past and present glory, certain regiments and divisions were designated as "guards" regiments and "guards" divisions after an old czarist custom; army grades were restored, uniforms became more fancy and rules about keeping them tidy became strict. Even Premier-Marshal Stalin donned an attractive one. Discipline throughout the army was tightened and saluting was made obligatory. Today the Russian Army salutes far more than do the American and British armies. Numerous military traditions from former days have been brought back into use and the political commissars, who came into being during the early days when the regime felt it could not trust the army officers held over from the Czar's army, have disappeared, to the satisfaction of all. Russian diplomats from the lowest category to the highest now wear uniforms as did their predecessors in the former regime. A new national anthem expressing patriotic rather than ideological feeling was adopted.

The new attitude toward the Orthodox Church and the teaching of religion are further indications that the revolution's books are closed. The church joined wholeheartedly in the Patriotic War, thus identifying itself with the new state. The established church had been so bound up with the czarist regime that it was difficult to distinguish between them. When the regime went, the Greek Church and all other faiths necessarily felt the wrath of the revolutionaries. The Greek Church during part of its history actually owned serfs, and at the time of the revolution it possessed some eighteen million acres of land. These things were rather far removed from pure religion, but in the turmoil, religion and church were confused as being one and the same thing. Religion hence was called a dangerous opiate and members of the Communist Party were forbidden, and still are forbidden, to practice religion or to belong to the church. But there are only two and a half million members of the party out of a population of 180,000,000.

The Orthodox Church since the October Revolution has been painfully working its way back. The Patriotic War gave it its great opportunity to display its fidelity. A column of tanks was purchased by the church and on the occasion of its presentation to the Red Army the Metropolitan Nikolai of Kiev and Galich had this to say:

"Dear brother fighters in the ranks of our glorious Red Army, I bring you greetings, gifts and blessings from the Holy Russian Orthodox Church and its head, Patriarch Sergius, whose call to the congregation of the Russian Church brought forth the funds to build this tank column. It gives me great happiness to be able to tell you that the days in which we collected funds for this sacred cause were a great festival for the entire Russian Orthodox Church. She takes pride now in the thought that the Dmitri Donski tank column will do its part in crushing the hordes of German bandits who have invaded our country.

"On behalf of Patriarch Sergius, and from the depths of my heart, I say to you, beloved warrior brethren: May the Lord be with you in the holy cause of the defense of our country! May these fighting machines driven by your stern will to victory bring vengeance and death upon the Fascist butchers who have drenched the sacred soil of our country in blood, upon these children of Satan, these enemies of the culture and happiness of the people, these foes of mankind unworthy to live on this earth! It is our earnest prayer that our arms may emerge victorious from the conflagration. Our faith in the final triumph of freedom, truth and peace; our faith in a speedy victory over the dark forces of Fascism, is unshakable.

"Forward warriors! Sweep the impious horde from our soil. Bring back to us the peaceful life and happiness of our people. In the name of our sacred cause, forward!"

The Patriarch, the Metropolitan and the three Archbishops of the Holy Russian Patriarchal Church previously had issued a statement in which they said:

". . . The Russian people and all those to whom the Fatherland is dear, have now only one aim—at all costs to smite the enemy. The hand of the true patriot shall not tremble in the destruction of the Fascist invaders. The heart of a Christian is closed to the Fascist beasts, it exudes only an all-destroying, deadly hatred for the enemy. . . ."

Such an attitude smoothed the way to reconciliation. High churchmen were named to sit on state commissions, and the Council of People's Commissars set up a Council for Religious Affairs to establish for the first time official contact between the Government and the various churches and faiths: Greek, Armenian, Georgian, Old Believer, Catholic, Lutheran, Moslem, Jewish and Buddhist. Church matters in which the state had to make a decision were to be cleared through this Council. The teaching of religion has been possible within the home when parents wished, but religious instruction may now be given to wider circles. More and more marriages are being performed in the church. They must, however, also be "performed" by the state. The system is much as in France where, if you want to be married by the church, you must first be married by the state. More and more persons, too, are attending church services. I attended a small church in Moscow on a Saturday evening, when the Orthodox Church holds its principal week-end service. The church was as packed as a Moscow subway train and that is a condition very familiar to the canners of sardines. There were a few soldiers in uniform and a few children, but 98 per cent of the congregation was composed of elderly persons. Church services take the elderly people back to their childhood days and to memories of their father and mother. The Russian woman with whom I went to the service said she normally attended only once a year, on Easter Day. She did not believe in God, she said, but she did want her ten-year-old daughter to believe. When I asked her why, she said she desired it because her daughter was absolutely fearless and she felt the daughter should learn to fear God for her own good.

The 1936 Constitution of the U.S.S.R. guaranteed freedom of religious worship, and many church doors were open long before the Patriotic War brought the distinct change in the atmosphere. A pamphlet published in Moscow by the Patriarchate of Moscow in 1943 said: "It is true, as everyone knows, that there is anti-religious propaganda in Russia. . . . It is also known that anti-religious ideology is the ideology of the Communist Party and certainly the Orthodox Church has suffered." Some of the changes I have noted have come since that pamphlet was published.

Religion, morals and spiritual life in general were uprooted by the Revolution along with the political and economic life; the October Revolution was a real revolution. A new political and economic regime replaced the old, but nothing was brought forward to take the place of religion. Gradually new moral standards developed until now they are puritanical by comparison to what they were immediately following the overthrow of old standards. The revolution emphasized the material aspects of life. Now, with the Orthodox Church giving signs of having sincerely accepted the shearing away of its temporal power and of being prepared further to support rather than oppose the new state, the church does not present the same concern that it did. Indications are that the state is moving toward a filling of the spiritual gaps left open by the revolution. But nothing new has been added to the Orthodox Church. It is the church of old, merely chastened and conditioned to carry on under the new circumstances.

Russia under Stalin has been cutting a pattern at variance with the pattern of twenty years ago. The word "revolution" is rarely mentioned in Russia today. Premier Stalin occasionally uses it in public addresses, but otherwise it is seldom seen or heard.

JOSEF STALIN, KREMLIN "ENIGMA"

Josef Stalin has been the guide of Soviet Russia for the past seventeen years. In tenure, he outdistances even Franklin D. Roosevelt. Most of that time, Mr. Stalin's influence was exerted from his post as secretary general of the Communist Party. He did not take the office of Premier until just before the German invasion in 1941. At that time he also became Commissar for Defense. Later he took a military rank, that of marshal, and cast off the very plain uniform he had been accustomed to wearing in favor of another more befitting a man who was directing one of the great defensive struggles of history.

Josef Stalin has been the directing head but he has not been alone. Russia stretches across the earth and contains at least something of everything. It is too vast for one man; it was too vast for a couple of million Germans. There have been able men immediately around the Premier and in the scattered Republics. Capable men are running the multifarious branches of the bureaucratic government, and the Premier has had competent generals during the war at his elbow. The Republics have self-government and either the elected officials or the party men in them keep the men on the banks of the Moscow River informed about local needs and local sentiment. This is beyond the representation that issues from the Supreme Council of the U.S.S.R., a two-chamber body, one elected according to population and the other according to nationalities. Thus, he who dwells behind the Kremlin's high walls and towers is not completely isolated from the people's needs and desires. Even if Mr. Stalin were a traveling man, he could not get around enough to find out all that he needs to know.

Different points of view exist within the Soviet Government just as within any other government. This in itself shows that Marshal Stalin seeks advice of many others, although he is usually thought of abroad as running his country singlehanded.

The world usually thinks of Stalin as a skeptic who believes only in that which has been proven before his eyes; it thinks of him as a hard-headed realist and thoroughgoing practitioner of the rule that a bird in the hand is worth two in the bush. Into this cocktail is thrown a jigger of slyness and a slice of certainty that he is capable of relaxing and being convivial and human only at a banquet table where the object is to impress distinguished foreign guests. And who cannot become human and convivial at a Russian banquet?

Men who have come into close contact with him in recent years, but who were not subject to his personal power, have given another view of him.

Mr. Stalin is of peasant stock, and the peasant the world over is born with a triple dose of suspicion in his being. Beyond that, Mr. Stalin was a revolutionist and if he had had no suspicion in his blood, it would have got there somehow as a result of his necessarily clandestine activities. Moreover, from the time Soviet Russia came into being, right down to the German invasion, it was in difficulty with the outside world. When a part of that hostile world then joined forces with the Union, a careful lookout was kept to ascertain whether the motives for the change were other than they seemed to be. Nobody ever gave the Soviets anything and the leaders do not expect anyone to begin giving now. Mr. Stalin has one guiding principle: it is whatever he thinks is good for the Soviet Union. No other rule or rules enter into the conduct of Soviet foreign affairs.

Yet Mr. Stalin has shown that he is capable of believing even when the proof is not exactly before his eyes. His record of predictions in regard to the long-debated second front showed him as being not quite the ultra-realist he is supposed to be. He thought he had reason to believe that a second front in the west would be opened before it was. He accepted what he was told so thoroughly that he committed himself to the Russian people, telling them that the help they wanted was coming soon, when, in fact, it was a long way off.

When Foreign Commissar Molotoff visited London and Washington in May 1942, communiqués were issued which said that the urgent task of creating a second front in Europe in 1942 had been discussed and that there was an understanding on the subject. The wording was ambiguous, but there was no reason for anyone reading the communiqués cold in his newspaper to think that the men who framed them were not of the same mind as to exactly what they meant. Yet there was a difference of opinion. President Roosevelt and Prime Minister Churchill, as events showed, did not regard the wording of the communiqués to mean a second front along the English Channel coast of the Continent, but Premier Stalin did. And the Moscow press began to talk about 1942 bringing the final defeat of the Hitler hordes. At that time, the North African invasion was in preparation; it was to be the substitute for action on the continent of Europe, as it was not yet considered possible to get into Europe.

Despite this misfire, again in 1943 the Premier assured his people that the second front was coming soon, although at the time he did so, he had nothing in hand any more reliable than he had had in 1942. Now, not even the head of a state where there is no vocal opposition likes to be caught making false promises. He neither likes it nor can he afford many such excursions.

The men I am citing found Mr. Stalin to have a particular dislike of those who indulge in slick deals. There is nothing of the diplomat in the Marshal: he gives it right from the shoulder and he likes men who give it right back the same way. If this trait of character had been realized in the United States, there would have been no demands for the recall of Ambassador William H. Standley in 1943. Such demands were made because, it was said, he had ruined his usefulness and disturbed American-Soviet relations by his undiplomatic act of calling in American correspondents in Moscow and complaining that the Soviet Government was being unfair in not telling the Russian people about the assistance they were getting from the United States through Lend-Lease. As a result of that undiplomatic act a generous amount of information about Lend-Lease receipts began to appear in the Soviet press.

Mr. Stalin loathes nebulous diplomatic phrases, and, again contrary to the customary view of him, he wants to be able to take a man's word without tying him down to a sworn statement. The Premier states what he wants in a straightforward way which some have described as blunt. To diplomats accustomed to having intentions concealed in phraseology, Mr. Stalin's manner would be blunt. But as one informant put it: "He is the right sort for anyone who likes to be looked straight in the eye and be talked to frankly without words being minced. There is nothing pretentious about him. His whole face lifts behind that mustache when he smiles, which he frequently does. He is not a grim, hard figure in spite of the long hours he puts in, and it does not take an official banquet to loosen him up. He likes a good joke and he can tell good ones."

THE "SOVIET STATE"

The present state is referred to as the "Soviet State," the state of "Lenin and Stalin," or the state of "workers, peasants, intellectuals and nationalities which consolidated itself through the Patriotic War." Since the war started there has not been so much harping on the theme of Capitalism versus Socialism, although occasion is taken from time to time to point out what the Soviet State has accomplished in building a victorious war machine. The absence of blatant attacks against capitalism may have been dictated by high policy, in view of the country's need for its capitalist allies. However, it is no longer so necessary to propagandize the people of Russia on this subject, for what the Soviet State has done in the factories and on the field of battle in this war is present for all Russians to see. The socialist state has proved itself in a great crisis.

Stalin has built the Soviet State by following day-to-day experience. Doctrine has taken a back seat whenever it did not meet current needs. But predictions abroad that compromises with principle are leading the regime to gradual adoption of capitalism appear exceedingly far-fetched. The Russians know that in order to build they must produce; that production is the cornerstone of material wellbeing. That would seem to be an elementary bit of economics—socialist or capitalist—and so it is; in fact, it is so elementary that it has been forgotten by large segments of the community in some capitalist countries, including the United States. Labor unions in the United States regard piecework as a relic of barbarism, but piecework in Russia is an important device for increasing production. The emphasis in the Soviet State is on output, not on wages, and there is no such thing as featherbedding. A worker's wages increase according to what he produces: "From each according to his ability, to each according to the work performed." An inexperienced youth and an elderly man working on the same factory bench receive an identical unit wage, but the pay envelope of the older man invariably is larger because he knows how to turn out more volume than does the boy.

Something for something, not something for nothing, is the Soviet way. "He who does not work, neither shall he eat," is a socialist principle and in wartime practice this has meant almost literally what it says. Food ration cards made this easy to accomplish. There are four categories of food cards: one for manual workers, one for white collar workers, another for children under twelve years of age and a fourth for non-workers. The non-worker ration is fixed close to the bare subsistence level and this has acted as an incentive to both men and women to become classified in the first category where the meat allowance, for example, is almost four times that of the non-worker category.

"From each according to his ability, to each according to the work performed," necessarily means that there are income differences. It is possible to gather "wealth" through individual enterprise. There are such things as a bank account and an income tax in Russia. There is plenty of money scattered among the workers now, but it does not mean much to them for consumption goods are almost nonexistent. Collective farmers, like industrial workers, have money in comparative abundance, realized from the sale at high prices of their produce. The farmers can grow vegetables, raise animals and fowl on their plots of land allotted to them, and they can sell as much of what they produce as they wish. Yet all means of production remain collectively owned through the state. There is no private business and there are no employees working for anyone except the state. Ownership of a home, but not the land upon which it is built, is the highest form of private property. There is no suggestion that this cardinal difference between capitalism and socialism is likely to be changed in the foreseeable future. On the other hand, there is no inkling that the Soviet State is an intermediary stage in communistic development, a way station on the road to the "ultimate" phase or perfect communistic society of which Karl Marx wrote. On the contrary, the successful outcome of the Patriotic War has entrenched Stalin's pragmatism.

It is of vital importance that the world should understand what the U.S.S.R. of today is and what it is likely to be tomorrow so that Moscow may cease to be "a riddle, wrapped in mystery inside an enigma," as Prime Minister Churchill once said.

14

COLLABORATING WITH THE SOVIET STATE

From a non-Russian viewpoint, collaboration with the Soviet State in the coming years will depend upon what Russia wants abroad. She has more neighbors than any other country. That is an old fact destined to assume great importance if the Union avails itself of the future that certainly lies in store for it. In one solid mass, Russia sprawls into Europe, the Near East and Asia, and thrusts a corner of herself into the Western Hemisphere. The wartime air route to Siberia and the Alcan Highway have made Main Street conscious that Russia is a near neighbor. The German-Japanese threat also has made Main Street think seriously about the problems of coöperation with the U.S.S.R.

Widespread fear of communism among the western powers was one of the major factors giving the Nazis their chance to become strong. They had the blessing of a large portion of public opinion in the west. No more than a short peace can be hoped for if, for any reason, Russia and the western powers again become antagonistic toward each other.

What, then, does Russia want abroad? As I have already said, there are good reasons to believe that international communism need not arise again to bedevil relations between the U.S.S.R. and other countries. Words, deeds and domestic needs combine to indicate that world revolution is no longer one of the aims of Soviet foreign policy. Soviet leaders may still believe thoroughly, as Stalin did when arguing with Trotsky, that capitalist countries will fall ultimately of their own weight. As long as such a belief is confined to the realm of theory, there can be no objection from the capitalist countries. The task of the capitalist countries is to prove the inaccuracy of the theory and not to belabor Russia for the form of government she chooses.

What the Soviet State wants above all is security on its borders. In the west it wants to make Germany so helpless that she cannot strike again. Soviet policy in the Balkans, in Poland and in Finland has been aimed at just that. Where Russia has not insisted on actual territorial adjustments, she has labored to create friendly governments. She desires to have around her frontiers precisely the same thing that any other country desires: strategical defense positions and accommodating neighbors. She may have proceeded in some instances in a manner displeasing to the United States and Britain. She holds that what she believes to be her needs on her frontiers is her concern and not the concern of the United States and Britain, just as they hold that what they deem to be their needs is none of Russia's business. She has given no signs of wanting to wander further afield than the immediate territory along her borders. What the Soviet State would want in case of victory, became evident early in the war.

Having consolidated itself in the Patriotic War, the Soviet State has every reason to desire domestic and foreign peace for many years to come. Putting it conservatively, there is a good half-century of constructive work to be done at home. At no time since the revolution has it been possible to turn the energy of the country loose, producing for prosperity. The years immediately following the revolution were filled with the task of liquidating the old regime and establishing the new socialist state. When the debris left by the old regime had been cleared away, a series of five-year plans were started for the purpose of endowing the country with a new industry and agriculture, and through them a higher standard of living. The first plan began in 1928. Heavy industry was to be developed under this plan so that consumers' goods would eventually find their way into the hands of the people. The plan was so concentrated and the goal was so high that it brought considerable hardship. The end desired, however, was regarded as so valuable that notwithstanding the cost, it was pushed through ahead of schedule. The objective of the planning, however, had to be cast overboard before the Second Five-Year Plan was long under way. The industry earmarked for making consumers' goods was shifted to making war materials and all of the new industry that came into operation had to be used for the same purposes. Japan had gone into Manchuria in 1931 and in 1933 Adolf Hitler took over in Germany. Hitler was frankly anti-Russian; he made no secret of his intentions to pursue the old German dream of acquiring the Ukraine. Beyond these hard facts was the fear that Europe might join in a war to crush the U.S.S.R., or at least sit smilingly by while Hitler tried to do it. As it turned out, the switching of the Plans from peace to war production well in advance of 1939 was one of the important contributions to the defeat of Germany.

Foreign developments, therefore, broke up the domestic program and forced a postponement of prosperity. The Russian people are eager to taste more of the fruits of the revolution, and the Soviet State is just as eager to demonstrate that it is capable of making life more comfortable. It wants to pick up where the Five Year

Plans left off. It now has even greater opportunities than it had before. The war has brought consolidation and it has also brought a remarkable increase in industrial capacity through the forced development of the rich mineral basins in the Urals and in Central Siberia. What the Germans destroyed in the Ukraine and elsewhere will have to be replaced, but when the reconstruction period is over, Russia will have producing power in such abundance that the State, if it wishes, can transform the face and habits of the country. The opportunities are so enormous that it is interesting to speculate upon what changes may take place in the people if a prolonged period of peace enables the Government to pull away from adversity.

The basis for post-war collaboration with Russia is twofold: the desire for peace and the desire for trade. The regime will need much from the outside world to assist in building up the country. Foreign materials and technical skill were used before this war, but the atmosphere between Russia and the Allies having changed considerably, a much more vigorous trading period should follow. Russia will need foreign credits as indeed will all of the countries struggling to reconstruct and return to working order again. Happily, there is no prospect of a repetition of what happened after the last war when the revolution was fresh in men's minds. The U.S.S.R. needed credits then, too, but instead of getting credits, it got a boycott because it had confiscated all foreign property. The boycott was attempted as a means of punishment. All countries in position to do so this time are going to welcome Russia's trade, and not the least of these will be the United States and Britain. Differences in trade practice which used to cause irritation should now be more easy of solution, if for no other reason than that there is a greater amount of good will on both sides.

During the past two years many doubts have arisen in the United States and Britain as to whether or not Russia down deep really desired to collaborate. Britain first, and then the United States, were brought into a working arrangement with the U.S.S.R. solely through a blunder by Hitler. It was dire necessity and not mutual affection that caused them to get together. Doubts of a similar nature about the sincerity of Britain and the United States were to be heard in Moscow. The years of conflict between Soviet Russia and the West could not be forgotten so quickly. From the Allied intervention in Russia on behalf of the Whites at the time of the revolution down through Russia's exclusion from Europe at Munich, there had been uninterrupted if not always open antagonism. The Munich deal meant to the Soviet Union that capitalism had turned Hitler eastward in hope that he would destroy bolshevism. Stalin slapped back very hard by signing the famous treaty of nonaggression with Hitler in August of 1939. That treaty, from Moscow's viewpoint, turned Hitler around and headed him west, although to go west he first went east for a short distance. What the treaty did was to reassure Hitler on his eastern flank while he went about his business in the West. The Soviet explanation today is that they knew full well what they were doing; they knew that Hitler was going to hit them as soon as he completed his job in the West, and that they wanted the intervening time to prepare themselves. In view of what Britain and France did to Russia at Munich, the Soviets had no compunctions about taking time for themselves at the expense of these countries. Despite some minor indications to the contrary, there is no reason to believe that the Kremlin really thought it had permanently turned Hitler westward. It was freely said in Germany at the time that Hitler wanted the treaty with Russia solely to keep his eastern flank quiet while he struck in the West and that in due time he would prove that he had not abandoned his anti-bolshevik policy. The Russians all along had been well informed about what was taking place in the Reich so they must have known what Hitler's real intentions were.

Behind the second front controversy during 1942-43 stood Soviet uncertainty concerning the intentions of Britain and the United States. Russia was getting Lend-Lease and the British were helping wherever they could in substantial ways, but all of this help was regarded as not enough of a sacrifice to prove conclusively that the capitalists had had a change of heart. Were not Britain and the United States giving the sort of aid that would keep Russians and Germans killing each other so as to get rid of nazis and communists in one fell swoop? Lend-Lease was looked upon by some (and this was a view not held exclusively in Russia) as a Yankee method of promoting business and getting rich from the war! Willingness to give Anglo-Saxon lives to the cause of defeating Germany was the touchstone of sincerity to the Russians. They had a narrow view of what giving lives to the common cause meant. The British had shown their determination in no uncertain fashion before the Russians were even in the struggle; the United States had shown its intention to fight in the Pacific, but to the Russians the Pacific was of little concern. At sea, both Britain and the United States were carrying on large-scale warfare from which Russia benefited; from 1942 on, Allied airpower began to show itself in strength over occupied Europe. But the Russians did not understand sea warfare nor did they believe in the efficacy of aerial bombardment. A well-known Russian said to me: "Only an old woman believes it is possible to win by bombing."

At the end of 1942 came the Allied landings in North Africa and the campaigns that were to push the Germans completely out of Africa. These campaigns the Russians regarded as side issues, engaged in to avoid the major task of assaulting the continent where the Germans were supreme. The Germans were on Soviet soil locked in a great land battle, and the Russians wanted a second front in the west that would draw enemy divisions out of their country. The multiple difficulties militating against the opening of a second front always offered by the Anglo-Americans were treated with skepticism. The Russians were doing the impossible and they felt that their Allies should do likewise if they were really sincere in their desire to defeat Germany.

Mr. Lazar Kaganovitch, the Commissar for Railways, with several other Commissars, crowded around the American Ambassador, Mr. W. Averell Harriman, at the Red Army Day reception on February 23, 1944, at Spiridonovka Palace.

"You're a railway man," Kaganovitch said to the Ambassador, "and I'm a railway man. Let's talk about railroads. I'm working three shifts. I'm crossing rivers that couldn't be crossed and in general doing things that were thought impossible. Why don't you do the impossible and open a second front?"

That goading of the Ambassador took place after the approximate date for the western European invasion had been decided upon at the Teheran conference. Premier Stalin knew the details, but even in the interim between the conference in December, 1943, and the opening of the land fight in the West in June, 1944, the agitation in Moscow continued, although in a lesser degree. It was to be concluded from this either that knowledge of the results of that conference was confined to a few of the very top men, or that having been misled before, Premier Stalin this time was willing to let the agitation for a second front continue as a constant reminder.

Jokes springing from the absence of the second front the Russians wanted were popular in Moscow. One of them went this way:

Boy: "Papa, what does 'second front' mean?"

Papa: "Never mind now, son. You'll find out when you grow up."

And a clown at the circus quipped:

"The clocks of Moscow tell the time. The clocks of London say it isn't time yet!"

Notwithstanding this agitation, in the spring of 1944 there was a touch of belief, or at least of hope, that Russia might be able to accomplish the stupendous task of winding up the war without a western land front. Red Armies were at the time driving brilliantly forward toward Poland and the Balkans. Every night Moscow's guns boomed out victory salvos and the streets of the capital were lighted by fireworks. Such a confident feeling was far removed from the expression Premier Stalin made to Henry Cassidy, Associated Press correspondent in Moscow, in October, 1942. Answering Mr. Cassidy's question as to what place a possible second front played in Soviet estimates of the military situation as it then stood, the Premier replied: "A very important place; one might say a place of first rank."

But it is doubtful that such a belief was shared by the highest levels, proud as they were of the Red Army's prowess. The Germans knew, or suspected, that a western invasion would come some time in the fore part of 1944, and they were in no condition, after the mauling they had had in Russia, to cover both fronts fully. They were obliged to accept shorter lines in the East. The Red Army's role so successfully played was to hit the Germans hard all along the line and keep hitting them so that as many Germans as possible could be destroyed and the withdrawal could not be made in orderly fashion. The constant pressure put upon the enemy also gave him less time to scorch the earth as he fell back.

The matter of a western invasion by the United States and Britain hence came to be treated in Russia more as a political than a military question. Had there been no such invasion to prove Anglo-

American good faith, the effect on the post-war world would have been disastrous. Russian suspicion of the motives of her Allies would have been confirmed; indeed, as it is, the delay in opening the front until the Russians had just about ousted every German from their territory has left a lingering feeling that the front could have been opened long before it was, and that it was planned to wait until the Red Army had exhausted the Wehrmacht. The English and the Americans, especially the former, did follow a policy of manpower conservation into which the arguments of the bomber generals that they could pound the Reich into submission fell nicely. But there were few Englishmen or Americans who entertained the notion that a land front would not have to be opened at some costly date; and there were certainly not many who thought that the delay in the West was uniquely caused by a desire to let the Russians bleed while knocking the Germans to their knees, whence we could easily push them the rest of the way.

That anyone should find it necessary to conserve manpower was another aspect of the war that the Russians could not comprehend. First of all, they had plenty of manpower, and secondly, they were fighting for their own land and there could be no question of sparing anything. Moreover, their attitude toward death does not accord with ours. This was brought out by an incident that took place at an air base in Persia where American fighters and bombers were turned over to the Russians. A Russian test pilot took up an Airacobra fighter and proceeded to put the plane through a number of daringly unorthodox manœuvres, to the amazement of American boys on the ground. When the Russian came down, one of the Americans said, "Gosh, man, don't you know you'll kill yourself handling that machine that way?" The Russian gave him a quizzical look and in his best English replied, "You afraid die?"

The Russians have not had a monopoly on doubting. Many times in the past two years doubts about Russia's willingness to move in harmony with Britain and the United States have arisen. Whenever Moscow took a step that did not appear to have the full approval of London and Washington beforehand, a chorus of doubts about Russia's motives were to be heard in England and the United States. Collaboration does not imply that on every issue there will be agreement, or that any of the parties to it will be subservient to the others. London has done things that Washington has not liked, and vice versa. London and Washington have sometimes acted in a manner displeasing to Moscow.

There are three aspects concerning our relations with Russia which we must understand.

The first is that no country relishes being isolated, however strong it is. They all want friends and allies, and when they do not have them, they are most uncomfortable. Russia's rulers are pleased to be among the United Nations after the long period of isolation between the two wars.

The second is that in so far as the U.S.S.R.'s security is concerned, the Russian General Staff knows what it wants, has stated it clearly and intends to bide with no interference. Russia has entered the game of power politics along with the rest of us; and because she fears that her present Allies may one day again turn against her, she is playing her cards close to her chest. This fear prevents her from becoming confidential with her newly found friends. Some party members are not convinced that, in the long run, it will be possible to avoid a clash with capitalist countries. Regardless of the form that the conflict might take, the underlying cause, as they see it, would be the nonexistence in Russia of private property. Such thinking, however, does not dominate present policy, but it is one of the elements contributing to Russian hesitation and suspicion. There is a direct connection between this sort of thinking and the questions asked in Moscow about the interest expressed by the United States in Finland, Poland and the Baltic States. That America's concern is placed on a high plane of morality is not accepted at face value, and this question is posed: As the archcapitalist country, is not the United States looking ahead to a possible future contingency when it will want to make use of Russia's western neighbors?

The third is that Russia is a country of nationalities and by no means all of them are western-minded. Methods and manners, therefore, cannot be expected always to conform to western practices. And when they do not, it does not necessarily indicate an attempt to wreck collaboration. The Russians can be as bewildered over some of our actions as we can be over some of theirs.

The first three months of 1944 brought a series of events that stirred American commentators into furious action. A Moscow news-

DAS REICH

> *Is there not some chosen curse,*
> *Some hidden thunder in the stores of heaven,*
> *Red with uncommon wrath, to blast the man*
> *Who owes his greatness to his country's ruin?*
> —ADDISON, *Cato*

15

IS HITLER GERMANY?

Of the decisive battles of history, one that took place in the Teutoburger Wald in western Germany in the year A.D. 9 deserves a place among the foremost. The German tribesman Arminius (or Hermann), who had been trained by the Romans, gathered his clansmen together and turned on the Roman general, Varus. The representative of civilization of the time was defeated. There was consternation in Rome when the news reached there, but the dejection was based on false grounds. The Emperor was downcast because he had lost several legions; but he could hardly have been expected to foresee that the loss of his legions was as nothing by comparison to what the consequences of their defeat were going to be.

Tiberius then sent Germanicus Caesar to repair the damage, and he, too, narrowly escaped Varus's fate. Finally, in the year A.D. 15, Tiberius recalled Germanicus and there ended the attempt to conquer the Germanic barbarians. The light of Mediterranean culture was carried no further into the land of the Germans.

Arminius is a great German national hero. In 1875 a huge monument, the Hermann Denkmal, was completed in his honor on

Grotenburg Mountain near Detmold. It was not so intended, but in reality it is a monument to ignorance and to the terrible misfortune that all Germany did not come under the influence of the civilizing factors of Rome.

An idea of what Germany might have been and of how different European and world history of the past century might have been, had the Romans been able to keep on going eastward, can be seen in the development of the Netherlands. Germanic tribes inhabited the Low Countries north of the Rhine when Julius Caesar got up there. They were of the same stock as the tribes in western Germany. But they felt the influence of the Romans and centuries later, they also were under further western influence. Their geographical position also exposed them to English thought. Consequently, Holland, although basically the same, acquired a far different outlook on life from that of other Germans, and to suggest today that a Hollander is a German is nothing short of an insult. The Hollander does not think as a German, he does not aspire to what a German does, he does not want out of life what the German does. Yet he is Germanic.

As far away from A.D. 9 as A.D. 1827, the great nonconformist Goethe said to Eckermann, "We Germans are of yesterday. It is true that we have acquired a considerable amount of culture during the last century; however, still a few more centuries may pass before enough enlightenment and higher culture will penetrate our fellow countrymen and become general, that they, like the Greeks, will show obeisance to beauty, that they may be enchanted by a beautiful song and that it can be said of them: it has been a long time since they were barbarians."

Any explanation of modern German behavior which ignores the differences between the political and cultural development of the Germans and the political and cultural development of their western neighbors, can be no more than a partial explanation. Economic and emotional maladjustments which followed World War I were immediate factors in the rise of National Socialism. But the course taken to rise above these maladjustments reflected the instincts of the people and their previous training and standards. In crises, nations as well as individuals show the true composition of the marrow in their bones.

About noon on January 24, 1712, a male child was born in Brandenburg. He was a fourth child and a princeling. Two other male brothers had been born and died, and it was rumored about the courts of Europe that the mother could not have healthy children. The fact that another boy had been born and the fear that he might not live, caused the rough and at times volcanic father, Crown Prince Frederick William, almost to stifle the boy with caresses before he was rescued by a nurse.

The boy was to become a great man in Prussia, Frederick the Great, and he was to leave his mark on Germany and on Europe. In the history books, the son was to cast such a deep shadow over the father that the latter could scarcely be seen. In reality, the father was more important than the son. Frederick William became the second King of Prussia a year after the boy's birth.

Frederick William's father, Frederick the First, was a crippled spendthrift. His stepmother was a melancholic, ill-natured person who could never be pleased and who eventually went partially mad. The court was filled with intrigue, pomposity and extravagance that exhausted the public funds. As the Elector Frederick, he was deeply hurt when he saw his neighbors advancing in the world faster than he was. The Saxon Elector August came by a kingly title through Poland and the Duke Ernst August of Hanover was trying to elevate himself to the rank of Elector while at the same time he was living in hope that he might become King of England. This called for action on the part of the Elector Frederick. He put pressure on the Kaiser Leopold in Vienna for seven long and anxious years, without result. He tried to buy a kingship. The bribe did not work, but there came a time when the Kaiser needed troops and he granted the title of King of Prussia in exchange for men to help fight in the Spanish Succession War. The coronation was a gaudy affair of purple cloth. It took place in Koenigsberg (East Prussia). Eighteen hundred carriages were used to make the trip across the four hundred and fifty miles of wilderness and corduroy roads that separated Brandenburg from Koenigsberg. Thus was born the Kingdom of Prussia.

His father's court thoroughly disgusted Frederick William. He did not get along with his stepmother, but more than that, the extravagance and ostentatiousness burned him to the quick. Frederick William was a thick-set, burly man with grave ways. He was quite unruly in his youth, when he took advantage of his strong physique. He loved soldiering and he formed a regiment of Potsdam giants which served as a model.

When he became King in 1713, he completcly reversed court procedure and lost no time doing it. As he went in to his father's deathbed, he was forced to pass through a collection of flunkies, courtiers and trappings of all sorts which he loathed. As he left the death chamber, he went straight to his own quarters, summoned the Court Chamberlain and told him the flunkies and other retainers could remain in service until after the funeral, but then from top to bottom, they were to clear out. He kept eight lackeys and eight assistants; three pages instead of dozens of them; thirty riding horses and a few teams instead of a thousand horses; and he abolished threequarters of the pension list and trimmed down the remaining fourth. He labored personally over state administrative and even household expenses until he had mercilessly cut them to the bone. He went through all government departments with the combined zeal of a budget director and an accountant, weeding out the phantoms that pad every payroll not closely guarded. He was arbitrary, crude, a worshipper of money as a criterion of wealth and of food for volume instead of quality. He saved huge piles of coins and stored them in barrels in the cellar of the Schloss. He made a treadmill out of the kingdom. He used to walk the streets and crack idle heads with his bamboo walking stick. "Go home and work," he would shout to the idlers. Dust he despised and therefore he would have no carpets or upholstered chairs. Bare wood benches were to his liking.

The King personally wrote out specific instructions as to how the young Prince was to be educated. These he gave to the tutors. The boy was to learn no Latin, for "what has a living German man and King, of the Eighteenth Christian Saeculum, to do with dead old Heathen Latins, Romans, and the lingo they spoke their fraction of sense and nonsense in?" He found it frightful how the young years of the European generation "have been wasted for ten centuries back; and the Thinkers of the world have become mere walking Sacks of Marine-Stores, Learned, as they call themselves . . . babbling about said Heathens and their extinct lingo and fraction of sense and nonsense, for the thousand years past!" The King doubted that the "heathen Latins and Romans" would be found great "if well seen into."

"I have heard judges say," he wrote on, "they were inferior, in real worth and grist, to German home growths we have had, if the confiscated Pedants could have discerned it! At any rate, they are dead, buried deep, these two thousand years; well out of our way; and nonsense enough of our own left to keep sweeping into corners. Silence about their lingo and them to this new Crown Prince! Let the Prince learn French and German, they will be of practical use to him.

"Let him also learn Arithmetic, Mathematics, Artillery and economy to the very bottom. And useful knowledge generally—history in particular—ancient history only slightly but the history of the last hundred and fifty years to the exactest pitch . . . and in histories most especially the History of the House of Brandenburg where he will find domestic examples which are always of more force than foreign.

"With increasing years, you will more and more, to a most especial degree, go upon Fortification, the Formation of a camp and the other War-Sciences that the Prince may from youth upwards be trained to act as Officer and General and to seek all his glory in the Soldier profession. This is whither it must all tend. You, Finkenstein and Kalkstein, have both of you in the highest measure, to make it your care to infuse into my son a true love for the Soldier business, and to impress on him that, as there is nothing in the world which can bring a Prince renown and honor like the sword, so he would be a despised creature before all men, if he did not live it and seek his sole glory therein."

The King also wrote out a weekly schedule for the Prince, hour by hour. He was told when he should get up each day, how many minutes he had in which to dress, how many to get his breakfast, how many to retrace his steps to his quarters, how many hours for study and when he should walk in the park for fresh air. It was so ridiculously detailed that it even had the seconds counted and provided that on certain days the Prince would have to eliminate a part of his morning ablutions.

It was under such regimentation that Frederick the Great was reared. He did not take to it for a long time; he did not like his father's Spartan methods any more than his father had liked his father's extravagance. Frederick William was hard on his son as he was hard on everyone. In the end, the young Prince came through a remarkable product of the treadmill. He took what his father had built, added to it, and set a precedent that has never ceased to be looked up to in Germanic lands.

Frederick the Great did not follow his father's advice in regard to the learning of Latin and the study of the ancients. Because they were forbidden, he studied them clandestinely in defiance of his father. But he absorbed very little of the full meaning of Latin civilization. Nor was Old Fritz's scorn of the ancients taken seriously by German scholars. The German classical period was coming into being already at the end of Frederick the Great's reign. During that period the classics were widely printed and commented upon in Germany, as they have been in later times. The Germans are excellent compilers. The leading figure of the classical period was the Saxon Lessing. He was alive during the time of Frederick the Great and hence knew first hand the sort of regime Frederick William had outlined for his son. In a letter written in Hamburg in 1769, Lessing said:

". . . Tell me no more of your freedom in Berlin, freedom to think and to write. It is only the freedom to air as many foolish statements against religion as one may like. And a righteous man will soon be ashamed to make use of that freedom. But just let a man once try in Berlin to write of other things as freely as Sonnenfels has written in Vienna; let him try to tell the truth to that rabble of court aristocrats just as Sonnenfels did; let someone appear in Berlin and raise his voice for the rights of the subjects against despotism and extortion, as is happening now even in France and in Denmark; and you will soon learn what country is most enslaved in all Europe."

Lessing saw and understood. Others in his day saw and understood. Others since his day have seen and understood. But none of them, regardless of his teachings, has changed the central idea of the power-state, based upon master and serfs with no regard for the rights of individuals, which Frederick William whittled out. For every Lessing, there have been at least three other teachers who lauded the power-state and ridiculed the ideal of liberty and equality toward which western civilization has striven. These latter are the prophets Germany has followed.

Frederick William laid the foundations for the totalitarian state of Hitler. It might be said that Old Fritz was behaving quite in accord with his times. Was there not a contemporary by the name of Louis the Fourteenth of France who said: "l'Etat, c'est moi" and who conducted his long reign on that principle? Louis's conception of the state perhaps was even worse than was that of Frederick William. The crux of the matter lies in this: Louis's doctrine did not sit well with the French and they did something about it, whereas the Germans took to Old Fritz's doctrine like ducks to water.

The history of the ruling houses of Prussia after Frederick the Great would seem to deny that he and his father had created a definite pattern. Frederick the Great's very first act upon becoming King was to steal Silesia from Austria. When he died in 1786, Prussia was no longer a pitiful kingdom on a sandpile. But for three-quarters of a century thereafter she had weak kings. Prussia was no trouble whatever to her neighbors and her efforts against Napoleon were none too brilliant. In 1848, the wave of unrest that swept over Europe even brought forth a democratic move in Germany. The National Assembly at Frankfurt in 1848 proposed a union of the German states under a democratic monarchy. It was during this period that democratically inclined Germans immigrated in large numbers to the United States. It is significant that they EMIGRATED to find the freedom they desired; they could not find it in the "heimat." Nietzsche once said: "All true Germans used to go abroad to live."

A delegate from Prussia to the Frankfurt Assembly was a man named Otto von Bismarck. He was from an old Junker family and he had his ideas as to what Germany should become. He wanted a united Germany under Prussia and he fought to keep Austria out of the Frankfurt meeting. Later, he used tools other than oratory and parliamentary manœuvring to keep out the Hapsburgs. Bismarck became Minister-President of Prussia in 1857 and immediately began his program of unification which became a reality after the Franco-Prussian War of 1870-71.

The foreign policy of Bismarck is usually misunderstood. He was an expansionist only in the sense that he wanted German states united under Prussia. He was against stepping over into other people's yards. He was not a colonizer. But he was devoted to the power-state idea. He was a learned man. He had studied the classics and had lived abroad. He had men about him who were trained in the classics. They were really educated men, whereas the almost sub-human Frederick William was not. But all this learning changed not a whit their notions about equality, freedom and the use of force. Bismarck is credited with being a pioneer in social insurance. There had been a shift in population from the eastern estates to the industrial west and workers were clamoring for assistance. Bismarck finally gave in, but his act was one of appeasement rather than one motived by a sense of social justice. By appeasement, he hoped to retain the old governing basis and he was successful in his effort.

"As an individual in private life, Bismarck goes to holy communion and tears roll down his cheeks," wrote Hugo Ball in his *Criticism of the German Intelligence.* "Yet it is not a question of the Mystery of Love, but of the state, for 'in the kingdom of this world it has precedence and right.' He holds prayer meetings with his preacher, but to Consul Michahelles he makes this testimony of faith: 'Yes, we all are in the hand of God and in such a situation the best consolation is a good revolver, so that at least one need not set out on the journey alone.' Through his extreme laws against the Socialists five hundred families lose their daily bread. The prison sentences pronounced by the courts are divided among the fifteen hundred persons and amount to one thousand years. But the famous social legislation, one of the greatest and most fateful attempts at corruption of all times, is a result of 'the real forces of the Christian life of the people' and an act of 'practical Christianity,' just as the standing army of the Great Elector was an act of practical Christianity and evidence of Protestant care for the poor."

Frederick William laid the foundation and Frederick the Great started the unification of Germany under Prussian aegis. Bismarck completed the cycle. The stage was set for William the Second, the last Kaiser. Bismarck and the new Emperor William did not see eye to eye. The trouble did not arise over fundamental principles; it was over what should be done with those principles. Bismarck did not want foreign expansion, William the Second did. The Iron Chancellor was ousted in 1890 and the Kaiser took over. That incident marked the beginning of trouble with the outside world. The Kaiser was ambitious for foreign conquests. He wanted colonies and he wanted to dabble in world affairs. He was pompous and conceited. He thought the German philosophy of life was the only worthwhile philosophy. He made the famous remark that, "Und es soll am deutschen Wesen auch die Welt dereinst genesen" (The world shall recover by adopting the German way of life). He twisted the words of Hoffman von Fallersleben's beautiful national anthem, "Deutschland ueber Alles" into meaning that Germany is above all others. Von Fallersleben was a liberal of 1848 and such a meaning was furthest from his thoughts. He meant "Deutschland First" in the same sense that a patriot puts his country first.

Frederick William made possible a Bismarck; Bismarck made possible a William the Second and a William the Second made a Hitler possible. The connecting line was the power-state with its officer-landowner (Junker) basis and a simultaneous lack of appreciation of the humanistic aspirations of western civilization.

THE JUNKERS

The Prussian concept was a medieval one carried over into modern times. It encountered no difficulties so long as there was no large industrial population. The Junkers were landowners and as such they had control over all of their peasants who labored in their fields. Until very recent times, the peasants were, in fact, serfs. When industry began to grow in the latter part of the last century and the first part of this century, there was a shift of population from the eastern section to the west where it became centralized. It meant that large sections of the population were evading the direct influence of landowners. It was a challenge to the basic structure of the country, but it was met without great difficulty. By 1933, when the Nazis came to power, there were only 14,000 Junkers of the old type. But something new had been added. A new type of Junker had arisen in the west, the industrial Junker. Eastern and western Junker had engaged in an orthodox struggle over the opposing interests of industry and agriculture, but by the time Hitler came along, they were merging their interests as a means of preserving the social structure. Between them, the two types of Junkers in 1933 controlled 90 per cent of the land wealth of Germany and the country's industrial strength as well.

The western Junker was an upstart without aristocratic background, and his roots were not embedded in the army and in state officialdom. But he had sympathy with both of them, the more so because of the labor unrest to which he was becoming prey. He had been willing to help house his workingmen quite well. In fact, German industrial workers were better housed than their English counterparts. Slum districts are not to be found in Germany. They are an offense to the German sense of cleanliness and sanitation; the German is a worshipper of spotlessness, come what may.

The industrialists belonged to the cleanliness cult, but when it came to giving their workers more say in how the country was to be operated, they found themselves to be blood brothers of the eastern Junkers. Together they worked to bring Hitler into office. They acted thus because they thought Hitler and his great National Socialist movement could be used to preserve the old Junker system. Moreover, they were thoroughly in accord with his nationalistic and expansionist ideas. However desperate they may have thought their position to be, making common cause with the fanatic Austrian was a brilliant example of political stupidity. That can be said today with a brave air of finality, but the stupidity of it was just as apparent at the time the forces were joined. It was intended that the old crowd would lead Hitler but instead he led them.

The core of the Junker system was the army. Families owning large estates furnished the highly developed officer corps and the state officials. The land, until recent times, provided the wealth which gave the officers and the officials financial liberty. The middle class in the cities ran their own affairs, but they doffed their hats in servility to the aristocrats and stood in awe of the army. The military managed to dominate without putting itself forward where it might become subject to controversy. The army was regarded as being an older unit of the community than the state. The army was a guardian of the "Volk" and stood above the state. Politics was something that took place within the state and so long as the men running the state did not interfere with the foundations of the army, the protector of the people, the army remained quietly in the background doing as it pleased.

This conception of the army's position was accepted by the community as a whole, even in the Weimar Republic. Some sincere Social Democrats raised their voices whenever they thought that they saw evidences of army influence, but generally speaking, Social Democrats, as well as all of the other parties with the exception of the Communists, looked over their shoulders to the army for guidance. In the last years of the Republic, open accusations were made in the Social Democrat press to the effect that the army was giving aid to Hitler's Brown Shirts, who were marching up and down the country creating turmoil. Competent military authorities indignantly denied the accusations and, indeed, a few years later, after the Republic had been buried, the army hierarchy and the Brown Shirts came into direct conflict.

Hitler's idea of the position of the army coincided with that of the staunchest supporter of the army, and other than opening the higher officer ranks to men of lower birth, he did nothing to destroy the old system. The colliding point between Hitler and the old army hierarchy was his insistence on directing the army as well as the state. At first he used his Brown Shirt para-military organization to back up his pretension. But a year and a half after he took office, he felt obliged to cut down his monster in cold blood: some of the top leaders in the Brown Shirts were beginning to threaten him as well as the army. At least he was told that he was being threatened and until it is otherwise proved, the General Staff will be suspected of having had a hand in conveying that idea to Hitler. The June 1934 blood purge effectively ended the Brown Shirts as a paramilitary outfit. The army was pleased. There quickly arose, however, a far more powerful weapon in the shape of the Black Guards and the Gestapo. Eventually the Black Guards put regularly organized and equipped divisions into the field. There was nothing para-military about them; they were the real thing and were capable of engaging the army in a local action. They played their part in persuading the army to accept Hitler as the boss, but more influential still was the fact that as time passed Der Fuehrer demonstrated that he had a firm hold on the country and that he really was the best friend the army ever had. He had differences with individual generals, but never did the officer corps as a whole refuse to follow him.

The Versailles Treaty stipulated that the German "Great General Staff and all similar organizations shall be dissolved and may not be reconstituted in any form." The men of Weimar who were supposed to have the desire and the will to build a Germany with a fresh outlook, did nothing to carry out that provision. All parties, including the Communists, favored a revision of the Treaty and most of them helped to undermine it whenever they could. The Treaty left Germany with a hundred-thousand-man army, and in 1920 the able Colonel General Hans von Seeckt was named to command it. It proved quite easy for him to put together a general staff and lay the foundations for the army that stepped into the light of day fifteen years later under Adolf Hitler. This General, who got his job under the Weimarians, expressed his philosophy quite clearly in a magazine article. He wrote:

"The Will is the highest point of man's spirit, the result of all of his many-sided and secretive forces. The Will is the endowed, creative power of man. Will makes him into the master of the world which this same Will created.

"War is the highest achievement of man's accomplishments. It is the natural, the final development stage in the history of mankind. War is the father of all things. . . . Will and war belong together. War is born through Will, is by it led and carried to its purest fruition. . . . How the superiority of the aggressive Will brings itself to bear upon the masses is a secret of nature. That the Will has this effect upon the masses is the proof of its strength. . . . The first opposition which the Will must overcome lies in the masses; it consists of indolence, men who know it all, envy, vanity, cowardice, fatigue, fear and stupidity. Here lie also the forces of average ability and medium wills which the greater Will must turn to its service. . . ."

"The Germans think that strength must reveal itself in harshness and cruelty," said Nietzsche, "then they submit with pleasure and with admiration. All at once they are rid of their charitable weaknesses, of their sensitiveness to all nonentities and can reverently enjoy the feeling of fright. That there is strength in gentleness and in quiet, they cannot readily believe."

In the middle of the last century there lived a German liberal poet named Ludwig Boerne. He traveled abroad, as did so many of his kind, where he found means of comparing his people with others. He was a sharp critic and in explaining why he chose to be so, he replied:

"When I say that Germans are like a crocodile, I naturally do not mean by that statement that they are like a wild, cruel, predatory animal, such as the crocodile is, and that they weep hypocritical tears. I have the exact opposite in mind. Germans are tame, good-natured . . ., and weep tears as sincere as those of a child who is whipped. If I have called the German people a crocodile, it was merely because of its body covering which is altogether similar to that of a crocodile. It has thick, hard scales and is like a slate roof. Whatever solids fall on it, glance off; whatever liquids, flow away.

"Now suppose that you wished to hypnotize such a crocodile; first to make it clairvoyant so that it can see into its own insides, recognize the disease, and hit upon the suitable remedies; secondly, to cure it of its weak nerves.

"What would you do? Would you stroke the armored skin of the crocodile with a warm, tender hand? Certainly not; you are too sensible for that. You would realize that such stroking would have as little effect on the crocodile as on the moon. No, you would trample on the crocodile, you would run nails into its scales, and if this was not enough, you would fire a hundred musket balls at his body. You would calculate that ninety-nine one hundredths of all this great force you have applied would be totally lost, and that the one one hundredth left would produce just the gentle, moderate effect that you intended with your hypnotization.

"And that is what I have done."

In the pages of history and literature is evidence of many burning hearts and earnest cries: the Prussian system was recognized by some for what it was. In every period since the system began, men stood out against it. The very last Reichstag provided stimulating evidence of this. But none of these burning hearts, none of these earnest cries of anguish disturbed the pleasant Sunday afternoon beer garden concerts. These burning hearts and these voices of anguish are not to be found in the main channel of German history. Once in a while, as in 1848, they collect together and are deemed worthy of a paragraph or so in the grand recital of that country's past. But no more than that; they have to be found in the fringes of German history.

Liberalism never took root in Prussia. Wherever it appeared, it soon disappeared like a puff of smoke. It was not understood, and it made the majority of the people most uncomfortable. The inexperience and naïveté of the Weimar Republicans were sad commentaries on the political and social climate. Western and southern Germanic peoples, who had come into contact with Roman culture and the later culture of the West, had greater respect for freedom and democratic principles than had the Prussians with their Slavic background. It was, however, a matter of degree.

History shows no era when any section of Germany ever developed a liberal ideal of commanding force. Even those sections where the soil was more or less propitious never became so wrought up over Prussia's philosophical conceptions that they fought to the last ditch to prevent being conquered by such "foreign" ideas.

Nowhere did liberal notions of national freedom and freedom of the individual come to a bud. Luther's Reformation customarily is used as proof of a strong underlying urge for freedom, but in fact, the Reformation was bound tightly with the personal fortunes of princes. Luther's protest concerned church practices: it did not reach down into the hearts and minds of the common people. The German church is a state church and its pastors are no more than civil servants. The nonconformism of England never touched the Germans. The church joined forces with the all-powerful state idea and became an integral part of it. The powerful "force" state was placed alongside God. Even pastors who called themselves liberals could not get away from that idea. Frederich Naumann, a pastor who took a leading part early in the Weimar Republic and who was once a Secretary of State, wrote that "Militarism is the foundation of all order in the State and of all prosperity in the society of Europe. . . . Hence we do not consult Jesus when we are concerned with things which belong to the domain of the construction of the State and Political Economy." Pastor Naumann in 1895 started a periodical which he called the "National Socialist Hilfe" and in it he preached such a doctrine. The name, "National Socialist" was a coincidence; other than possessing similar ideas about militarism and the place of the state, Pastor Naumann and Hitler had nothing in common.

A rebel of 1914, Georg Nicolai, who at war's outbreak was teaching at the University of Berlin, wrote in his book, *The Biology of War* (which he had to have published in Switzerland): "The renaissance, which caused a revival of liberty and civilization and culture throughout Europe, later led indirectly to a diminution of the church's power in Europe. But in Germany, because of her strong religious bent, it all passed off in religious disputes; and the humanists, properly so called, never had much influence there. Hence in Germany, all the liberalizing tendencies of the new era were from the very first driven into a side channel. Men were so taken up with religious liberty that they forgot there was any such thing as civil liberty; and so busy were they about spiritual affairs that they forgot all about intellectual matters. Above all, however, Germany got into the habit of considering the world on which she, after all, depended, as something far away above the clouds and everything 'on this side' or 'here below' as of small moment.

"In his comparative indifference to terrestrial concerns, the German did not expect anything on this earth to be complete or perfect, and accordingly he frittered away whatever individuality he still possessed in all manner of absurd trivialities."

Germany's economic development, too, was effected through other than liberal media. State protection of production and distribution and even state ownership showed themselves early in the process of unification. The great German cartels had their roots deep in the practices of the country. If this same philosophy had not permeated all phases of German life, one would be inclined to take little notice of the importance of the power idea in the economic development. Germany came along late in the lives of European countries and when she began to expand her industry and commerce, she found she needed protection in order to do it. Britain at the time had switched or was changing from mercantilism to the liberalistic policy of free trade. Germany could not follow free trade and build her own industries at the same time.

In that courageous Parliament of Frankfurt of 1848, numerous liberals poured out their hearts and presented their wishes for facts. There were statements such as this one by a participant named Arnold Ruge: "I propose that the thinking German nation should take the initiative in the great idea of general disarmament and in enjoining this idea on the other nations . . . In every phase of our entire development, even during the period recently passed through, we have shown that we are adverse to militarism; all our revolts were revolts against the military, much more than against the power of the Government and of the monarchy. They were revolts against the Junkers, the landed aristocrats in the army. They indicate the German spirit . . . that we demand liberty of the subject, and not militarism."

Herr Ruge was dreaming very wild dreams. There never had been a revolt of any sort, and the one which came after Herr Ruge's day, at the end of the last war, was a phantom. Militarism and all of its disgusting trappings have had a special place in the consciousness of a vast majority of the German people. There was a natural revulsion against war after the defeat in 1918. But it did not last long. The revival of the German spirit came through a reawakening of the old consciousness. The Junker-army system has made a deep impression. I found many German prisoners in this war sick and tired of fighting and some were quite disillusioned. But their disillusionment emerged from the fact of defeat and not from a realization that their country had committed a wrong. In the early days of the Weimar Republic an effort was made to educate the Germans to become good Europeans. Germans could be heard talking about becoming "World Citizens" and reconciliation of the nations was taught in some schools. At the same time, however, the old forces were at work behind the scenes. Even the motives of Gustav Stresemann, the man who stood out as the apostle of a Germany working in harmony with the rest of Europe, have since been called into question. How the military spirit accomplished its work under the noses of the Allied control commissions was proudly related after the Nazis came into the open with their military program.

Dr. Karl Waninger, an engineer of the Rheinmetall-Borsig Company in Berlin, in April, 1943, told how his concern had managed to confound the Allied Military Control Commission and circumvent the Versailles Treaty. He said:

"The reconstruction after the World War, which had smashed up everything and dispersed our 200 artillery construction engineers, is particularly interesting. We saved what we could, and above all we transferred the designs and construction models to various places in central Germany. We managed to find employment for a number of elderly and experienced artillery construction engineers in our own works, where they got busy manufacturing locomotives, wagons, mining apparatus, enamel ware, agricultural machines, etc. The firm of Rheinmetall was appointed to meet the demand for guns for the German Reichswehr, up to and including the 17 cm. guns, and in the course of years it was able to equip workshops for this purpose and set up the machines sanctioned by the Inter-Allied Military Control Commission. The workshops could naturally be equipped only extremely modestly because of the small quantity of equipment permitted to the German Reichswehr.

"The fact that any new development of guns was prohibited in Germany led to a cautious and farsighted measure when, in July, 1921, at the demand of the Reich Naval Command, the firm opened up a construction office in Friedrichstrasse in Berlin, which was disguised as a wagon construction office. Six months later, as the result of an anonymous advertisement, a member of the Inter-Allied Military Control Commission made attempts to locate the Artillery Construction Office. These naturally met with no success; for we had disguised ourselves as a wagon construction office. But the firm realized that the setting up of a construction office in Berlin was hardly practicable and withdrew its two construction engineers to Duesseldorf early in 1922. It was here that the construction office took on a few more collaborators under the very eyes of the French occupation authorities. In the middle of 1922, when to remain in Duesseldorf did not appear possible any longer, four engineers moved into our artillery-range in Unterluess in the Lueneburger Heide.

"Here the office was divided into two sections, one for naval construction and the other for the manufacture of army guns. The periodical meetings with the board of directors in Duesseldorf were extremely difficult. One of these strange consultations was held at the time of the murder of Schlageter in the French prison in Duesseldorf, where the French had meanwhile imprisoned two members of the board. Rheinmetall was at that time the only factory which went ahead with the development of artillery under enemy rule, making use of all the tricks of camouflage.

"One must have lived in Duesseldorf in those days in order to realize what the words 'We were busy with the further development of German artillery' really meant. In the meantime, a new and small gun factory was set up and was able to start work in the summer of 1925, despite all manner of drawbacks and difficulties. The first artillery order actually carried out by Rheinmetall after the World War was destined for the new so-called K-cruisers, *Koenigsberg, Karlsruhe* and *Koeln* and the cruisers *Leipzig* and *Nuernberg*. This was the first time that we had to build turret guns for ships. We carried out this task to the complete satisfaction of the German Navy, at the same time creating a precedent in the construction of triple turrets in Germany. Meanwhile the construction section for army equipment had considerably increased and moved to Duesseldorf in 1927. After a decline in development in the field of artillery in Germany's years of distress, the construction offices grew continuously after the foundation of the Third Reich. Rheinmetall was without a rival in its original field of activity, that of the manufacture of mine-throwers and other weapons used in close fighting. It also took a decisive part in equipping the artillery with guns up to the heaviest calibre. Afghanistan, the Argentine, Bulgaria, Estonia, Greece, Holland, Roumania, San Salvador, Turkey and Hungary were among the nations which we supplied after 1933.

"Rheinmetall-Borsig has thus made a name for itself as a first-class arms factory, not only in Germany but throughout the world, thanks to the strengthening of Germany by the Fuehrer, Adolf Hitler."

This pattern of deception was duplicated in everything having to do with the rebuilding of the military establishment.

As long as the Germans cling to their tribal conception of the army's place in their society, they will always find a form of government that will do justice to it. The 1919 Constitution was doomed from the start. Reichstags and cabinets under the Republic were weak. The state form had changed from monarchy to republic, but nothing else had changed. The army remained in its privileged position. The peacemakers at Versailles thought they had effectively disposed of the military establishment by abolishing the high command, stripping the country of its arms stocks and reducing the size of the army to a mere policing instrument.

The program of the Social Democrats, the largest party in the Republic, was anti-imperialist, pacific and in favor of collaboration.

The program of the Center Party, which had less than half of the strength of the Social Democrats, was likewise pacific. All cabinets between 1919 and November 1923, with two exceptions, were formed with these two parties as a basis, and after 1923, either together or singly, they figured in every cabinet. Although their total strength throughout the life of the Republic never reached a majority of the Reichstag, they were in position to make their influence felt. Yet in spite of their written programs, they did not take advantage of the opportunity afforded them by the Versailles Treaty to bring an end to the dominating position of the army. On the contrary, they resented the attempt to weaken the army and either gave active help in circumventing the Treaty or closed their eyes when they knew others were undermining it. The army was allowed the freest possible latitude.

In spite of its program, the Catholic Center had a distinguished Junker in Franz von Papen, the political "genius" who helped to bring the Nazis to power. In the middle 1920's, the world outside Germany pinned great hope for peace on Gustav Stresemann, the leader of the People's Party. He signed the Locarno Treaty and was the chief advocate in Germany of Franco-German rapprochement. Yet in one election the head of the People's Party ticket in Magdeburg was none other than the reorganizer of the Reichswehr, General von Seeckt, whose notions about the meaning of the army to the German people already have been quoted.

It was his aggressive militarism and his expansionism that won Hitler the wide support he undoubtedly had. Apart from the forces working behind the scenes, the people as a whole took to Hitler because they liked and understood his martial spirit. Doubt has lingered abroad as to whether he ever had a majority of the country behind him. His "plebiscites" were regarded as being of no indication whatever, it was thought that they were held under duress and that there was falsification to make the percentage in his favor appear almost unanimous. Duress and falsification existed, but they did not alter what most certainly was a fact: that the overwhelming majority of the people favored the Nazi regime in so far as it was bent on building up a huge military machine and carrying the Reich forward to a great destiny. Equally true was the fact that on the other multiple points of the National Socialist program, Hitler probably did not have a majority of the people behind him. He knew his Germans and he knew what they liked most of all.

A Latin, Frenchmen excepted, likes a gaudy uniform pinned full of ribbons and silver and gold medals, but it is the decorative aspect that appeals to him, not what the uniform stands for. A Swede has the same attitude toward a uniform as a Latin has; a policeman's uniform in Sweden is as glamorous as a naval officer's. A Frenchman, on the other hand, despises any uniform; he is by nature against the man in uniform. A French crowd will take the part of an arrested man regardless of the issue involved; it will defend a street car passenger in an argument with the uniformed conductor, and again regardless of right or wrong. The uniform represents authority and the French do not like authority.

The German, as he is in Switzerland, also loves the uniform; but in his case it is the badge of honor and liberty. It is through the uniform that he feels he is protecting his liberty. He does not look upon the uniform as does his relative, the German in the Reich, as a means whereby he may gain world recognition; he loves it so that he may have liberty at home. Switzerland has always been a militaristic nation, but her citizen is not a militarist.

The German loves the uniform and he loves authority. Without them, he is a helpless, miserable soul; his whole being sinks into a state of chaos. Rank and titles are an obsession. Everyone strives to have some rank by which he may be called, however low the rating may be. Janitors want it, farmers want it, businessmen want it. The extent to which the university degree of "doctor" is carried is an amusing commentary to this obsession. There are more "doctors" of this sort in Germany than in any other country. And when a man has more than one doctorate, he takes great pride in advertising the fact. If he has two doctorates, his calling card reads this way: Dr. Dr. Hans Schmidt. If he has three such degrees, it is: Dr. Dr. Dr. Hans Schmidt!

The Swede has taken over this German love of titles and has carried it perhaps to an even greater extreme. A foreigner throws up his hands in bewilderment trying to address Swedes by their proper and complicated titles. But their love of titles has no special meaning.

Commenting on Germany as a country of differences in rank, Georg Nicolai, in his book, *The Biology of War*, from which I have already quoted, says that "The nobility of all countries used, indeed, to lay great stress on questions of etiquette; but whereas in the rest of Europe the knights ceased to have any importance as a separate class as early as the fifteenth century, in Germany they continued as a recognized class into the nineteenth century. Moreover, ordinary citizens used to ape the nobility; guilds and corporations flourished; and everyone endeavored to obtain some rank, position, title or order which would confer on him a distinction, albeit a trifling one, above his fellows.

"The ordinary Philistine, therefore, satisfied his yearning 'to be somebody' by acquiring stars and titles, while the cultivated German found satisfaction for his aspirations in philosophy, which accordingly began to develop along specific lines. Thus, while British and French philosophy turned increasingly toward practical questions, German philosophy became more and more abstract. What German genius needed was that in the free world of thought each person should be a law unto himself, while, as a matter of fact, in the actual world he was forced to bow the knee to his superiors.

" 'Do or die' is a German proverb, and the pleasing saying, 'Well, if you won't be my brother, I'll bash your head in,' has become another German proverb. And the German thinks this is the formula by which he can redeem the world."

The German lives in the abstract. He finds it most difficult to comprehend that other peoples may think differently from his way, and he therefore is unable to picture for himself how a neighbor might react to a given German act. The Czechs, for example, were branded as plain idiots because they did not want to be absorbed by the Reich. Why there should be a strong tie between Britain and the United States is likewise baffling. The German explains our participation in the last two wars by maintaining that a small clique of English parentage has been powerful enough to swing the nation. To him, nothing more fundamental than that was involved. The German has majestic ideas and he conceives of grandiose plans and schemes. He labors over them carefully and patiently until he is certain that they are mathematically perfect; he selects good material, trims the edges, sandpapers the flat surfaces, caulks the joints and administers three coats of paint. Thus he has produced something perfect to the eye and satisfying to his soul, and that leads him to conclude that he has a grasp on perfection. That there might be invisible flaws does not occur to him. He is, therefore, dumbfounded when the inevitable flaw puts in an appearance. In his perplexed state, he does not look within himself for the source of the flaw; he looks rather for some devil whose sole purpose is to ruin him. Such a mentality easily accepts excuses for failure.

The stab-in-the-back explanation for the defeat in 1918, which Hitler so successfully propagated, but which he did not originate, is an example. The German people were told that the plans for the last war were brilliant; the army did not falter. The trouble, they were told, was on the home front which weakened in the crucial moment, and Wilson's Fourteen Points, which were sheer propaganda, aided in the breakdown. Hitler believed that, and one of his principal tasks was to steel the people so that they would not buckle again. Prevention, if possible, of a repetition of such an absurd legend after this war made the Allied demand for unconditional surrender so necessary. No inducement to surrender could be given this time. It was also advisable to pursue the German armies to the very heart of the country so that every German could see for himself that the German machine was thoroughly beaten. It was impossible to prevent the German mind from soothing itself by discovering a rationalization of some sort, but it was possible to eliminate a repetition of the old stab-in-the-back canard.

We know how the Germans are going to rationalize their defeat in this war. They can see that they were defeated on the field of battle, but that has not brought them to an admission of inferiority. Nor would the occupation of every hamlet and stream in the country bring them to such a pass. What they tell themselves is that their enemies were not superior, but that they, the Germans, lacked sufficient material. They convince themselves that if they had had equality in arms, they would never have been defeated. Thus the unconditional surrender policy, although justified, will not be gratified.

The Germans likewise have compiled their story of the responsibility for the war. Dr. Friedrich Stieve, historian of the Foreign Office, produced it in 1940. Here it is:

"Germany's enemies maintain today that Adolf Hitler is the

greatest disturber of peace known to history, that he threatens every nation with sudden attack and oppression, that he has created a terrible war machine in order to cause trouble and devastation all around him. At the same time, they intentionally conceal an all-important fact: they themselves drove the Leader of the German people finally to draw the sword. They themselves compelled him to seek to obtain at last by the use of force that which he had been striving to gain by persuasion from the beginning: the security of his country. They did this not only by declaring war on him on September 3, 1939, but also by blocking step by step for seven years the path to any peaceful discussion.

"The attempts repeatedly made by Adolf Hitler to induce the governments of other states to collaborate with him in a reconstruction of Europe resemble an ever-recurring pattern in his conduct since the commencement of his labors for the German Reich. But these attempts were wrecked every time by reason of the fact that nowhere was there any willingness to give him due consideration, because the evil spirit of the Great War still prevailed everywhere, because in London and Paris and in the capitals of the Western Powers' vassal states there was only one fixed intention: to perpetuate the power of Versailles."

Dr. Stieve then ran through the many peace "offers" Hitler made and related sorrowfully how every last one was rejected. He concluded:

"In the face of this series of historical facts is there any need for further details as to the question of why they did so? They had created Versailles, and when Versailles threatened to collapse they wanted war in order to follow it with an even worse Versailles. The reproaches which they make today to Adolf Hitler and Germany, recoil one and all on those who make them, and characterize their actions. They are the disturbers of peace, they are the ones who meditate the forcible oppression of other peoples and seek to plunge Europe in devastation and disaster . . ."

The German has an astounding belief in miracles. That was another weakness that Hitler exploited successfully.

Germans who were in the last war have told me how, when everything was crumbling at the front and the armies were in retreat, officers persisted in refusing to see the handwriting on the wall. They believed that something would turn up to bring victory. The same attitude was evident in this war. The frantic search for miracle weapons and the propaganda that went with the search responded nicely to German character. For more than a year, Dr. Joseph Goebbels, Hitler's propaganda genius, played the theme of mysterious weapons that would bring victory. Dr. Goebbels knew his people very well indeed.

The German desperately wants the world to like him. His soul tortured because the world does not render unto him the full measure of devotion to which he deems himself entitled, he turns to the absurd: he tries to force the world to like him. He seems incapable of realizing either that friendship cannot be forced or that his scientific, industrial and musical achievements, of which he is abundantly capable, are sufficient to bring him the acclaim he desires.

Military might is what he understands best. The army is a part of his very soul; when it is not strong, he is fretful. Hitler's reinstitution of compulsory military training (abolished by the Versailles Treaty) was greeted with extraordinary relief and satisfaction. It brought a light to the eyes of youth. National Socialism's marching formations were one of the most welcome aspects of the Hitler regime. I have seen university teachers and paunchy government employees in their forties and fifties march off on Sundays in brown uniforms happy as lambs. They went to the outskirts of Berlin where they crawled on their bellies with loaded packs while "playing" at war. Behind them as they marched out, an ambulance slowly moved for the benefit of those who faltered in spite of their will.

Ordinary Americans and Englishmen who used to travel to Germany found it difficult to believe that the pleasant, orderly, cleanly Germans they knew could possibly behave in the way that they have, unless they had been caught up in forces far beyond their control. American and English businessmen feel the same way: they like to do business with the Germans, who are known for honoring their commitments and for dealing in a straightforward manner. For social and business contacts the Anglo-Saxon would choose the German above all others on the Continent. The Anglo-Saxon would do so because, in spite of his connections, he never comes to an understanding of the workings of the German mind. It does not occur to the Anglo-Saxon that a man with a clean collar and with a distinct odor of freshly used soap could be such a fool politically. The Anglo-Saxon assumes that the German's mind is like his (he has had every reason to think it so) and he therefore is astonished when he is told that there is something wrong with his friend the German. This Anglo-Saxon misunderstanding of the German has wrought enough havoc in the past to warrant a change of method. The English and the Americans should try letting general policy toward the Germans be determined by those who know the German mind more intimately: the Norwegians, Netherlanders, Poles, Belgians, French, Czechs, Danes and Russians.

Hitler was not the first of his kind to rule Germany; he was merely the worst.

16

THE WAY THE GERMANS SEE IT

Frederick William's antics, after he assumed the throne of Prussia in 1713, were a source of amusement to all of Europe. Jokes about his exceedingly crude ways and his Potsdam giants were a dime a dozen. Brandenburg-Prussia was looked upon as an unfertile country quite inferior in all ways to other German states and, of course, in no way to be compared with Russia, France and Britain. Brandenburg for generations had been called the "sand box of the Holy Roman Empire." A short time before Frederick William, the Electress Dorothee (whence came the name of Berlin's Dorotheenstrasse of today) had kept a dairy farm and a market garden on ground that is now the heart of Berlin. She was even suspected of being part owner of Berlin's biggest beer hall.

The Prussian court was considered distinctly low class. That hurt Frederick William, as it had also touched the pride of several of his immediate predecessors, but Frederick William feigned indifference; he appeared to be the last man on earth who cared what others thought about him. While other courts were laughing, he went about pulling Prussia out of the sand. He had his eye on the day when there would be no more joking about Brandenburg-Prussia.

Financially, economically and militarily he made his kingdom strong. He instructed the Prince's tutors to impress upon the Crown empire was formed, in one of his conversations with Eckermann. Says Eckermann: "The latest copy of the 'Globe' lay beside him (Goethe). He picked it up. I was speaking with Frau von Goethe about young Englishmen whose acquaintance I had made in the theater.

" 'What people they are, these gentlemen of the "Globe," ' Goethe said with some animation, 'how they grow in stature daily and are motivated as by one mind is almost inconceivable. In Germany, such a paper would be utterly impossible. Each of us is a particularist; agreement between us cannot be thought of; each one has the opinion of his province, his city, even of his own individuality and we may have to wait a long time before we achieve a sort of general cultural penetration of ourselves.' "

Unfortunately for the world, Goethe's "long time" was not long enough.

Most of the states were anti-Prussian. Many a Hanoverian of today, for example, can recall how his father used to say to him: "Son, remember always that Prussia is your greatest enemy." Prussia was the aggressive state ever crowding the others, before the empire and after it.

As Bismarck's opposition to Austria was not based on solid ground, so this opposition to Prussia among the German states was not very deep. A great deal of it came from loyalty to the ruling houses which had been built up over the centuries. Some of it, indeed, was cultural, but all of it was more or less swept away by a rising tide of Germanism. The German states allowed themselves to become Prussianized and to be caught up in the craze known as "Deutschtum." Prussia unified Germany politically, and in the wake the other German states took on Prussian characteristics.

Today, as far as the main problem which interests the world is concerned, all Germany is Prussian. It is one unit in its desire for political unity and in its belief in the militaristic power-state. "Deutschtum" has a mystical force that grips the German, no matter from what part of the Reich he comes. It is bound up with the superiority notion and the determination that all Germans everywhere in the world, in South America and South Africa as well as in the Sudetenland, must belong to the same Reich.

There has been widespread belief abroad that the old states would welcome separation from Prussia; that all liberals and laborers, even those in Prussia, would support such a division. The separatist movements after the last war are pointed to as an indication of this. These movements were not, however, very serious and their real origin still lies somewhat obscured. It has never been clearly established how important foreign money was in the separatism. The despair of defeat could very well breed genuine separatist movements this time, but the development of the unity idea into a passion and my own observations of how the Germans feel, lead me to the conclusion that any such movement, in all likelihood, would be temporary. With the first shock over, the old urge would come back and there would be agitators galore whipping up sentiment. A good portion of the people, in fact, would turn against the peace settlement on that score even if they had no other objections. Romantic pan-Germanism has a spiritual force which can scarcely be realized by anyone who has not witnessed its manifestations. Even if the divisions were so sound economically that the populations were assured of prosperity, this spiritual force would retain its vigor.

Union of all German peoples is desired not by one group but by all groups: liberals as well as Junkers, Rhinelanders as well as Bavarians. It must not be forgotten that the populations of the old states have been diluted. They are no longer strictly Bavarians, Hessians or Saxons. The Nazis consciously labored to break down the barriers of old; they shifted people about indiscriminately. But long before Hitler, the process had started in a noticeable way. It began with the industrialization of the Rhineland in the latter part of the last century. Eastern Germans—Prussians—moved westward to the factories.

Union of all Germanic peoples means also union with Austria. The democrats of the Weimar Republic were as favorable to "Anschluss" with Austria as was Hitler. They firmly believed in it and they tried to bring it about by means of Wilson's self-determination principle. But the League of Nations denied them that right. Pan-Germanism has been much stronger in Austria than responsible quarters in the United States and Britain would like to believe.

World War I embedded the idea of unity into the German mind

more firmly than ever, and there is no reason to suspect that World War II has not further proved to the Germans that they have to put forth their all to maintain it.

17

THE GREAT DILEMMA

The search for an explanation as to why the untutored fanatic Adolf Hitler was able to master Germany so completely has brought forth many reasons from the "sound" and "unemotional" thinkers of today. Some of the reasons advanced have been: Allied stupidity in not giving more support to the Weimar Republic, Germany's six million unemployed, and reasons of similar nature. They place the blame largely upon the victors of the last war and conclude that a Hitler would not have been possible had the Versailles Treaty not disrupted German economy, creating a large mass of unemployed.

Modern war is disruptive and the victor can no more escape it than can the vanquished. It does not take a Versailles Treaty to create the trouble. That Treaty, in fact, does not warrant the recrimination that has come its way. Its financial and economic provisions were senseless—but they were never fulfilled. The remainder of the Treaty, with few exceptions, was by no means vicious. The post-war inflation in Germany, that did so much harm to the middle class, and mass unemployment were definite factors in Hitler's rise, especially in so far as they helped to frighten the Junkers into supporting the National Socialist Movement. Distressing times create a climate in which crackpots can flourish; more people are then apt to embrace radicalism. But regardless of how revolutionary the atmosphere, no crackpot can command an entire nation unless he goes far beyond the distress of the day and appeals to fundamentals in the character of the people.

That is what Adolf Hitler did. He tapped the deep well of militaristic nationalism and resuscitated the longing to assert the great qualities of the German people. What he said was music to the ears of those who believed that Germany was not defeated in the war, and they comprised the majority of the people, whether they were accepting the Weimar Republic or not.

"Germany," said Hitler, "will either be a world power or she will be nothing," and "For me and every true National Socialist there is only one doctrine: Volk und Vaterland."

The point of his attack against the Versailles Treaty was aimed at the limitation placed on German arms and the classification of Germany as an inferior country. "Ehre und Gleichberechtigung"— honor and quality—was his slogan. His attack against the economic phases of the Treaty was distinctly secondary and even then was linked with nationalism. He spoke of economic independence and freedom from "international finance," which he said was manipulated by Jews who were at home in any of the world's capitals; international finance was not German finance so it must be abolished, just as all international influences must be eliminated.

Hitler's lack of interest in economics was demonstrated in the very beginning of his career. He proudly tells about it in *Mein Kampf*. Many different political, social and economic groups sprang up in Munich immediately after the first World War, and Hitler went from one to another to hear what they were preaching. One night he attended a meeting of the "German Workers' Party," the leading figure of which was Gottfried Feder, an economic theorist who later was to impart to Hitler what little the future Fuehrer knew about economics. Feder made a long speech that night which bored Hitler. He was about to leave when it was announced that there would be a free discussion from the floor. Hitler says he did not think the discussion would produce anything more fruitful than Feder's speech had, but still he was moved to stay on a while longer. Suddenly, a professor arose and made a speech about the necessity for Bavaria to break away from Prussia and join with Austria. Such a step, the professor said, would make peace more possible.

Hitler jumped to his feet and demanded the floor. "I could do nothing else," says Hitler, "but . . . tell the learned Herr my opinion about this point." Hitler denounced in violent terms the idea of breaking Bavaria away from Prussia while "astonished faces" listened avidly. The professor, he says, sneaked out of the place before "I had hardly finished."

Feder's economics had left Hitler cold but when the unity of the

Reich was called into question, it was like waving red before a bull.

Later, Hitler did become interested in Feder, and the two threw in their lot together. Hitler was a man of action; Feder was a theorist. That accounted for much of Hitler's boredom at his first meeting of the "German Workers' Party." One point Feder made caught Hitler's attention: the necessity to abolish the "thraldom of interest."

"When I listened to Gottfried Feder's first lecture on breaking down the thraldom of interest in June 1919," Hitler wrote in *Mein Kampf*, "I knew at once that here we had a theoretical truth which will be of immense importance for the future of the German nation. . . . The campaign against international loans and finance has become the chief point in the Program for the German nation's struggle for independence and liberty."

It did not, however, become the chief point in the National Socialist program; the important thing about Hitler's remark was that he took from Feder only that part of his economic theories which could be used in his campaign against foreign influence. Feder went much further than that, but he faded from the scene a decade and a half later, after Hitler had come to power and had dealt with international finance. Feder and his other theories were forgotten, as we shall see, although they were written into the official program of the National Socialist Party.

In 1920, Hitler asked Feder to dress up a party platform. The engineer-economist put twenty-five planks into the platform. He put in his own pet ideas but the first three planks set the tone. They said:

"1. We demand the union of all Germans, on the basis of the right of the self-determination of peoples, to form a great Germany.

"2. We demand equality of rights for the German People in its dealings with other nations and abolition of the Peace Treaties of Versailles and St. Germain.

"3. We demand land and territory (colonies) for the nourishment of our people and for settling our surplus population."

Of the twenty-five points, not a single one demanded that an end be put to the Versailles Treaty because its economic provisions made it, or would make it, impossible for Germany to live. The program was written in 1920 and at that time, of course, the economic consequences of the Treaty were not yet fully visible. In later years, party orators shouted loud and long against the Dawes Plan, the Young Plan and the efforts of those who said the Treaty obligations could and should be fulfilled. In 1930, after the full effect of the Treaty was visible, a party manifesto about agriculture was published. But again it was international financiers who were charged with driving Germany deeper and deeper into debt.

"The reasons why farming is no longer profitable," the manifesto said, "are to be sought:

"1. In the existing fiscal policy which lays excessive burdens on agriculture. This is due to Party considerations, and because the Jewish world money-market—which actually controls parliamentary democracy in Germany—wishes to destroy German agriculture, since this would place the German nation, and especially the working class, completely at its mercy;

"2. In the competition of foreign agriculture which enjoys more favorable conditions and is insufficiently checked by fiscal policy, which is hostile to German agriculture;

"3. In the extravagant profits of wholesale trade which thrusts itself in between the producer and consumer of agricultural produce, and of which the greater part is today in the hands of the Jews;

"4. In the oppressive rates which the farmer has to pay for electric power and artificial manures to concerns mainly run by Jews. . . . There can be no hope of any sweeping improvement in the desperate position of the rural population, or of the revival of agriculture, as long as the German Government is in fact controlled by the international money magnates, with the help of the parliamentary-democratic system of government, since they wish to destroy the national strength of Germany. . . . Economic assistance under the present political system cannot produce any sweeping improvement, for the poverty of the German people is rooted in its political enslavement, from which only political means can liberate it. The old political parties, which were and are responsible for the national enslavement, cannot be our leaders on the road to freedom. . . .

"The battle for freedom against our oppressors and their taskmasters can be fought successfully only by a political movement of liberation, comprising the German-conscious of all ranks and classes, and fully acknowledging the importance of the rural population and agriculture for the nation as a whole."

Hitler's appeal throughout his rising years was to nationalism and equality with other countries; as soon as he came to power in 1933, he moved swiftly to build up the army and to seize not only equality, but superiority as well.

This man was low class and by prevailing standards unfit to associate with the proud Junker officers of the Reichswehr or with their landowner families in the eastern part of the country or even with the less aristocratic industrialists of the West. The Junker President von Hindenburg long held out against Hitler because of a personal dislike. Yet the Austrian appealed to every other instinct they possessed. He was strongly nationalistic; he favored a strong military machine as an instrument of national policy; he was violently anti-Bolshevik. He argued that his party was the one element of stability in the country. It was true that the 1920 party program contained proposals which would have hit the landowners very hard, if they did not completely annihilate them, and which would have been thoroughly contrary to the interests of the industrialists and the capitalist class in general. Among these proposals were the abolition of incomes unearned by work; nationalization of all businesses which have been amalgamated into trusts; profit-sharing in the large industries; a land reform "suitable to our national requirements"; abolition of interest on mortgages and prohibition of all speculation in land.

Those were largely Feder's ideas. They were a part of the basic party program, and a wing of the party constantly harped on them. Hitler, however, rarely mentioned them. Were they dead letters? Some industrialists obviously had discussed this point with Hitler and were satisfied with the answer. For at a critical period in the financial history of the party, money from industry and bankers saved him, and money from the same sources was at his disposal right up to January 30, 1933, when he became Chancellor.

Oddly, one of the factors that played a large part in the final complicated manœuvring that ended by Hitler's being called to the Chancellorship by President von Hindenburg, was a land reform plan which General von Schleicher, the last Chancellor before Hitler, wished to carry out. The eastern estates were heavily in debt and von Schleicher announced his intention to take over bankrupt estates and divide them. This brought the leaders of the Junker "Agrarian Association" a-running to old von Hindenburg, who was a landowner. Von Schleicher happened to be a non-landowning general. The President was horrified that the General would propose such a policy and that effectively ended von Schleicher's influence with von Hindenburg.

Prior to the attempted "betrayal" by the General, there had been another unsettling episode, and in this, too, President von Hindenburg acted with despatch. Chancellor Heinrich Bruening, who was only once removed from being von Schleicher's immediate predecessor as Chancellor, also tried to do something about the East Prussian estates. Dr. Bruening wanted to cut them up and parcel them out to the unemployed. Old von Hindenburg used his presidential powers to stifle that threat: he dismissed Dr. Bruening and called in the trustworthy (as far as the army and the Junkers were concerned) Franz von Papen. To the landowners, Hitler could be no worse than a Bruening or a von Schleicher.

After Hitler had obtained full reign as the head of the government, some of the Nazi underlings talked about land reform, but Hitler took a practical view and did nothing. Nor, on the industrial side, were businesses nationalized, nor profit-sharing introduced into industry, nor interest on mortgages abolished. But there were developments as the Nazi state grew which displeased the big fellows in the West; they ultimately became little more than state functionaries, in so far as they were directly concerned with the armament industry, and that included about all of heavy industry.

Not all of the western Junkers were enthusiastic about Hitler during the years before 1931, but for the most part they became converted to him during the years 1931, 1932 and 1933 when they were in trouble. When the United Steel trust, a huge organization, got into difficulty, the Bruening Government rescued it by buying its shares. That left the management largely as it was and kept open the possibility of later repurchase, for the Bruening Government's purpose in buying the shares was not socialistic but nationalistic; it did so to prevent control of the important steel concern from passing into foreign hands. Other large concerns likewise fell into difficulty; the way out seemed to be through government action. If Hitler could be relied upon, his strong nationalistic sentiments made him the sort of leader who could do what these industrialists in difficulty wanted.

The results of the parliamentary elections in November 1932 cast the die. The Nazis lost two million votes and their seats in the Reichstag were reduced from 230 to 197. On the other hand, Communists gained eleven seats in the election, rising from 89 to 100. Hitler then turned his face toward the West and shouted: "If the National Socialist party collapses, there will be another ten million communists in Germany." That was such a telling argument that a sufficient number of the western Junkers fell into line to bring Hitler in.

Thus an electoral defeat actually served to bring victory to Hitler.

The mechanics of how he received the senile President von Hindenburg's mandate to form a cabinet were complicated and the whole story of what went on behind the scenes has not yet been told. Certain it is, however, that the schemers intended to keep Hitler in check by forcing him to agree to maintain a cabinet in which he did not have the majority. Hitler had previously refused to form a government which was not strictly a National Socialist Party government, but the 1932 elections and rumors that ex-Chancellor von Schleicher, with Reichswehr backing, was planning a coup in which both Hitler and von Papen would be arrested, caused him to look differently upon the matter. That is, it caused him to turn away from his announced intention to capture the chancellorship by constitutional means. He readily gave his promises to von Hindenburg, but he broke them as soon as it was feasible, eventually forming not only a one-party government but also a one-party state in which he held the combined offices of president and chancellor under the title of Fuehrer and possessor of all wisdom.

The development was not what the "clever" industrialists and bankers intended it to be, but Hitler did not sweep them out. He saved them and made use of them in building the power-state he wanted and in the raising of Germany's might in the world. With all of the nationalistic and expansionist motives, they were in accord; their only differences concerned details.

Hitler's treatment of the officer-landowning Junker class paralleled that of the western industrial Junkers. The army stood out foremost in his plans and in his beliefs; in the early days of his government, he needed the good will of the landowning officer corps. He was a politician after the heart of the general staff. He did not break up the big estates with which the officer corps was so closely linked, but eventually he did interfere in the army's affairs to a greater extent than the officers wished.

The great purge of the Brown Shirts and sundry other elements (including the shooting of von Schleicher and an attempt to kill von Papen) in June 1934, was a Reichswehr victory. A revolutionary army was eliminated, as such, by ruthless action and the regular Reichswehr took its place as Hitler's right arm. From then on, the army got everything it wanted. Its military geniuses had only to ask in order to receive. Hitler cut all of the Versailles Treaty bonds which had forced the legally abolished general staff to work in the dark. He remilitarized the Rhineland, reinstituted military training and in every way urged the Reichswehr on to do more than even some of its own officers desired.

All was not harmony, however, for the army had to maintain constant vigil against the fanatic wing of the party as represented by the Black Guards under Heinrich Himmler. Himmler did not trust the generals; he was forever attempting to work "sound" Nazis into high posts in the army. By the time Himmler became a threat to the army, Hitler had climbed to a position of esteem and power, far above the tumult. He was the arbiter and usually he decided in the army's favor. It was not until the war machine actually started to roll that Hitler and the generals came to serious disagreements. Der Fuehrer had made it abundantly plain before just who was boss in the Third Reich. Two excellent chiefs of staff of the old school had had to step out because of disagreements with him. Hitler also had tried to pry open the closed caste system so that more boys with no land behind them and no "vons" before their names could have an opportunity to rise in the army. But these incidents did not shake the army's foundations. Hitler's interference with the army could not be called anything more than a nuisance. What he did to build up the military establishment far outweighed petty annoyances. The

German General Staff was one of those rocklike institutions that perpetuates itself through taking the long view of events.

Once the machine began to roll, however, Corporal Hitler became convinced that he was even a greater strategist than a sergeant and then the fun began. From 1933 on, Hitler took political steps against the advice of the General Staff. The army's opposition to reoccupation of the Rhineland militarily and the provoking of the Czech crisis stemmed purely from the fact that the General Staff did not think it was yet capable of coping with the forces that could be thrown against it, should the French and British react violently. But Hitler obeyed his intuition and went ahead. When it came to actual military operations, he again called upon his intuition and convinced himself without a struggle that he knew more than did his generals. Therein was the source of friction, but Hitler was master and he weeded out the generals as he desired, putting in their stead Nazis and second-rate men from the army itself. There always had been army officers who were ideologically Nazis and these men got their chance when the top notch field marshals were unable to carry Der Fuehrer's fantastic plans to successful conclusions.

Reversals on the field of battle brought with them complete Nazi domination of the army; the Nazi Party had to assure itself that the army was in the hands of men who would fight on as fanatics and not as men trained in military science. The General Staff became nazified and Heinrich Himmler, the deceiving-looking man whose cold-blooded crimes were countless, was placed over the entire military establishment to conduct a reign of terror.

The philosophy of might and the power-state ideal led the Junker officer corps straight into the maelstrom. The General Staff was a vast organization comprising the military brains of a great militaristic country—without doubt it was the best general staff in the world. Hitler was a tremendous boon to it. Its disagreements with him involved personalities and relatively petty matters, not fundamental principles. A great deal of the best personnel of the military establishment was eliminated by nazification, but the organization and military tradition with all that that implies—the framework—remained. The system of Frederick William and Frederick the Great was not destroyed. As long as the system remains, the personnel can again become high class: names do not have to have "vons" before them to make their owners first class military men.

And how can the system be changed?

The answer to that question is not so simple as it might seem to be. A sure way to change it would be to break up Germany as a state and scatter a good proportion of her inhabitants to the four winds. But this is neither physically, politically nor morally possible. Physically, an entire country cannot be wiped off the face of the earth in the way that the Germans eliminated Lidice and other towns. Politically, the disastrous pre-war fear of Communism in the West and fear of capitalism in Russia, in spite of the wartime comradeship in arms, are still strong enough to prevent either West or East from desiring to remove the Reich entirely. Morally—can anyone conceive of American and British public opinion permitting a deliberate act smacking of cruelty?

Mere partitioning of the Reich would not be tantamount to destruction of the system; partitioning would not wipe out the Will, which is the real foundation of the system. Rather than destroying the desire of the Germans for unity and a power-state, partitioning most certainly would intensify that desire for it would be, to them, one more added proof that their geographical position in Central Europe demanded a power-state. Cutting them up would not be taken as a signal that old methods had failed and that something new should be tried.

Whatever is done to topple the German temple, if the Will to keep that temple erect still burns furiously in the German soul, a way eventually will be found to reconstruct it in some form. Can that Will be weakened by reëducation from abroad? The answer is an emphatic "No!" Nationalism is too strong in all nations to permit extension course instruction from the outside. In direct form, instruction would be discounted as propaganda and mental and physical barriers automatically would be raised. None can convert the German people but the German people themselves, and that cannot be a ninety-day, evening school process.

In every period there have been "good" Germans—but they have been so few, and so, incapable of carrying the nation along with them. It would be criminal for the Allies to turn the nation over to them and come away thinking that the job had been done. If the historical explanation of German behavior is the correct one, then history may bring a change in its own good time. But history more often than not is quite slow in forcing an entire people to alter its notions of where its salvation lies, especially when history itself has been the teacher. We are now, however, concerned with the present and the next half-century; we are concerned with what can be done to protect ourselves while the Germans are coming to their senses.

The Will is the real foundation of the power-state system but the more obvious bases are the landowner-officer clique and heavy industry. This time it seems certain that the older of these will be removed once and for all: the world is about to hear the last of the landowning Junkers. Their stronghold was in East Prussia, Mecklenburg and Pomerania where more than 50 per cent of the farming area belonged to them and was directly operated by them (although big landowners in the Reich as a whole held but one-fifth of the total agricultural land). Those large estates in these three cradles of Junkerism which escape being shifted to Polish jurisdiction certainly will be liquidated through land reform. All of East Prussia and at least a section of Pomerania are a part of German territory which it is proposed to transfer to Poland.

The happy prospect of getting rid of the Junkers, who for so long have been the backbone of the soldier-state, at first glance, would seem to go a long way toward solving the German problem. But this extraordinary class leaves a strong legacy in what it taught the German people to believe. The people were good students and the legacy is embedded in the national outlook. Until the nation becomes convinced that the power-state system is fundamentally wrong, substitute reservoirs of officers, to replace the Junkers, will be found. Hitler, in fact, has already blazed the trail.

The big industry arm of the power-state presents an entirely different problem. Modern warfare is impossible without tremendous production and for that reason, since the experience of World War I, the western Junkers have caused Germany's neighbors more anxiety than have the eastern Junkers. Germany's production capacity, in its broadest sense, so far surpasses that of any of her immediate neighbors, or of any combination of them, that it is a constant nightmare for central Europe. Nothing is more natural, therefore, than that proposals should be put forward for the reduction to impotence of the tangible parts of that capacity. Why not?

The German nation deserves the worst fate that can befall it. To hold in this day and age that the people of a literate country are not responsible for the sort of government they have is anachronistic indeed. If a majority of a people disagrees with its government but does nothing about it (either through the ballot or old-fashioned revolt), such a people are unworthy of special consideration.

In settling accounts with the Germans and in looking to the future, however, it cannot be a question of attempting to discover what the "worst fate" could be. Rather than centering attention on what the Germans deserve, the victors must concentrate on the sort of punishment they can *afford* to administer. Can the victors afford to destroy Germany's production capacity?

Getting devastated Europe back on its feet again is a multiple task that will try the intelligence and patience of statesmen for many years to come. None of the affected countries can pull itself back from the brink without assistance from abroad, and there will be constant social fermentation until such assistance is forthcoming in quantities ample enough to give peace of mind and peace of stomach to the masses. German industry is a dynamo close to the very heart of the continent and it has been one of the tragedies of Europe that the Germans have shown themselves incapable of using it for constructive rather than destructive means. Logically, German industry is a perfect complement for the agriculture and raw materials of the Balkans and central Europe.

Moreover, Germany's geographical position makes her a continental trading center. Already in the middle ages the Germans had become a great merchant people. The Hanseatic League was an outgrowth of this favorable trading position; the produce of the eastern part of the continent was traded in Germany for the products of the more industrialized western part. German rivers were a natural means of communication, and a good railway system was built in the latter part of the nineteenth century to improve these communications.

The Germans have tended to look upon their location as placing them in a dominating post, rather than in a post of service to the continent as well as to themselves. All efforts of other countries to resist domination have been interpreted by the Germans as pure jealousy. This was the attitude in 1648 when Sweden, through the Treaty of Westphalia, got control of the mouths of the Weser, Elba and Oder rivers, and it again was the attitude adopted toward the Versailles Treaty. The Germans believed the latter treaty was a calculated attempt to rob the Reich of God-given fruit. Seventy-five years after the Treaty of Westphalia, the Swedes were pushed back to the north, but it only took the Germans twenty years to spring out from underneath the Treaty of Versailles. The feeling that Europe was jealous was extended to include the whole world, after the great advance in industrialization at the end of the last century.

To destroy Germany's industry deliberately, would be folly of a sort the victors can ill afford, if they propose to try to bring Europe (and the world) out of the morass. Some of that industry has been destroyed and more of it has been damaged by the course of war. But experience has shown how remarkably fast it is possible to put damaged plants back into at least partial production, if labor is used at wartime tempo. The immediate post-war approach to the problem of German industry should be one of trying to find means whereby the dynamo can be put into the service of Europe's economic and social rehabilitation. That means rehabilitation of Germany, too. We will not be overly anxious to apply ourselves to Germany's welfare; others will demand, and be entitled, to be served first. Germany will get the leavings, but enough for subsistence will have to be provided, if for no other reason than that the personal well-being of Allied occupation troops will require economic action to allay popular unrest. Use of German industry in Europe also would be a contribution to world recovery, for Asia, especially China, will be bidding against Europe for available assistance of all sorts.

Successful direction of German industry to this end calls for a high degree of intelligent international control. This control could not be carried on indefinitely, but it would be possible to maintain such close supervision as long as United Nations' troops are in the country to enforce it. It has been suggested that occupation troops should stay in Germany for twenty-five years, or even longer, but it is extremely unlikely that they will, even though it is intended that they should when the occupation begins. They are likely to stay, however, long enough to make it possible to use German production capacity for the good purpose I have suggested. The occupation period after the last war was fixed at fifteen years, but it lasted only ten.

The larger problem of how to prevent German heavy industry, as a pillar of the power-state system, from again being turned to war production will arise once the occupation troops are withdrawn. A suitable formula either for choking key war-making industries or for keeping tab on them so that it would be known what they were doing, could be devised. Despite all of the subterfuge employed to shield armament preparations in the Weimar Republic and the Third Reich, the broad facts were fairly well known in Paris and London as well as in Prague, Warsaw and Brussels. It was not German cleverness in covering up tracks that enabled the Reich to come back with such revengeful fury; it was the unwillingness of the ex-Allies to act. The French and the Belgians acted in 1923 by occupying the Ruhr territory when Germany defaulted on certain reparations payments, but by so doing the two countries incurred the ill-will of a world inclined to agree with the German thesis that the act was illegal. Nowhere was condemnation of the French and Belgians stronger than in Great Britain and the United States. Thereafter, intervention was never seriously considered until 1935 when Hitler remilitarized the Rhineland, in defiance of the Versailles Treaty. By that time, the ex-Allies were so divided among themselves and so confused in their thinking that they could not reply effectively to Hitler's challenge.

There would appear to be an easy way to deal with this industrial problem. If the three areas where heavy industry is concentrated were placed under the full sovereignty of other countries, the German capacity to make war would be almost rubbed out. It would not be difficult to shear them away, for all lie close to other countries—the Saar to France, the Ruhr-Rhine to France, Belgium and Holland, and Silesia to Poland and Czechoslovakia.

Annexation would do away with complicated and hard-to-maintain international control, but it is not as foolproof as it appears at first glance. Assuming that the victors could agree among themselves as to who was to get what, if the entire German populations were not moved out, the annexing powers would be in for real trouble. With the German populations remaining, annexation would be akin to partitioning and as has already been pointed out, partitioning is bound to have the effect of whipping up the Will of the German people again to pull themselves up by their bootstraps. If, on the other hand, the German populations were transferred to the interior of the Reich, they would have to be dumped down where there is no room for them. Such a transfer would involve at least five million persons. The Germans shunted helpless hundreds of thousands of persons around Europe with complete disregard of human factors; they turned human beings out to die of cold and starvation—and for so doing they won the strong condemnation of the United Nations. Dare the United Nations turn around and emulate the terrible acts of the Germans?

The answer is that they dare not lower themselves that far and they will not do it. Here again it cannot be a matter of what the Germans deserve; it can only be a question of what the victors can afford, and they cannot afford knowingly to create an economic and social cancer in the heart of Europe. Even without transferring the populations, such a dangerous condition would most certainly result if all of the important industrial regions were taken completely away from the Reich.

Conditions in Germany today are far different from what they were after World War I. The collapse of the Monarchy did not bring with it a total collapse of the political structure of the country. The form of the state disappeared, but government remained. Political parties and a Reichstag were still in existence; there was an Opposition. This time, there is only one political organization, the Nazi Party, which is at once the state and the government. Political opposition managing to survive underground has had no influence, although much is likely to be claimed for it. The Allies, therefore, will be hard put to find responsible acceptable persons with whom to deal. A certain number will come forward proclaiming their hatred of the nazis and professing their willingness to coöperate with the conquerors. They will be vehement in their denunciation of the nazis; they will have many horrible tales to tell and they will be hankering to get their hands on individual members of the nazi band. Among these, some will be sincere, but most of them, like so many million others who do not make themselves conspicuous, will be hating the nazis simply because the nazis dragged the country to defeat instead of gaining the promised victory. It will be next to impossible to weed them out.

Those who will express their delight in being rid of the nazis will come from all classes, but the workers will be the most vociferous. Among them will be communists—and it will be surprising if those communists (there were many of them), who hastily climbed into Brown uniforms between 1932 and 1934, are not at the head demanding priority for a "good fight" they will claim to have waged all these years within the nazi ranks. The question of the amount of support to be given leftists carries with it seeds of trouble among the Allies. The Russians have given no indication that they want to make a communist state out of Germany, but they do want a Germany friendly to the U.S.S.R., and they might conclude that the best way to obtain it would be through supporting communists. It is a foregone conclusion that the British, Americans and French will shy away from anything smacking of communism, even though the communists represent themselves as being the most democratic element in the country, which, in truth, they are most likely to be.

The Russians have not been fighting an ideological war. They have bent over backward to give the German people the idea that communism did not figure in the war. Hitler put an ideological mask on his war. He was fighting, he said, to keep communism out of western Europe. The Russians refused to accommodate him by fighting back on that basis. They tried to destroy that Hitler argument by setting up a Free German committee of captured generals and officers. If communism were the aim, a puppet government of refugee German Communists would have been created in Moscow, instead of a committee of bona fide German generals who could not be suspected of having communist leanings. The propaganda going to Germany from this committee told the Germans it was imperative that the nazis be overthrown in order that Germany might live. The Germans were not urged to set up a communist state in order to live, and as a bold touch, the Germans were told that Russia had no desire to prohibit Germany from having an army.

Occupation troops went no further than the Rhineland after the last war, but this time the entire Reich must submit. Russian, British, American and French zones have been established, but it has been agreed that a central mixed commission should fix a common over-all policy for all zones. Each power, however, will be responsible for the governing of its zone and there may not be a central German government for several years. Differences in tactics are certain to exist with four nationalities, of varying temperaments and outlooks, doing the governing. The stress will have to be on local governments with the military commands sitting at the top, administering law and order.

Both politically and economically, the nazi state was highly centralized with Berlin as the hub. The tall political superstructure can be dispensed with, without great repercussions, but regardless of the consequences, it will be thrown out, for one of the objectives of the war is to get rid of it. The economic superstructure is quite another matter. In Hitler's totalitarian state, the economic and the political were scarcely distinguishable, one from the other. One of the major tasks of the occupying powers will be to unscramble the two, for the economic ties that bind the Reich are so complicated that they cannot be brushed aside easily. Politically, the four occupying powers should be able to get along with a minimum of central control, but economically there will have to be a large amount of collaboration and management among the zones.

The Reich, even before Hitler, was a cartelized country and the state had large industrial holdings. At the end of the Weimar Republic, for instance, 50 per cent of the national dividend belonged to the state and that percentage increased under the nazis. The state's industrial and banking undertakings are controlled through a holding company known as the Vereinigte Industrie Unternehmungen A. G. in Berlin. The Reichs Kredit Gesellschaft of Berlin, one of the five largest German banks, is state owned, as is the Vereinigte Aluminium Werke, one of the largest aluminum producers in the world. The state also owns a remarkable variety of concerns such as power companies, metal works, shipyards, nitrogen plants and even bedstead and bicycle companies. These companies are scattered all over the Reich and hence will not be in any one of the military occupation zones. As for cartels, with their production and distribution agreements, there are between fifteen hundred and two thousand of them, not counting syndicates in some of the basic industries such as coal and potash. Either cartels or syndicates exist in every sphere of production.

What to do with the banks and how to prevent inflation will be one of the hardest problems to solve. The banks are glutted with paper whose sole value rested upon the existence of the nazi state and that state's ability to produce more and still more. The nazis had no gold: their currency backing was the sweat of the worker and the farmer and their dreams of the future. German finances are in a bewildering condition, to put it mildly. A minimum amount of reconstruction of damaged homes and businesses will require a new credit structure, and this cannot be built satisfactorily on a local or zone basis. The Reichsbank, the central banking institution, was a complete tool of the party-state. The president of the Reichsbank and the minister of economics were the same person and the bank's directorate could not veto any act of the president.

On top of what might be called the normal amount of economic centralization, the nazis erected still another story for war-making purposes. This story housed an extremely intricate supervisory mechanism for production and distribution. This top story was superficial, depending entirely upon the authority of the nazi state. Its disappearance will be automatic. It is the interlocking arrangements closer to the fundamental producing capacity of the country which are important in keeping the country from sinking out of sight. Chaotic conditions are bound to prevail for some time after defeat and they cannot be checked without making use of the country's "normal" centralized machinery on a national rather than zone basis.

Germany will be so exhausted after this war that nothing whatever would have to be done to prevent her from rebounding militarily within at least a decade. Military occupation of the country will be in the nature of a double guarantee. But after the troops leave, what will happen?

Such a virile organization as the Nazi Party is certain to go underground and make itself felt sooner or later. Hitler did not labor for his lifetime alone; he looked ahead to a Thousand Year Reich. Eventually, new men with hardy anti-Nazi programs will be found to take the lead, but unless the German people have changed during their latest ordeal far more than the observer can see, the new regime will not be violently anti-Nazi in its foreign policy. Nazi foreign policy was not a peculiarity of a single party, it was not a product of Hitler's diseased brain. It was distinctly a German foreign policy and on that score the German people backed Hitler to the hilt. Among the more astute Germans, including the old General Staff, there was disagreement with Der Fuehrer over execution of that policy, but very few indeed were not in sympathy with its aim. As the Germans look back in the cooler times of the future, they will see that Hitler could have achieved the domination they want, if he had been temperamentally able to make haste just a bit more slowly.

The great German dilemma is this: no matter what course the Allies pursue within Germany, it is certain to be wrong, for no lasting solution can come from the outside through imposition. The Germans have to save their own soul and they cannot hurriedly be shoved into trying to do it. Enlightened exterior aid for the purpose of creating an atmosphere, in which the few "good" Germans could propagate their kind of course, would be helpful, but no more than that.

It is what the United Nations do among themselves that will determine whether or not the Germans in another generation or two will break out again as the enemy of humanity. Can the United Nations remain united long enough? Until the Germans have evolved from their present state, they will try again and again to break out. The only way to hold the damage to a minimum is for the world to keep itself materially and spiritually capable of prompt and vigorous action.

PEACE IN OUR TIME?

> Whoever thinks a faultless peace to see,
> Thinks what ne'er was, nor is, nor e'er shall be.
> —Pope, Essay on Criticism

18

ACHTUNG MINEN!

When American and British soldiers went into Normandy they found a profusion of board signs with the German words **ACHTUNG MINEN** and skull and crossbones on them. The signs were attached to wire fences, nailed to trees, or they had stakes of their own and were just stuck into the ground. They were all along the coast. The Germans had put them up by the thousands to indicate mine fields. The mines had been laid long in advance of the Allied landings, hence the "Beware Mines" caution was necessary to protect German troops and French civilians. It was too bad that the enemy had to be told just where the mines were, so in order to create as much complication as possible under the circumstances, the Germans did not always lay mines where they put up signs. Sometimes there would be but one mine in a field of several acres and sometimes the Germans merely planted pieces of old iron. But wherever there was a sign, our mine-detecting squads were obliged to comb the entire area and that took time and men.

In the field of peacemaking, detecting squads are going over the vast ground in an effort to determine where the mines are. There, also, many signs have been left by the failures that piled one upon another during the first World War, and between it and the second World War. Some of these signs, too, are real, some are only partially real and some are entirely misleading. The difficulty is that regardless of the time and men used, the political detector, unlike the scientifically constructed one the boys used in Normandy, never accurately determines where all the mines are and where there are none.

Throughout the world there is a much more sober view of what peace will bring than there was at a similar period in World War I. Nowhere in the world today is there a Woodrow Wilson firing the imaginations and hopes of men with a prospect of eternal peace. The hopes Wilson created were too cruelly dashed for any statesman to come forward so soon again with a similar lofty program. To be sure, there is the Atlantic Charter with its "desire to bring about the fullest collaboration between all nations in the economic field" and its belief "that all of the nations of the world, for realistic as well as for spiritual reasons, must come to the abandonment of the use of force." But the Charter is a mere expression of "desire," a guidepost; it is not a fiery program of action such as Wilson attempted. The Charter, in fact, is not a charter at all: it neither grants nor guarantees anything, and these two things are the essence of a charter.

The masses, exhausted by the most thoroughgoing war of all time, hope that something can be done. They know that that "something" must be in the field of international action, but they have not fastened upon any method. They are not at all sure that a method can be found, but they hope that it can. In this respect, the Charter is a reflection of a general feeling.

Sails have been greatly trimmed as a result of the failure of Wilson's ideas. There has been a distinct return to the past: this war has produced no new idea. Official thinking has turned to the past for inspiration. With pre-1914 practices of world powers as a guide, governmental efforts to construct a world security organization have centered upon remedying faults in the Covenant of the League of Nations. It has been deemed realistic to bow to power politics, which Wilson tried to destroy, and to patch the old League in the light of power politics tenets. This was the spirit of the Dumbarton Oaks proposals.

Private organizations and individuals have presented plans for carrying world organization beyond the Wilsonian conception into the realm of a World State, but such plans have been confined entirely to the United States. None of Main Street's neighbors has been thinking in terms other than those which are called practical. It is important that the citizens along Main Street should understand the limited scope of what is taking place, so that there will be no deception later on. Inasmuch as the United States must remain in the thick of international collaboration, hopes that the war now drawing to a close will bring an end to all wars should not be allowed to mount high enough to make possible a dangerous reaction against coöperation.

The search for security is as old as man, and man has always tried to find it in alliances and balances of power. Yet alliances and balances of power have never brought him more than temporary security. Alliances inevitably have turned sour and power balances have become unbalanced. Real and presumed national interests have stepped in to undermine such structures.

The future being planned for us rests upon this bankrupt method. Wilson, the idealist, tried to get away from this principle in the League of Nations by establishing universal collective security; old style alliances would not be necessary because the world would be united in one grand alliance with all members pledged to join against an aggressor. But it was soon demonstrated that the power to make the organization effective rested with those countries which possessed the greatest physical strength. The others could exert moral force (moral force did play an important role in minor matters), but it was by no means powerful enough to be decisive in major matters. The League itself had no armed forces at its disposal to carry out its decisions; it was dependent entirely upon the arms which members might wish to use on the League's behalf in each given instance. The universality idea received its first blow when the United States rejected its own President's proposals, but many of the League's vicissitudes could have been avoided if its two most powerful members, Great Britain and France, had not worked in opposite directions—almost from the time the war ended.

With the League shattered, the fresh hunt for security started by taking heed of the League's failures. Germany and Japan being the latest peace-breakers, attention centered upon how to prevent them from striking again. That raised the question of where the power resides to keep them bottled up, and incidentally of how to prevent breaches of the peace from other quarters. Thus the Dumbarton Oaks proposals emphasized the role of the five powers regarded as most likely to possess the means of accomplishing this end. But neither Russia nor Britain nor the United States was willing to agree to use its national arms upon the desire of a majority vote of all of the nations members of a future world organization. This led right back to the alliance method hardly disguised; in fact, the Dumbarton Oaks proposals provided for regional agreements and they are but another way for countries to express their anxiety lest the world organization should not give them the protection they want. European members of the League of Nations turned to regional alliances as soon as they began to doubt that the League would stand the test. Regional agreements were concluded as insurance policies.

Hence, whether or not there is to be a "lasting peace" depends upon the ability of the Big Five—the United States, Britain, Russia, France and China—to remain united in peace as they were in war. A multitude of influences will draw them from this unity, and the further we move away from the horrible experiences of this war, the less necessary that unity will appear. We shall certainly have peace as long as those who hold the power are of a mind to give it to us. But history solemnly rears its head and asks: "How long can they remain of one mind?"

This question will recur over and over again as long as the people of the earth are content to interpret their personal interests in terms of nationalism. The nations refuse to yield a single bit of their national sovereignty in the interest of peace, which they all profess to desire above everything else, yet that sovereignty to which they cling has proven itself unable to bring peace. The citizens of a community surrender a certain amount of their personal rights in order that they may live in a law-abiding community. Laws are made, courts are established and a police force is set up to enforce the rulings of the courts. When Joe Griffiths on Pine Street is alleged to have broken the law, his neighbors do not come together of their own volition and decide whether the law has been broken and if so, how and if he is to be punished. The police force and the courts take care of that according to laws which recognize no difference between rich and poor; it is out of the hands of Joe's neighbors, and that fact represents what they have yielded or delegated in order to have an orderly community.

The international community still follows the bloody course of primitive methods. The neighbors still demand the right to decide in each case whether anyone is to be punished or not and they refuse to create a police force standing above all and empowered to keep the peace regardless of who breaks it. In international life, the wealthy (that is, the largest and most powerful countries) insist on meting out justice as they see it, and they have never been able to agree upon what justice is, for any great length of time.

There has always been crime and crime there always will be, but that fact does not render useless the manifold efforts to reduce the volume by preventive means. Attempts to remove the causes of war are an essential part of the search for peace, but the primary hope for world peace lies in educating the peoples of the world to a point where they will accept a civilized international order in the same way that they have accepted community life.

In centering attention on peace plans, we put the cart before the horse. A workable scheme could be found overnight if the peoples of the world were really ready to demand an international regime regulated by laws rather than by treaties. It is wrong to focus attention on a "lasting peace" for that gives the idea that war can be conveniently and even comfortably outlawed, when in truth we can no more rid ourselves of war than we can of crime or fire.

Prince that there is nothing like the sword to bring a Prince renown. One fine day the rest of Europe suddenly stopped laughing and began to wonder what was going on among the "Sandhaufen." The old miser had pinched everything for the benefit of the military establishment which he expanded to an alarming degree. His army grew to 83,000 men and in it were husky six-footers corralled from all over Europe. Only Russia and France had armies larger than that.

The army was the center of Frederick William's boundless activity; his spartan economy was but a means to an end. His officers he got from the nobles, his soldiers came from the farmers (and foreign mercenaries), and the money for their upkeep he squeezed out of the townspeople.

Frederick William not only turned over the first sod for the totalitarian state, but he also gave expression to a feeling that, since his day, has got the Germans into terrible muddles. The tough old King was going to make Prussia liked and he was going to do it by the only means he knew how—by military force. By the time of William the Second, the last Kaiser, that feeling of inferiority had become one of superiority. It was more than a feeling: it was a belief and it was not confined to the ambitions of a ruling class. Philosophers and teachers offered the solid background for the belief and the masses wallowed in it. Wherein was the German superior? The answer to that touched the nebulous and the ridiculous but to the ordinary person it usually translated itself into something like this: we are a disciplined people capable of bringing order out of chaos; we are "sauber," and cleanliness is one of the principal marks denoting civilized man; we have great technical skill; we know how to organize and to raise low people from their sloth; our forefathers were men of excellent blood and throughout history the worth of northern men has been proved as against southern men; our beneficent efforts will most certainly be appreciated and welcomed. The ordinary man's thinking usually did not go much further than that. Indeed, it is possible to find the same sort of beliefs in almost any country, if the comparison between northern and southern men is omitted. The people in almost every country feel themselves to be superior to at least a fraction of the rest of mankind and that fraction is usually the next door neighbor or neighbors. But this feeling ordinarily is not a part of the basic philosophy of the country and hence does not crop out in virulent form.

But it was sufficient for the German to believe. When a William the Second and a Hitler talked about Germany's world mission, therefore, they were speaking about something in which the German, upper class, middle class and worker, believed. Bismarck was not a "world missionary" but he was a devout adherent of the militaristic power-state which he buttressed as much as possible and handed down to his successors. It was only through such an instrument that the superiority nonsense could become a menace to the world. Frederick William's philosophy of "Like me or I'll bash your head in" remained studded in German character.

The German does not understand how anyone in his right mind could object to his, the German's, tailored ideas which the German is positive are constructed of the very finest elements. His mental life in the world of romanticism shuts him off from actuality and perverts his thinking. None but a German could take the attitude assumed by the German air attaché in Norway at the time of the German invasion of the Scandinavian country. As told by C. J. Hambro, the former president of the Norwegian Parliament, in his book, *How to Win the Peace*, the air attaché, after helping to prepare the treacherous attack while covered by diplomatic immunity, took the lead of a motorized German force which was trying to capture the King and the Government who were fleeing. A Norwegian bullet hit the attaché, whereupon he cried out with great moral indignation: "Why, this is murder!"

I myself have witnessed many similar exhibitions of this peculiar working of the German mind, both inside and outside the Reich.

During the low times of the Weimar Republic, this superiority feeling remained to gnaw at the German soul. It came forth again with fury under Hitler. Superiority of the German way of life was, in fact, a theme Hitler constantly drilled into the people. He did not have to convince them; they were already convinced. What he told them was that he was going to prove it to the world or bash in the thick heads that could not grasp it. The Germans liked that.

As the German sits at home in the center of Europe he looks out and complains of the treatment the world has accorded him. The grand coalition against him in the last war proved to him not that he was wrong, but that almost the entire world was determined to keep him down. Why did the world want to keep him down? Because of his genius; because he was so far superior to other peoples that they turned heaven and earth to prevent him from exercising his great gifts. The world was afraid of his ability, it was jealous. That it took a world coalition to down him was adequate proof of his superiority. No single country or small alliance could cope with him: it took a grand alliance to do it, and even then Germany would have won had there not been treachery on the home front! He is proud of that.

In this war it took another coalition to beat him. And once more he came near to victory. That is an invitation to try again.

History books, even before Adolf Hitler had an opportunity to touch them up, drummed the idea of Germany's "Mittellage" into the youth. A history used in the upper grades during the Weimar Republic began with a dissertation on Germany's geographical situation and from it a good idea can be gained of how the Germans feel they are and have been assailed from all sides.

It said that Germany, unlike many other European countries, did not have natural boundaries and that the open borders in the East and West had made Germany a theater of war. "All foreign forces strike this land of the center and it was only when Germany was strong and able to carry arms that this pressure could be adequately offset; when on the other hand she was internally disunited, when she had not collected her strength together, Germany was forced to become a football in the hands of her enemies. But despite all misfortunes which have descended upon Germany as a result of her 'Mittellage' in the course of time, the country of the European Middle could not be destroyed, its power never completely broken. Time and again it produced from its slumbering strength the means for a new rising. . . .

"When the Reich was again united by Bismarck, Germany's industrial power grew with her trade to such a height that before long all of the industrial and trading countries of the world set themselves against us. The wealth of Germany's sub-soil treasures, especially of coal and potash, was the foundation of this development; the diligence and skill of her inhabitants, along with a higher education for the masses, assisted it."

Under the subheading of "Germany's Task," the history book went on to say that "When we have brought our strength together and firmly united it, we shall regain our former political, economic and spiritual positions among the people of Europe, which the advantage of our 'Mittellage' commands."

The book wound up its basic survey with four paragraphs on the subject of "national states," the burden being that Germany's state borders did not coincide with the territory inhabited by Germanic peoples. After World War I, it said, the enemy talked about self-determination of peoples and while the principle was applied to some parts of Germany, the Germans of Alsace-Lorraine, Posen and Austria were not given an opportunity to express their desire to belong to the Reich; "force was placed above right." In this way, it said, the German people in the heart of Europe were separated into two states with only an artificial border between them. Then the students were told:

"We have duties as 'Volksgenossen' as well as citizens of the state. We must never forget that the Germans who live outside of our state also are our brothers from the same stem and the same blood, joined with us through common language and sentiments."

While Bismarck was not a "world missionary," he was a unitarian. He completed the cycle which Frederick the Great began, by forging the modern German Empire in 1871. After Bismarck, unity became involved with the superiority folly through the idea that in union there is strength. Bismarck, however, violently opposed joining with Austria-Hungary. He fought a war to keep the Hapsburgs from meddling in the affairs of the German states. But his opposition was that of one dynasty against another; he was a Prussian minister and he intended to see to it that Prussia became the dominant power in the empire he envisaged.

No fundamental economic or political principle was involved in Bismarck's action, and between him and the advent of Hitler, although the German states were then a part of the same empire, they showed the same characteristics they had before the Empire was formed. That is, they were fully conscious that they were Germans but they were at the same time "localists." They were Hessians, Bavarians, Saxons and Prussians instead of empire Germans.

Goethe spoke of this localism as it existed in his day before the